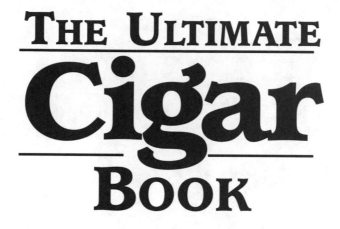

THE ULTIMATE
Cigar
BOOK

THE ULTIMATE
Cigar
BOOK

by
**RICHARD
CARLETON
HACKER**

Autumngold Publishing™

Beverly Hills, California

Second Edition
Third Printing

Other Books by the Same Author

Die Welt der Zigarre (German Edition)
The Ultimate Pipe Book (U.S. Edition)
The Ultimate Pipe Book (British Edition)
Die Kunst Pfeife zu rauchen (German Edition)
The Christmas Pipe
The Muzzleloading Hunter

Videos

The Ultimate Pipe Video (Premiere Edition)
The Ultimate Pipe Video (Collector's Edition)

Audio Tapes

CigarQuest - Conversations In Smoke

Printed in the United States of America.

Library of Congress Catalog Card Number: 96-84667

ISBN No. 0-931253-05-5

∂❧

To my lovely and long suffering wife, Joan, who has encouraged and nurtured the passion I have for cigars. Never once has she shown the slightest hint of jealousy.

∂❧

"Gentlemen, you may smoke."
— King Edward VII

"If I cannot smoke in heaven, then I shall not go."
— Mark Twain

"I am sure there are many things better than a good cigar, but right now, I can't think of what they might be."
— Richard Carleton Hacker

Table of Contents

Foreword

Just as it takes more than one leaf to make a cigar, so has it taken a number of people to help me bring this book to fruition. Originally the first edition of The *Ultimate Cigar Book* was to have premiered back in 1989, well before the current cigar craze had been publicly acknowledged. But world events, sociological changes, and the unbelievable number of "new breed" brands that were beginning to emerge upon the cigar scene at that time inspired me to delay publication of the first edition of this book until 1993; the winds of change that I felt were carrying an ever-increasing aroma of cigar smoke. During that time span, I revisited many of the cigar making factories that I had formerly been to, re-interviewed many of the people I had already talked to, and in essence, re-did all of my research in order to make this the most complete book of its type that had ever been written. I am proud to say that my goal was achieved, as born out by the fact that the first printing sold out within three months. Five subsequent sold-out printings and a foreign language edition have continued to carry the information contained within these pages, most of it never revealed before, to tens of thousands of fellow cigar smokers the world over.

Now, with this greatly expanded second edition, an even wider expanse of information is brought forth. Just as the previous edition was the first to chronicle such ground breaking subjects as the counterfeit Cuban cigars and the dreaded *Lacioderma* beetle, so does this new edition unveil the latest trends of collectable cigars, the emergence of women smokers, and the

i

proliferation of smokeasies, just to name a few of the many discoveries that await you.

Of course, no book such as this can ever be completely up-to-date. New brands are appearing almost daily while others are fading away. Blends change, trends change, world situations change, and the cigar industry changes as a result. In spite of years of travel and interviews and countless rolls of film and audio tape, one can never presume to capture it all. Ironically, up until recently, Cubatabaco had been having the very same problem in trying to reconstruct the past history of their great Havana brands. Part of the reason for this difficulty is the fact that many of the original cigar-making families fled Cuba when Castro came into power, taking their precious records and memories with them. Consequently, today the history of the Cuban cigar is spread throughout the Dominican Republic, Jamaica, Honduras, Spain and other parts of the world. Fortunately, I was able to recapture much of this material through my long-standing friendships with many of the original cigar makers and their families. As a result, you will discover information throughout this book that has never before been published. I am proud to say that even the Cuban government has used this book as a reference for helping to reconstruct some of their own cigar making heritage. Keeping that thought, it is my hope that the International Compendium of Cigar Brands in Chapter 9 may somehow help to bring the cigar world together again.

Just as I felt the need for a worldwide listing of cigars, so did I find myself blazing other new paths in a jungle where I found there were no roads. The lack of an all-encompassing cigar rating system caused me to embark upon and then abandon the notion of starting my own (which I finally realized was an impractical idea, as we all have different concepts of "flavor"). Instead, I created the Highly Prejudiced HackerScale, as a measure of strength, rather than taste. And even the HPH is subjective. After all, it is each individual's perception of a particular cigar that determines whether or not it is worthy of being smoked.

Indeed, both cigar smoking and cigar making are very people-oriented endeavors. Throughout the research and writing of this book, I have encountered numerous individuals who, like the cigars they make, are of the finest quality, with a consistency that is never disappointing. Most of them you will meet via their products, which are depicted throughout this book. But a few deserve special mention.

First, I must thank Carlos (Carlito) Fuente, Jr., for his unbridled enthusiasm when he first discovered I was writing *The Ul-*

timate Cigar Book, and for going out of his way to open so many doors for me in the Dominican Republic. Likewise, Consolidated Cigar Corporation's Dick DiMeola was a living embodiment of his pledge to "do anything that will help promote cigars." Equally responsive was Danny Blumenthal of Villazon, who shared his experiences from a lifetime in the cigar business. I am also indebted to Frank Llaneza, one of the most respected cigar makers today, for so openly sharing his invaluable insights and knowledge. That same openness was readily found with Benjamin Menendez (General Cigar), Hendrik Kelner (TABADOM), and Manuel Quesada (MATASA) in the Dominican Republic. Likewise, the late Larry Weinfeld and his son Brad, who continues on in the respected family tradition of guiding Hollco-Rohr, were never too busy to answer my many requests concerning this book. And I must pay tribute to Robin Philpott of Alfred Dunhill Ltd., who holds the unabashed title of the Fastest Fax in Great Britain. A request instantly became a deed the moment it reached his desk. Nor must I forget Simon Chase of Hunters & Frankau and his invaluable insight into the Havana cigar smoker's role in England.

International borders have never been a barrier to cigar smoke, and so it was that Heinrich and Monika Villiger not only opened up their cigar-making operations to me, but also volunteered to act as my liaison with Cubatabaco, thereby permitting me to disrupt their German offices with my barrage of correspondence. And over in Holland it was Peter Zwart and Bernard Prenger who were more than helpful with my many Rothmans-oriented requests, just as Dr. Herbert Rupp was with Austria Tabak and their history and products. I will never forget the day when Herbert said to me, "As long as you are in Vienna, do you want to see some 100-year-old Cuban cigars?" You'll find the photos in this book.

Back in the States, on the retail side, Hugh Getzenberg of Century City Tobacco Shoppe in West Los Angeles proved more than willing to provide cigars for testing that might otherwise not have been available. And Jimmy Hurwitz of Gus' Smoke Shop in Sherman Oaks, California unselfishly made his humidor available for storage, so that the cigars I was saving for testing and photography would not unravel or go stale over the long course of writing this book. I must also thank Victor Migenes, Jr. of La Plata Cigar, one of the last of the handrolled cigar makers in Los Angeles, for his friendship and assistance. I would also like to pay tribute to the memory of his father, Victor Migenes, Sr., who was never too busy in the late 1960s to answer a multitude of questions from a young advertising executive who stopped in once a week to pick up a handrolled "Hacker Special," and watch the cigar makers at work in the back room.

I am also indebted to the multi-lingual talents of longtime friend Isabelle, Countess Cowley, for her unselfish assistance with my international communications. By now Lady Cowley is probably one of the world's most well-versed nonsmokers on cigar lore.

And finally, saving the best for the last, I am forever grateful for the editorial support and unwavering faith and dedication of my wife Joan, who, upon smelling the aroma of my hastily extinguished cigar on our first date (in what seems like not-so-many years ago), nonchalantly said, "Your car smells just like our living room at home." It seems that her dad was also a cigar smoker.

There are many other individuals who have helped make this book a reality, but if I tried to list them all it would seem like an Academy Awards producer's worst nightmare. Suffice to say, it is because of *people* that we have some of the finest cigars the world has ever known, and, taking inflation into account, they are one of the most affordable pleasures we can enjoy today.

I am fortunate in being one of the few writers who has been able to visit all of the major cigar producing countries in the world. And in having smoked a substantial percentage of all of the cigars being made today, as well as a few that have been out of production for quite awhile. It is my hope that, through this book, you are able to share some of those adventures and discoveries with me. So pull up an ashtray, fire up a favorite cigar, and join me as we travel the smoke-filled pages ahead.

Richard Carleton Hacker

photo: Domingo Batista

Chapter 1

In The Beginning...

October 12, 1492. We all know the date. It's been branded into our brains ever since grade school. They even made a couple of movies about it. That was when Christopher Columbus miscalculated by half a hemisphere and accidentally discovered the Americas. But what they don't tell you in school is that seventeen days later, on October 29th, Chris and his flotilla of three sailed into the protected waters of Cuba's Bahía de Gibara. Not knowing just what to expect, he sent two sailors ashore: Rodrigo de Jerez and Luis de Torres. It was here — and not on the Bahamian island of San Salvador as has been so often and erroneously chronicled — that the two Spanish conquistadors discovered native men and women smoking what may very probably have been the New World's first version of the cigar. And they were Havanas! Of course, they were not the cigars that we know today; these were made of raw, twisted leaves of uncured tobacco. Dried corn husks were used for wrappers, and it is safe to surmise that they weren't shade grown. Estimated ring size was as big as your arm. It was recorded that Rodrigo actually took a puff or two, thus becoming the first European cigar smoker in history.

Eight days later, on Tuesday, November 6th, fall guys Rodrigo and Luis were again put ashore, this time on the island of

San Salvador, and again they found the local natives, who had by now been labeled "Indians" by Columbus, who still didn't know where he was, smoking the same crudely made cigars.

Columbus took this information, along with some tobacco leaves, back with him to Spain, where Rodrigo de Jerez decided to show off by smoking this unusual weed in public, just as he had done in Cuba. Rod paid a high price for lighting up in an historic no-smoking area. He was tossed in the slammer for three years. Yes, even back then, what has come to be the most gentlemanly of pastimes was being persecuted by anti-smoking factions. Or in this case, the Spanish Inquisition.

But Rodrigo's suffering was not in vain, for soon cigar smoking became the *nouveau culture* of Spanish society. A short time later, this New World custom was taken up in Portugal. However, because of the cost of tobacco, it was reserved for the upper classes and trendsetting people of style, an image that has remained with the handrolled cigar to this very day. For whatever reasons, the Spanish decided to keep their discovery of tobacco for themselves, and cigars were seldom seen beyond their borders for the next three hundred years.

Nonetheless, by the 18th century the making of cigars had become big business in Spain, and in 1731 the "Royal Manufac-

An early 19th century European "cigar boutique."

2

turers of Seville" was established to organize this growing industry. With the help of Dutch traders, by 1750 the cigar eventually made its way to Holland and then to Russia. There, Empress Catherine II had her cigars decorated with delicate silk bands so that her royal fingers would not become stained while she was smoking. This simple yet ingenious device would subsequently inspire the cigar bands that we know today.

But it took a British naval officer, Colonel Israel Putnam, to bring cigar tobacco to America. In 1762, upon returning to the Colonies after King George III's war with Cuba, "Old Put" (as he was later called during the American Revolution) brought back three "donkey loads" of Havana cigars. Of course, the rebellious Americans were already enthralled with their own native tobacco, which was being smoked in pipes. Cigar smoking would remain largely ignored in the new republic until the early 19th century, and would not come into its own until the 1850s.

Although the British only occupied Cuba for one year — 1763 — that short time frame was sufficient enough to open the door to Europe and let in the sweet, earthy aroma of Havana to-

A gentleman's accessory from the last century: when the knobs are turned the doors swing out, each holding a cigar.

3

bacco. It was a taste and sensation that few people on the Continent, other than the Spaniards and the Dutch, had ever experienced before. The lure of this pungent perfume was further intensified in 1803, when France invaded Spain and Napoleon's soldiers discovered Cuban cigars firsthand. Of course, this was not the first encounter the French had with Havanas. In 1793, while fighting the British, Antoine Depierre commandeered a Dutch merchant vessel en route from Havana and brought it into port. On board were — you guessed it — cigars! They became an instant hit with anyone who was fortunate enough to obtain one. Recognizing a good thing when they saw it, France eventually created a government tobacco monopoly in 1811, but did not start making cigars until 1816, after their war with Britain. After all, they did not want *their* cigars being unwillingly towed into some foreign port!

By the beginning of the 19th century, cigar making had spread to Italy and Switzerland. And finally, in 1810, the first cigar factory was started in America. Of course, this was still the era of the clay pipe and snuff, the latter of which was garnishing most of the best grades of Cuban leaf. Although the cigar was a much more convenient way to "take tobacco," it took a while for it to become socially acceptable. But through the gilded elegance that was to become the Victorian Age, the cigar gradually assumed an aura of prominence and respectability. In 1823, only fifteen thousand cigars were imported to all of Britain. By 1840, that number had jumped to thirteen million. Clearly, cigar smoking was on the rise. And because a cigar was much more expensive than a bowl of pipe tobacco, it was also becoming the symbol of elegance and wealth, a literal smoke signal that you were among the more successful inhabitants of the civilized world.

By 1845 tobacco had replaced coffee as Cuba's principle export, and many of the small tobacco farms that had been started by Spanish colonists were being annexed and combined into large plantations. In 1855 alone 360 million Havana cigars were exported. As Cuba's prosperity continued to climb with the ever-growing fame of Havana tobacco Spain began to fear that she might lose her "New American" province. And indeed she might. During the early 1850s there had already been a movement afoot in the U.S. to annex Cuba (no doubt propagated by a group of governmental cigar smokers), and in 1854, President Franklin Pierce actually tried to buy Cuba from Spain. Had he been successful, our nation's 14th President might have been better remembered, at least by American cigar smokers if not by historians.

Towards the middle of the 19th century, cigar bands came into their own, and many of the bands that we see on today's legendary brands, such as Punch, Partagás and Romeo y Julieta, remain largely unchanged from those embryonic years. It soon became fashionable for wealthy smokers to have their portraits put on their cigar bands, an affectation the cigar makers of Cuba, America and Europe were only to happy to oblige. But it didn't stop there; non-Cuban manufacturers began taking liberties with some of the better known Havana labels as well. These early forms of counterfeits became so prominent that in 1870 the Havana Cigar Brands Association was formed in order to protect the names of Cuban-made smokes.

A worldwide recession in the late 19th century caused many European countries to start developing their own cigar industries, a revenue-producing move that effectively began reducing the number of Cuban cigars being imported to these nations. Nonetheless, by 1873 France was selling one billion cigars a year, of which ten million were imported. By this time, England had be-

From the collection of the Austria Tabak Museum in Vienna comes this salesman's cigar sample case, enabling customers to order by simply pointing, rather than by leafing through pages of a catalog.

come *the* market for Havana cigars. Consequently, the latter part of the 19th and early 20th centuries saw new shapes evolve, inspired in part by some of Britain's most prominent smokers. During the 1880s, London financier Leopold de Rothschild instructed the famous Hoyo de Monterrey factory in Havana to make a short cigar with a large ring size so that he could enjoy the richest flavor possible without having to take the time to smoke a full length cigar. As an aside, when the first Honduran-made cigars were brought into the United States after the Cuban embargo, it was Hoyo de Monterrey that reintroduced American smokers to the famous Rothschild shape. Today, the classic Rothschild (4½ x 52) is still being made, not only by the same Hoyo de Monterrey brand that originated it, but by countless other cigar companies as well, many of whom have sought to honor this century-plus old shape by giving it new names, such as Robustos (Davidoff), Romanos (Dunhill), Pluton (Pléiades) and Consul (Joya de Nicaragua). British-inspired shapes continued into the 20th century, when the Earl of Lonsdale commissioned Havana's Rafael Gonzales factory to create a special shape exclusively for him, with the Earl's portrait placed prominently on the inside label of the opened box. For a while, the new Rafael Gonzales Lonsdales were the most expensive cigars to come out of Cuba. Today, the Lonsdale still remains one of the most popular shapes among cigar smokers, whether they are titled or not. And the earl is im-

Often mistaken for pipes, these Victorian cheroot holders were extremely popular during the late 1800s. The cheroot holder on the right was specially made for Colt's Patent Firearms Company and is dated 1877.

mortalized by still having his photo and signature on the inside of every Rafael Gonzales lid.

Meanwhile, cigar making was gaining momentum in America, and aficionados like Civil War hero Ulysses S. Grant and humorous writer Mark Twain were helping to focus attention on both the Cuban and the American-made products. One-man cigar-making rooms and larger multilevel factories began springing up in almost every state in the Union. Many of these factories were built on an East-West line, so that the leaf graders and cigar rollers would always have northern light, just like an artist's studio. But many early American cigars were not always works of art. It wasn't until after 1875 that ongoing experimentation with improved strains of filler leaf began to give U.S. cigars a taste and a character of their own. Soon, the best U.S. tobaccos were coming from Pennsylvania, New York, Ohio, Wisconsin, Florida, and, of course, Connecticut.

With better tobaccos, American cigar making began to take on new momentum, aided by a steady flow of skilled immigrants from Cuba and Europe who had worked in cigar factories in their homelands. Seeking a new life in the New World, they were also helping to solidify a new American industry. Spain, now fearful of losing Cuba to American imperialism, unwittingly furthered the cause by creating a stranglehold of taxation, which resulted in the Cuban Revolution to free herself from Spanish rule. So intense were the atrocities committed by Spanish soldiers, thousands of Cubans fled their homeland en masse and sailed for the nearest shore, America. Or more specifically, Key West and Tampa, Florida, which soon became known as "Little Havana." Meanwhile, over in Europe, Otto von Bismarck's controversial plans for German unification caused many skilled printers to flee the Fatherland and head for America, where they brought their unparalleled skills of chromolithography, a technique that virtually revolutionized the cigar label business by permitting as many as 30 different colors to be printed on a single sheet (today, these early labels are highly collectable). Soon America's cigar-making centers were concentrated in New York and Florida, the two main entry ports of immigration.

By 1890, "Made in Tampa" had become a tremendous selling point for any U.S. cigar, as it was naturally assumed that only the most skilled Cuban workers were making cigars there. A Tampa-made cigar was almost the same as saying a Havana cigar. In fact, most American cigars were made with Havana tobacco, either used as filler with American wrapper and binder, or made with 100% imported Cuban leaf for wrapper, binder and filler, in what came to be called a "clear" (or totally Cuban leaf) Havana cigar.

A popular cigar-making subdivision of Tampa was Ybor City, which was started in 1885 by Vincente Martínez Ybor, a "free Cuba" sympathizer who was forced to flee to Florida during his country's revolution. By 1898, there were over 500 cigar factories in the Tampa, Ybor City, and Key West areas, and another 7,000 factories in the rest of the country. Indeed, America had become a cigar-making/smoking nation! At one point, the annual sale of cigars was used as an indicator of the country's economic condition: on October 9, 1899, a New York newspaper stated that "the rise in the sale of stogies, being a workingman's smoke," was proof that the economic depression of 1880-90 was over. As for Cuba, even the four-month long Spanish-American War of 1898 did not noticeably affect sales; although exportation of Havana cigars dipped by 25%, enough had been stockpiled during the embargo (yes, this was the *first* Cuban embargo) so that smokers did not even notice a shortage. However, the embargo of 1898 did force American cigar makers — who by now were buying practically all of the leaf and cigars that Havana was export-

A wooden Henry Clay cigar cabinet from the 19th century. Each cedar book slid out of the cabinet and opened to reveal an assortment of sizes.

8

ing — to start seriously considering another type of tobacco for their wrappers. Thus, the excellent quality of our homegrown Connecticut broadleaf finally came into its own.

During this time a good American-made cigar, using Havana leaf, cost five cents apiece, while an imported Havana cigar would set you back ten to fifteen cents each, depending on the brand and the size. On the other hand, you could still pick up a stogy for a penny. Of course, supply and demand had a big effect on costs, and during the Alaskan gold rush of 1898, a tobacco-starved man in Dawson paid $750 for a box of cigars that very likely were not the best.

By the early 20th century, the cigar store Indian had become a familiar figure in America. This one was photographed around 1907 in New York City.

photo: Herb Peck, Jr.

9

As it has done since its inception, the cigar was having its effect upon society. During the Victorian era it was generally considered impolite to smoke in public, and especially in front of women. In fact, in 1880, Boston passed a law prohibiting anyone from carrying a lit "seegar" on the city streets. Of course, this was not the first anti-smoking law, and it certainly would not be the last. Hence, the smoking room came into being, and it soon became a much-coveted ritual for the men to retire after dinner and partake of a good Havana and a glass of port while the ladies were left to their own endeavors.

An ardent cigar smoker, Edward, Prince of Wales (shown here in an 1875 photo), achieved everlasting fame upon his succession to the throne in 1901 by uttering his famous phrase, "Gentlemen, you may smoke."

photo: Swisher International

Although cigar smoking was immensely popular during Victorian times, it was publicly kept in the shadows, largely due to Queen Victoria's adamant disapproval with anything even remotely connected with tobacco. Thus, it was literally an enlightened world when her son, King Edward VII, uttered these now famous words in 1901, after his coronation: "Gentlemen, you may smoke." Small wonder that King Edward is still one of the most popular cigars in England, as the sense of history so prevalent in that country will not let them forget the sovereign who publicly lit the smoking lamp. But that gratitude was not confined to England alone; by 1940, King Edward was the number one selling cigar in the world.

Another immortal quote was made on American shores in January 1920, when Thomas Riley Marshall, Woodrow Wilson's witty Vice President, grew tired of listening to an oratory in the Senate about what America needed. "What this country needs," Marshall told the Senators, "is a really good five cent cigar." It is perhaps the plague of vice presidents throughout our country's history that they are often ignored. Consequently, although many people have quoted this line, few knew where it came from. Now you do.

Vice President Marshall got his wish; by 1921, five cents bought a quart of milk, a cold beer, or a good cigar. Unfortunately, the necessity of keeping cigars humidified was not universally recognized, and part of the reason Tampa cigars were so popular (in addition to their tobacco and construction) was the fact that Florida's humid climate kept them fresher than cigars that were made and shipped from inland locations. Tobacconists normally kept their cigars out in the open, in glass display cases so that customers could see the variety of brands and shapes that were stocked. Later, when electricity became widespread, sealed boxes were kept in a humidified storeroom, but single cigars were still sold "out front" from the cases. Back then, a good box of cigars cost anywhere from five to ten dollars.

One of the first companies to recognize the need for humidification and the importance of aging cigars was Alfred Dunhill of London, who opened his Duke Street store in 1907. After

Mass produced nostalgia — King Edward, Optimo, and Marsh Wheeling. Although the boxes have not changed since their inception, the cigars inside have all given way to machine manufacture and the use of homogenized leaf. King Edward remains the most popular cigar in England, Marsh Wheeling is the oldest, having started in 1840, and at one time Optimo was all-Havana.

11

arriving in England from Havana, most of the Dunhill cigars were aged in special cedar-lined "holding rooms" for a minimum of ten months before they were permitted to be sold to a customer. Later, in 1920, Dunhill began offering their cigars in hermetically sealed tins, which their catalog claimed was perfect for preserving the freshness of cigars for "...the Traveler, the Yachtsman or the Smoker resident abroad..." Dunhill also maintained "customer gift cabinets," containing anywhere from 500 to 3,000 Havana cigars. Those were the days when, if you got a gift like that, you knew who your friends were!

World War I had seriously impeded (but never stopped completely) the flow of Havanas to Europe. But America had a self-contained industry, as tobacco was grown and cigars were made right within our own country. However, after Armistice was declared, the cigar world was dealt a far more devastating blow by the growing popularity of cigarettes. Cigar sales began to decline in the 1920s as more and more people turned to the less expensive, mass-produced cigarette. Clearly, something had to be done to lower prices, increase production, and win back customers. Taking a clue from the cigarette factories, mechanization seemed to be the answer, and by the 1930s, the cigar-making machine was being adopted by many companies. Some firms, such as

The magnificent, Havana-filled maturing room at Dunhill's in London, circa 1928.

photo: Alfred Dunhill, Ltd.

British resolve was never more evident than on April 17, 1941, when Alfred Dunhill manned the "customer service" desk the day after his famous shop at 30 Duke Street was leveled in The Blitz. Although much of London lay in rubble, you could still buy cigars at Dunhills.

photo: Alfred Dunhill, Ltd.

Cigars were a favorite treat to send to U.S. troops during World War II. Here, a group of G.I.'s in the jungles of the South Pacific gather around a freshly opened box of King Edward cigars.

photo: Swisher International

Cuesta-Rey and Swisher, were pioneers in this endeavor and began producing machine-made cigars much earlier. (As an aside, the original cigar-making machine was invented by Oscar Hammerstein, grandfather of the famed lyricist of that same name.) The machine-made cigar was not an American phenomenon, however, for this technique was also being used in Europe. Quality did not suffer, for these were all-tobacco cigars, many of them still being made with Havana leaf. And production was increased; by the end of the 1920s, Jno. H. Swisher & Son, one of the largest cigar companies in the world, was turning out one hundred million cigars a year.

Tobacco was still relatively inexpensive, and with the new mechanized mass production in place, the price of cigars dropped just in time for the Great Depression. Cigars could now be purchased three for a nickel and boxes were being made out of cardboard instead of wood. Suddenly, almost everyone could afford at least one cigar a week, and the golden image of the elegant, sophisticated cigar smoker quickly tarnished and faded as it became a smoke for the everyday working man. Only the expensively handmade Havana still retained its attraction for the connoisseur.

But even the Havana cigar was not immune to the ravages of World War II. Cuba suddenly found itself unable to sell cigars to England, one of its biggest markets, because of a freeze on the U.S. dollar (Cuba's medium of exchange) by Great Britain. England, desperate for cigars, shifted its attention to Jamaica, a crown colony in the Caribbean. That meant the British pound sterling was legal tender. Although expensive, Jamaicans were the only full-sized cigars England could get. Otherwise they were limited to the small Dutch-type cigars made with tobaccos from Burma, India and Brazil, or a scattering of homegrown brands such as Carvallo, Manikin and King Six, produced by the few cigar-making companies in England. But the British have always been known as great cigar smokers, not cigar makers. The course was clear. Jamaican cigars soon came into vogue in Great Britain, not only during the war years, but afterwards as well. In fact, it wasn't until 1953 that England finally began importing Havana cigars again. Of course, this was the best thing that could have happened to the Jamaican cigar industry, which had been started by some entrepreneurial Cubans in the 1850s but had been languishing until now. Suddenly, brands like Temple Hall, El Caribe, and Flor del Duque were in the smoker's spotlight. In addition, a group of cigar makers from Cuba opened up new factories of their own in Jamaica (using Jamaican leaf for the filler and binder but importing real Havana for the wrapper), and kept them in operation until Castro forced them to get rid of their holdings after the revolution. Of all the original Cuban brands that were made in Jamaica during the war years, the only one still being made there today is Macanudo.

After World War II, things began to change, not only for the world at large, but for the world of cigars. Even after the importation of Havanas was resumed, many British smokers continued to appreciate the flavor of good Jamaican tobacco. In postwar America, the first cigar price rise occurred; they went up to ten cents, and then twenty-five cents apiece. The increased use of high speed machinery was tearing the delicate wrappers on some cigars, and homogenized tobacco leaf (HTL) began to be used on American-made cigars (even those still using Havana tobaccos), initially just for binders, but eventually for wrappers as well. The totally machine-made, mass-produced cigar had been created. Even Cuba, anxious to be competitive with the sudden appearance of these low cost products, began producing machine-made cigars of her own. This dramatic change in manufacturing literally cut the price of a Havana in half, and the smoker who agonized over buying a handmade Cuban cigar for seventy-five cents now found that he could buy a machine-made Havana for half that price. The average man could finally afford a Havana! This, more

By 1946, Winston Churchill had become one of the most visible cigar smokers in the world. With cigar in hand, he looks as if he is about to pause and inspect the boxes of "Churchills," being offered.

photo: Churchill Cigars, Switzerland

than anything else, is what made the Havana cigar popular in America.

Unfortunately, the American smoker's love affair with Cuban cigars was to be short-lived. The Cuban revolution started on July 26, 1953. Six years later, Fidel Castro came into power. Those who knew of his Communistic leanings foresaw trouble. But others did not. After all, America had supported Castro's overthrow of the Fulgencio Batista regime. And Havana tobacco was an integral, one hundred-year-old tradition in U.S. cigar making. For many, it was unthinkable that there should be any rift in American-Cuban relations. Still, those who read the newspapers knew that President Eisenhower was demanding an embargo. But it took President John F. Kennedy to pull it off.

In 1962, President Kennedy declared an embargo (which the Cubans continue to refer to as a blockade) on all imported Cuban goods. But twelve hours before he made that world famous announcement, he gave his press secretary Pierre Salinger orders to purchase one thousand H. Upmann Petit Coronas. Salinger went over and above the call of duty by actually rounding up twelve hundred of the small Cuban cigars for the chief executive.

By 1977, when this photo was taken, Fidel Castro was feeling the effects of the Cuban embargo, a political act that has dramatically changed the cigar industry today.

photo: David Hume Kennerly

16

The embargo caught many cigar makers and cigar smokers off guard. Havana tobacco, always inexpensive, suddenly soared in price. Prior to the embargo, Cuban-grown tobacco sold for $150 a bale. By the end of 1962, the price had shot up to over $1,000 a bale, when one could be found for sale. Panetela panic set in. Smokers snatched up what remaining stocks of Cuban cigars they could find. But some companies had planned ahead, and had stockpiled huge stores of Cuban leaf. As a result, for many years after the embargo it was still possible to purchase cigars made with Cuban tobacco. As late as 1971, I can remember buying Honduran Hoyo de Monterrey cigars that were still being made with pre-embargo Havana filler. This helped many companies survive the immediate post-embargo shock and gave them time to rethink their roles in the new era of the non-Havana cigar. And although the embargo destroyed a great many brands, it also helped build others. Bances suddenly became one of the most popular cigars in the country because, although it was made in Tampa, it was an all-Havana cigar, thanks to pre-embargo stockpiling by the company. Even today, Martinez y Cia Havana Blend cigars are being made with short-filler Cuban tobacco from 1959; originally the filler was 100% Havana, but with ever dwindling supplies, it has now dropped to 20%. Nonetheless, this modest brand remains one of the last Havana-filled cigars that can still be legally purchased in America.

But even back in 1962 everyone knew that what little stockpiled Havana tobacco there was among a few companies was not going to last forever. And an all-tobacco, long filler cigar that was made in America by hand would be much too expensive to produce. The low-wage, handcrafted days of the 19th century were long over. Cigar companies had to frantically search elsewhere. The same problem confronted many of the Cuban cigar-making families who were fleeing their homeland in the wake of Castro's socialized takeover of their properties and their industries. With Cuba closed off to the American market — previously the biggest customer for both leaf and cigars — where could the cigar makers go? The Spanish provinces of the Canary Islands, rising out of the Atlantic Ocean off the northwest coast of Africa, suddenly became the immediate mecca that many sought. Of course, there was no cigar tobacco grown there, but that didn't matter; tobacco could be shipped over from plantations already established in Jamaica, Honduras, and the Dominican Republic. More important was the fact that, since the 17th century, the people on the Canaries had been making cigars for Spain. The factories were already in place. The expertise was there. And the workers spoke

Spanish, so communications with the Cubans would be no problem. Thus, with the appearance of Montecruz, Don Diego, Don Marcos and later, the first non-Havana H. Upmann, was born the saga of the Canary Islands cigar, handmade on a rocky island that had to import its tobacco.

Cigar makers were also casting renewed and amorous glances across the waters towards Jamaica, which had the same lure of skilled workers and preexisting factories, but with the added charm that this country grew its own tobacco. In fact, it was Jamaica, with its ever-popular Macanudo, that eventually helped start the cigar maker's exodus away from the Canary Islands.

Other areas in the Caribbean were being courted as well. The Dominican Republic was especially alluring. The ancient Taino Indians of this vast and tropical island had been growing and smoking tobacco since B.C. (Before Columbus). Local cigars had been manufactured since 1902. And more recently, a thriving cigar-making industry had flourished in the village of Moca from 1930 until 1960. Many of the original workers from Cuba, as well as Central and South America, were still there. Many more had relocated to the nearby city of Santiago. But of even greater significance was the fact that the verdant Cibao Valley, bisected by the waters of the Rio del Yaqui del Norte, harbored some of the most fertile and productive soil for tobacco farming than any other area in the vicinity, with the possible exception of Cuba. In fact, the unmistakable quality of Dominican-grown tobacco was already finding favor and flavor in many of the Canary Islands cigars. The only problem was, the Dominican Republic, like so many of its Caribbean cousins, had a penchant for revolutions. With a charter membership in the Dictator of the Month club, it would be a problem trying to establish a new industry when the government itself was not established. Nonetheless, the modern day Dominican cigar started to become a reality by 1972. Today, with a democratically inclined government now proudly in place, the DR has become the world's leading producer of premium cigars, exporting more than eighty million handmade cigars a year (most of which go to the United States), and another eight million machine-made cigars.

With the rebirth of the cigar industry in the DR, coupled with the unfortunate timing of Spain pulling back on subsidies for tobacco products made on the Canary Islands, many cigar manufacturers began moving their operations to the Dominican Republic. But the DR wasn't the only gold nugget in the cigar industry's newly discovered Mother Lode. Off to the west, and in the same tropical temperate zone, lay Honduras. Like the Dominican Republic, Honduras had its share of unrest. But it also had a very unique quality of soil, an attribute that was apparent to tobacco growing experts who visited the mountainous jungles as early as 1960, when the possibilities of a Cuban revolution and a subsequent embargo were first being discussed. Consequently, by 1962 pioneers like tobacco expert Angel Olivas and cigar maker Frank Llaneza were combining their talents to produce cigars in Honduras, assisted by experienced expatriate Cubans eager to resume their trade. But for many years, the development of Honduran cigars was hobbled by a nationalistic law that forbade the use of anything other than Honduran tobacco. Fortunately, this shackle was cut in the mid-1970s. Thus, the full potential of the Honduran cigar was realized with the discovery that tobaccos from other parts of the world could grow, and grow well, in Honduran soil. The new rules also permitted tobaccos from other countries to be imported and used in the cigar-making process. A new government, realizing the importance of this burgeoning industry and receptive to the marketplace, established a free zone similar to ones that had already been set up in Jamaica and the DR, enabling cigars to be made for exportation without the hindrance of heavy taxation. The result is that today Honduran cigars can compete in quality and price with any cigar in the world. Moreover, they have their own distinctively rich taste that has made them the second most popular cigar in America, with more than fifty three million being exported annually, of which over thirty five million are high-grade premiums for the U.S. market.

On a lesser scale, but equally impressive in the excellence of its tobacco, Nicaragua holds the potential for producing some of the best cigars in the world. Specifically, the soil that straddles the borders of Nicaragua and Honduras is as close to the rich red earth of Cuba's Vuelta Abajo as anyone has seen. Unfortunately, political problems keep getting in the way of cigar progress. The 1979 revolution did not help much either, nor did the U.S. embargo of 1985—1990. And in spite of a new government and valiant attempts at trying to heal decades-old wounds, the recovery process in Nicaragua is painful. As an example, in Honduras I talked to a farmer who had burned his Nicaraguan tobacco crop rather than pay the Sandinistas the tax/protection money they demanded. A brave and noble thing to do, but this unfortunate situation caused everyone to lose: the farmer lost his crops, the cigar makers lost badly-needed premium tobacco, and you and I lost what very probably could have been some very excellent cigars. Hopefully, this situation will change with the government's establishment of the Nicaraguan Tobacco Corporation in 1993 and its employee-owned factories. After all, there is plenty of good tobacco-growing land that only has to be cleared and planted. And there is an abundance of rollers, with pioneering cigar making families like Padrón and Placentia to help show the way. Six new privately owned factories were started in 1996 alone. But most of the tobacco is controlled by Tabacalera Agro Industrial de Nicaragua (TAINS), S.A., a government monopoly. (For additional background, see Joya de Nicaragua in Chapter 9.) Nonetheless, cigars like the new Joya de Nicaragua, MiCubano and Padrón have clearly demonstrated the excellence that this country is capable of producing. But with less than four million cigars produced in 1995, Nicaragua still has a long way to go.

Up until the mid-70s, most of the cigars being made in these "newly discovered" countries by Cuban exiles were purposely given new names (see Chapter 9 for specifics on your favorites), as it was assumed that when the cigar makers left Cuba, they forfeited the use of their original Havana brands, which were now being made by the Castro regime.

But in 1975, in a landmark case involving ownership of the Upmann name, the U.S. courts ruled that many of the cigar-making families and former owners of the Havana factories still retained the U.S. rights to the brand names they had either inherited or purchased prior to Castro's takeover. From that moment on, we began to see a reemergence of what has since been called the "exile brands" — famous name cigars that are still being made in Havana, but are now being made in other countries as well. Which is why today we have both Cuban and Dominican versions of Romeo y Julieta, H. Upmann, and Partagas, for example, and Cuban-Honduran pairings of famous name brands like Hoyo de Monterrey, El Rey del Mundo, and Punch. This dilemma is made substantially less confusing for consumers by the fact that no competing "exile brands" are allowed to be sold alongside Cubatabaco's products. In Switzerland, for example, you will not see a Cuban Por Larrañaga and a Dominican Por Larrañaga being sold side by side. The Dominican brand would never be permitted into that country. However, the Dominican brand could simply change its name while keeping the same filler-binder-wrapper blend. Thus, while the Honduran Punch cigar cannot be sold alongside the Havana brand with that same name, the Honduran-made San Pedro Sula is the exact same cigar with just a different name. Hence, it now qualifies for

European sales and is one of the top non-Havana cigars currently being sold in Germany.

Of course, this dual-nationality of identical cigar brands is entirely academic for American smokers, as entire generations have now grown up never having seen or smoked a Havana cigar. But many Europeans, especially those who travel to the U.S. and have access to both Havana and non-Havana versions of the same brand, sometimes find the situation confusing and have to be careful in what they buy. Just glancing at the label isn't always enough, as identical artwork is used by both the non-Havana factories and Cubatabaco on boxes and bands. Only special stampings on the box (as we shall discuss in Chapter 4), the word "Habana," and of course, the price (non-Havana cigars are noticeably less expensive than Havanas) can properly identify which cigar is from what country without actually lighting one up and tasting the difference. But even taste is not the ultimate test, for many of today's finest Dominican and Honduran cigars often equal or surpass some of the present-day Cuban products.

Unfortunately, this was not always the case; in the 1970s the quality of some Dominican and Canary Islands cigars began to suffer as factories relocated to different countries, and problems with workers and poor harvests manifested themselves on tobacconists' shelves. Moreover, a number of Third World companies would occasionally make a limited run of cigars, give it a Spanish-sounding name, and sell it to an anxious importer in the United States. The problem was, if you liked that cigar, you could never find it again. This situation still occurs today, with alarming frequency, due to the ever-accelerating cigar boom. But today's experienced cigar smoker is usually much more selective in choosing a brand that has staying power, and in today's highly competitive world, nobody wants to lose a customer.

By the 1980s cigar smoking had dipped from its heyday in 1964 when the Surgeon General's Report first told people it was healthier to light up a Corona than a cigarette. In that year alone, cigar sales jumped from 7.2 billion to 9 billion units. But other notable things — besides the embargo and a favorable health report for cigars — were happening in that fateful decade. In the late 1960s Dunhill had reintroduced their own brand of Havanas for the European market, and that *grand maître* of sophisticated smoking, Zino Davidoff, had been granted permission by Cubatabaco to start his own brand of exclusive Havanas. But by the end of the '80s, the romance with Cuba was over for both companies. It all began in 1989, when Cubatabaco abruptly canceled their contracts with every exporting firm with which they did business. New rules were suddenly imposed, whereby Cubatabaco insisted on a 51% ownership with anyone who imported their cigars. With the cost of Havanas rising almost yearly, it was felt that Cuba was not getting its fair share of the market price. In addition, Cuba was adopting a new policy of no longer making other people's cigars. With farmland at a premium, they wanted to preserve their limited supply of precious tobacco for their own brands.

Dunhill responded by amicably phasing out their line of Havanas, and concentrating solely on their newly introduced aged Dominicans for the world market. The Davidoff organization was a little more dramatic. On Wednesday, August 23, 1989, headlines in newspapers around the globe screamed that Davidoff, long a champion of Havana's finest, had just voluntarily burned 130,000 of their Cuban cigars — roughly three million dollars' worth. A lack of quality was the reason given. The cigars were no longer fit to bear the Davidoff band. Thus emerged a new line of Davidoff Dominicans and Zino Hondurans, which freed up even more precious Havana leaf for Cubatabaco. Still, both Davidoff and Dunhill retained huge pre-1989 inventories of their Cuban cigars. When visiting the Davidoff warehouses in Basil, Switzerland in 1989, I mentally inventoried what I estimated to be a three-year supply. When meeting with Cubatabaco in 1992, I learned that, even though there were still a few Davidoff Havanas left on the island, by contractual agreement none could be sold after December 31, 1992.

Aside from the dissolution of these two famous Cuban brands, which did much to draw the cigar connoisseur's attention to the excellence of the Dominican product, the 1980s were noticeable for one other questionable hallmark in the annals of cigar smoking. After almost five centuries, "health warnings" were finally mandated in America for cigars. George Burns, who outlived the doctor who told him to give up his El Productos, must have laughed. And so must have the spirits of other long time cigar smokers, such as Don Arturo Fuente, founder of the company that bears his name, who smoked twenty-five cigars a day and lived to be eighty-five years old. Oh yes, one more thing happened in the 1980s: Castro stopped smoking. Which no doubt freed up even more Havana tobacco for the sixty million cigars Cuba was now exporting annually.

The 1990s have not been kind to Cuba. The collapse of Russia left the island, never truly prosperous in recent times, in economic chaos. Today, everything is rationed, including food, clothing, and gasoline. And while there are ration coupons, there are no goods to exchange them for. Vegetables are available at the agro-market, but they carry a premium price due to their scarcity. Beef is a government controlled monopoly. Moreover, Cuban people are only permitted to have one roll of toilet paper a month, and one box of matches. And one small cigar, a subspecies of Havana that is loosely rolled and harsh tasting, hardly fit for smoking, let alone exportation. Ironically, some people in Cuba are actually able to save money because there is nothing to spend it on. Naturally, a thriving black market exists for all the necessities of life, including cigars. Once, while walking the streets of Havana, I was stopped by a young boy on a bicycle who offered me a box of Bolivars at a fantastically reduced price. Of course, I had no way of ascertaining that these really were Bolivars, and not some left-over leaf cuttings that someone had stolen from the floor of the cigar factory's warehouse and then rolled in a back room by candlelight. But the most interesting thing about this encounter is that it took place right outside of the Cubatabaco offices. Needless to say, the Cubatabaco official who was with me at the time was highly embarrassed.

Even in good times, Cuba has always had a problem being able to supply enough leaf to meet world demands. In the 1980s, Cuba was exporting 90 million cigars. By the early '90s that num-

The Partagas factory in downtown Havana.

23

ber had dropped to 60 million handrolled cigars (with an additional 20 million machine made cigars being exported). By 1996, the number of handrolled cigars had only risen slightly. And up until recently, a great many acres of their coveted tobacco farms have been converted to growing more food for a starving nation. However, realizing that cigars were now their fourth most important export, in 1991 an additional 17,000 acres of tobacco were planted in the Vuelta Abajo, a 17% increase over the 1990 acreage. This translated into more emphasis on wrapper leaf, which, after harvesting and aging, would not be ready until 1994. But then came Hurricane Andrew in 1992, which virtually destroyed many of Cuba's precious aging barns full of the winter harvest of tobacco, which was scheduled for cigars that were to be made through 1996. To compound the available tobacco problem, Cuba is now selling Havana leaf to other countries, such as Germany and Austria, for the manufacture of Havana cigars in Europe. In Germany, the best examples are the machine-made Saint Luis Rey and Romeo y Julieta small cigars and cigarillos, which are made of 100% imported Havana leaf. Havana cigars are also being produced in Australia, as well as in Canada, where a machine-made all-Havana Bances is made for that nation only.

The world still has an almost insatiable thirst for the coveted Havana cigar. In spite of all of Cuba's internal problems, Havana cigar sales were up by 26% in 1994 when compared to 1993, with foreign sales bringing in more than $100 million per year. To help in their marketing efforts, in 1994 Cubatabaco turned the responsibility of their foreign sales over to Habanos S.A., a private company. Cubatabaco, however, has decided to retain control of all sales in Spain, Britain, and France, the three largest markets for Havana cigars. It is interesting to note that of an annual production of approximately sixty million cigars, ten million of them are estimated to end up in the U.S., where they are illegal. Of course, these are not always of the best quality, and many of them are rolled outside of the five government-controlled factories (be sure to see the section on counterfeits in Chapter 4).

Because of the ongoing problem of not being able to get enough Cuban cigars to meet demand, some countries, like England, Germany and France, are starting to import cigars from the Dominican Republic, Honduras, and Nicaragua. This becomes significant when one realizes that France alone imports 7.2 million Havanas a year. But now, alongside the Bolivars, Quinteros and Quai d'Orsays, for example, there are cigars from Fuente, La Aurora, Joya de Nicaragua, Juan Clemente, and of course, Pléiades.

Germany, by comparison, only imports approximately one million Cuban cigars (not counting those sold in duty-free shops and the small German-made Havana leaf cigars). But in what is becoming a European trend, Germany is also gradually becoming familiar with the Caribbean product, and her one million cigar smokers are starting to become acquainted with the likes of Dunhill, Henry Clay, Royal Jamaica, Excalibur (a slightly revised nomenclature for the Honduran-made Hoyo de Monterrey so as not to be confused with the Havana cigar of that same name), and the Dominican cigars of John Aylesbury. In England, long the Havana stronghold, cigars like the DR's Santa Damiana and San Pedro Sula (a renamed Honduran Punch) are making their appearances, as are bundle cigars. And of course, we must not forget the United Kingdom's own premium Dominican brand, Dunhill.

This is not to imply that the Havana cigar is losing favor in England and Europe. Far from it. The Havana is still looked upon as *the* cigar for connoisseurs. But there are problems. For example, in September 1992 the Appellate Court of Paris issued a ruling that forbade Cuba from selling some of its most popular brands — Montecristo, H. Upmann, and Por Larrañaga — in France. Cubatabaco responded by substituting their Fonseca, La Gloria Cubana, Rafael Gonzales and Rey del Mundo cigars, but French connoisseurs wanted their old brands back. Many of them crossed the border to buy their favorites, especially the best-selling Montecristo. But many more did not, with the end result that since 1993, Havana sales have slipped dramatically in France. In the summer of that same year, a similar situation occurred in Spain, which again resulted in the withdrawal of some of Cuba's most popular cigars from their number one marketplace. To fill this void, Dominican and Honduran cigars are gradually making inroads. An additional lure is the fact that these non-Havana cigars cost substantially less than their Cuban counterparts. Consequently, a serious cigar smoker on the Continent may now elect to light up a Dominican-made cigar during the week, while saving Saturday night for a Havana, which, by the very nature of its higher price, is smoked sparingly. Even in England, where 30% of cigar smokers favor Havanas, average consumption is only twenty-five Cuban cigars a year, due to the exorbitant tax-inflated price. And these are mainly smoked after a special dinner and at Christmas, a traditional cigar-smoking holiday in the U.K. The rest of the time, the cigar of choice will be the small dry Dutch cigars. So the humidified non-Havana cigar is a new venture, as it looks like a Havana but doesn't taste like a Havana. To be sure, there is a definite education of the palate that most Europeans must go through when first smoking Dominican, Honduran, and Nicaraguan cigars, as each country's tobacco has its own distinctive flavor.

Unfortunately, in America — as in certain parts of England and Europe — prejudicial laws have taken away much of the impromptu pleasures of enjoying a favorite cigar whenever and wherever we want. No longer can we nonchalantly light up a Churchill after dinner in a restaurant to soothe the gastronomic juices. Nor can we casually puff on an elegantly shaped Lonsdale as we stroll through most shopping malls. Smoking in office buildings is now forbidden. Even lighting up on the city streets is more than likely to garner a wrathful gaze from some rude anti-smoker. And as unfathomable as it may have seemed just a few years ago, in many cities today you may not smoke a cigar in an open-air sports arena!

Many Europeans are shocked that the United States, the beacon of individual freedom, has such vehement anti-smoking restrictions. Conversely, among Americans there is the erroneous belief that Europeans are totally free of the rabid anti-smoking paranoia that has plagued the United States for so long. Unfortunately, this is far from being true. In 1990, the French Parliament banned all smoking in public places. Three years later they banned tobacco advertising. This, of course, was in direct violation of the Rights of Man, which was sanctified for all time (or so it was thought) by the French Revolution in 1789. Not to be outdone, England took a giant step backwards in 1990 by copying the Americans and demanding that a health warning be put on all of their cigars, Havanas or otherwise. And in 1991 they, too, banned all forms of tobacco advertising from the airwaves. The X Generation will never know what it was like to see Edie Adams holding a Muriel cigar in her delicate hand while her sultry voice invited us to "pick one up and smoke it sometime." Even Cuba now has anti-smoking laws.

I find it unbelievably ironic that cigars are maligned — or at best, ignored — by the very countries that they have helped to promote and to prosper. As an example, some of the most popular Dominican Republic tour books do not even mention the great cigar-making industry of that beautiful island republic. But perhaps now that this book is being read throughout the cigar smoking world, this gross oversight will be corrected, and the historic cigar-making industries of the Caribbean and Central America, as well as Mexico, Holland and other areas of the globe, will finally get the recognition they deserve.

Of course, cigar smokers are no strangers to prejudice and discrimination, as our noble pastime continues to be irresponsibly lumped into the general category of "smoking" by a misinformed media and government mis-representatives, oblivious to the fact that cigar smokers do not inhale, and that the product contains only *natural* tobaccos with no chemical additives. In an era of environmental awareness, has anybody ever mentioned that cigars are biodegradable? Nor is there any official acknowledgement on the part of medical science as to the very real benefits of a good cigar after a bad day. As it is, nonsmokers are already befuddled by the fact that a great number of premium cigars are being smoked by many of the same people who exercise, drink bottled water, and watch what they eat. But then, who else but another cigar smoker could possibly realize that a cigar can both stimulate the brain and relax the body at the same time.

"It's mental health, there's no doubt about it," says David A. Boska, M.D., a physician whose list of cigar-smoking patients encompasses numerous entertainment and sports celebrities, as well as government officials, including John F. Kennedy when he was President. "Cigar smoking is a very pleasurable thing," the doctor says. "You don't get hooked on it like you do with some relaxant drugs, which usually don't last very long anyway. It takes a while to smoke a cigar. And gratification is instantaneous. I also happen to think that group therapy is very beneficial if you happen to have a few friends that you like to smoke a cigar with."

Perhaps that helps explain the sudden resurgence of the Victorian Smoker, an event that started in 19th century England to create a safe haven for cigar connoisseurs, where they could escape the wrath of nonsmokers and enjoy their tobacco in peace. The Gentleman's Smoker (although more and more women are attending, I am happy to report) or "cigar night" as it is often called, has become a national trend in America, with such events occurring at least once a month (and often more) in virtually every major U.S. city. Some of these smokers have become legendary, such as the elegant black tie affairs held at the Ritz-Carlton hotels and the celebrity sports-smokers of the Friar's Club of California. I am often asked to be a speaker at these events, to audiences that range from fifty to one hundred and fifty people. This cigar smoking phenomena has not reached such epidemic proportions in Europe yet, but they are starting to catch on in countries such as England, Switzerland and France, as more and more people discover the joys and camaraderie of smoking good cigars with good friends. A Smoker is simply a gathering of cigar

27

aficionados who share an appreciation of life and all that it can be. These Smokers can be either formal or informal, and often center around a dinner, or a wine, bourbon or cognac tasting. Often times they serve as fundraisers for charities. Or they can merely be a simple gathering of friends with gently swirling clouds of blue-grey smoke as the only common bond necessary. Very often a local tobacconist will have a Smoker to introduce a new cigar. Or a sympathetic restaurant owner will organize a Smoker on an "off night." You don't really need a purpose to have a Smoker. All you need are a few people and a lot of cigars. Whatever the reason, the unbelievable number of special "cigar nights" that has now established itself as part of our culture is ample proof that we, as cigar lovers, are not alone.

And indeed we're not. Although anti-smokers are quick to point out that total cigar sales have dropped from nine billion in 1964 to 2.3 billion in 1992, the majority of this decline was (and continues to be) in the area of mass market, machine-produced cigars. Quite conversely, ever since 1975 there has been a steady rise in the number of premium cigar smokers who have been dis-

David A. Boska, M.D., believes in the medicinal benefits of a good cigar.

28

covering this old/new pastime that Victorian and Edwardian gentlemen knew so well. Today, premium cigar sales are increasing by 40% annually in the United States, with 132 million of these high-grade cigars sold in 1992 alone. In that same year, cigar sales totaled more than $705 million. By 1995 that figure had risen to $780 million. In 1992 there were 8 million cigars smokers in the U.S., more than 405,000 of whom were smokers of premium cigars. By 1995 those numbers had climbed to over a million smokers of premium cigars. Clearly, premium cigars are on the rise, a situation that was dramatically acknowledged in the U.S. by the appearance in 1992 of an upscale lifestyle magazine called *Cigar Aficionado* and in 1994 by the publication in Switzerland of an elegant German language magazine entitled *Cigar*. There is also the information-packed Austrian magazine *Cult-Cigar-Journal* and from France *L'Amateur de Cigares*. September of 1995 saw a bold new American magazine, entitled *Smoke* and in April 1996 a French magazine entitled *Cigar Passion* made its debut. Obviously, cigar smoking is starting to be recognized as playing an important role in the modern man's everyday life.

But not just men. Women, too, are now exploring this former male-only bastion. They are attracted to cigars for the same reasons: enjoyment and relaxation from the daily stress of life. But there is another element of cigar smoking that is unique to women: By learning to correctly smoke and appreciate a good cigar, they find that they are on an equal level with men. This can prove invaluable for businesswomen and others who must interact with their male counterparts on a regular basis. On a personal note, it also helps women understand and appreciate a man's fascination with cigars. Thus, communication and understanding between the two sexes is enhanced. And the ranks of cigar smokers are increased even more.

Pulitzer-prize winning cartoonist Jeff MacNelly often gets a good word in for his fellow cigar smokers via his syndicated comic strip, "Shoe."

And yet, while the number of premium cigar smokers continues to multiply, the number of premium cigars does not always follow the same percentages of increase. The reason, of course, is that today's cigar connoisseur is only consuming an average of three cigars a day, far less than our counterparts of even a few years ago. The obvious conclusion: we are smoking less but smoking better cigars and enjoying them more.

In retrospect, the Cuban embargo was the best thing that could have happened to the cigar smoker of today, not only in America, but throughout the world. Directly or indirectly, it has enabled us to discover the enjoyment of cigars that might otherwise never have existed: the mildness of a Connecticut wrapped Dominican, the spicy fullness of a Sumatra cloaked Honduran, the rich, sweet earthiness of a Havana, or the heavy undertaste of a Mexican Maduro. In addition, both new brands and old have fostered further refinements, such as the appearance of carefully aged vintage cigars, the creation of smaller shapes for those moments that do not always lend themselves to a lingering smoke, and the welcomed trend towards bigger ring sizes for fuller flavor. Moreover, prices of premium cigars, although relatively high in comparison with mass market cigars, are comparatively inexpensive when judged against the pleasures they provide. Just as it did back in the 1920s, a good cigar can still cost as much as a quart of milk or a bottle of imported beer. Besides, where else can you buy up to an hour's worth of peace and relaxation for so little money?

Just prior to the publication of this book, a reporter from ABC News asked me to comment on the phenomena of this tremendous new increase in cigar smoking. It was an easy question to answer: The world we have created — or that has been created for us — is a much more hectic place to live than it ever has been before, filled with stress, problems with our lives, our jobs, the economy, and the environment. We are all looking for a haven, a fortress where we can be free — even momentarily — from the dragons and demons that we must fight daily. The cigar has become that fortress, a sanctified place in time where we can regroup our internal forces. With just a single cigar, we can escape from the cares of the world.

That is the beauty of cigar smoking. That is the legacy we have inherited, and the secret of life that we all hold.

Chapter 2

Cigar Making:
From Seedling To Cedar

One of the more fascinating things about cigar making is that its basic art of construction has not changed in well over one hundred years. That is why a handrolled cigar is the perfect complement for those of us who appreciate the artistry of hand craftsmanship. Even machine-made cigars must still rely on various degrees of hand labor. Premium cigars however, are an anomaly, for even though each one is individually made by hand, we do not want them to be different. If anything, we want them to be the same. To fully understand the intricacies of a good cigar, we must first go to the very roots of cigar making. And those roots literally emanate from the tobacco plant itself.

Each geographic area in which a tobacco seed is planted will give that plant — and the subsequent leaves that ultimately end up as a cigar — a very unique and distinct characteristic. That is why a Honduran cigar tastes different from a Dominican cigar which tastes different from a Havana. However, given the world as a whole, there are extremely few areas that have the perfect combination of soil, temperature and rainfall to produce a tobacco crop worthy of making a high-grade cigar. Most of these micro-climates are in the Caribbean or in the nearly identical latitudinal regions of Mexico and Central America.

Certainly one of the most famous tobacco growing and cigar-making areas today is the Dominican Republic, a fascinating island paradox that is home to both the 10,000 foot high Pico Duarte mountain and the crocodile infested Lago Enriquillo which lies 144 feet below sea level. It is a land where they produce cigars worthy of an emperor's humidor, and yet the government periodically — and without warning — shuts down the power system to entire areas of the country in order to conserve electricity. Consequently, the large scale Fuente factory, for example, has

CIGAR TOBACCO: Primary Growing Regions

learned to keep a diesel generator with 20,000 gallons of fuel on standby at all times, so that their cigar making operations will not be interrupted.

In the Dominican Republic, which produces the majority of the world's premium cigars today, there are just two fertile valleys for tobacco, the Real, which was named by Columbus and means "Royal" in Spanish, and the Cibao. These valleys, which posses a variety of soil textures, yield two of the most luxurious, long leaf filler tobaccos ever rolled into a cigar. Specifically, they are Olor Dominicano (a native Dominican seed), and Piloto Cubano, a strain that originated with precious Cuban seed that was transported to the DR by cigar makers fleeing Castro. Thus, when you hear about "Dominican-grown Cuban seed," or "Cuban seed Dominican tobaccos," they are referring to Piloto Cubano. There is also a lesser quality Virginian tobacco grown in the Dominican, but this is mainly used for local consumption and doesn't apply to high-grade cigars.

Ironically, up until 1993, the incredibly rich growing areas of the Dominican Republic only produced filler and binder. And for the most part, there is still no major supply of Dominican

CIGAR TOBACCO: Primary Growing Regions
*No cigar tobacco is grown here. For location only.

wrapper, as the right combination of soil and seed has yet to be found on a continuing basis. That is why most brands made in this famous tobacco-growing country must import their wrappers from other areas, such as Connecticut in the USA, Cameroon from Africa, and with growing frequency, Java and Sumatra from Indonesia. The quest for a Dominican-grown wrapper goes back to the 1980s, when there were attempts by General Cigar Corporation to grow Connecticut seed wrapper in the Dominican for some of its flagship brands. Unfortunately, this exercise did not prove commercially viable. However, in 1992, I witnessed the first experimental planting of Cuban seed wrapper in the Cibao Valley by the Arturo Fuente family. This historic moment was captured in the photo you see elsewhere in this chapter, showing 35 to 45 day old seedlings being planted in the fields. Of course, no one knew it was going to be an historic moment at the time. But as it happened, 1992-93 was an especially good growing season in the DR, and even though some plants were lost in heavy winter rains, enough were saved to eventually create excellent rosado wrappers that have since become the Fuente Fuente Opus X, the first Dominican cigar that can finally be called a "puro." That is, a cigar in which the filler, binder and wrapper are all grown within the borders of a single country.

To the west, across the Caribbean Sea, is Honduras, second largest producer of non-Havana premium cigars in the world. A rugged country, with jagged, prehistoric-looking mountains covered with jungle, one would not be surprised to encounter the outlaw inhabitants of Jurassic Park roaming this tropical wilderness. Only 16% of the land is cultivated, but it is here that some of the world's richest tobacco is grown, primarily in the Jagua and La Entrada valleys. Yet it has only been fairly recently that Honduran cigar makers have been allowed to grow and import tobaccos that are not native to this land of the Mayan civilization. Thus, we are now able to enjoy rich Honduran cigars whose flavor is given additional subtleties with wrappers, binders, and fillers from other countries.

Honduras' sometimes argumentive neighbor to the south is Nicaragua, the largest republic in Central America (roughly as big as England and Wales combined), a land of volcanos and other eruptions of an even more violent nature. In Nicaragua there are two fertile valleys, the Jalapa and Esteli, where some of the world's most exquisite filler, binder and wrapper are grown. This area is located near the Nicaraguan-Honduran border, and possesses soil that many farmers say is as close to Cuban earth as you can get without going to Cuba. That is why, when

Nicaraguan and Honduran cigars are good, they are very good. Therefore, it is frustrating to realize that there are some potentially fantastic tobacco growing regions in Nicaragua that cannot be cultivated because of ongoing tensions in the area. Hopefully, this situation will soon change.

Mexico also has areas capable of producing some excellent tobaccos. Perhaps the most famous is the valley of San Andrés Tuxtla, located in the State of Veracruz, southeast of Mexico City and one hundred miles south of Veracruz Port, on the Gulf of Mexico side of the country (I tell you all this in case, after smoking a Cruz Real down to the band and tossing back a few Herradura Añejo tequila "shooters," you suddenly become inspired to visit the birthplace of your cigar). Here you'll find the oldest cigar factory in Mexico, La Prueba de Balsa Hermanos, which was started in 1852. Cigar tobacco is also grown on the Pacific side of the country, in the neighboring state of Oaxaca's Valle Nacional. To the north, in Guadalajara, is the well known Ornelas factory. Another tobacco growing region is in Nayaret, near the coast above Puerto Vallarta. Mexico is noted for its superb binder leaf, as well as producing a sturdy and spicy wrapper that lends itself ideally for Maduro. Of course, the country grows filler tobaccos as well. And it is a good thing they do, for the government requires all cigars to be made of 100% Mexican grown leaf, although a new law may eventually permit Havana cigars to be made in Mexico for the first time in history.

Although the United States produces tobacco in numerous areas of the country, two of its most celebrated crops come from Connecticut, specifically, the Housatonic Valley region. Here, the finest shade wrapper (100 acres), and broadleaf (800 acres) is grown, and a comparison of these two acreages will give you the ratios of both tobaccos for an enthusiastic world market. Because of the unique sandy soil in this one area, Connecticut shade-grown wrapper has an unforgettable taste that has never been duplicated in any other part of the world, not even in Cuba, where the seeds have now been planted on an ongoing basis. The entire growing area of the Connecticut River Valley, which stretches from Hartford north to the Massachusetts state line, possesses a two-mile wide strip of incredibly rich topsoil, deposited there centuries ago by an ever-narrowing river. Because of the richness of this farmland, Connecticut shade has become one of the most popular wrappers in modern times.

In spite of all these excellent tobacco growing regions, the fantastically fertile island of Cuba, the largest in the West Indies, continues to shine like a star jewel in the cigar maker's crown.

Located just ninety miles south of Florida, Cuba has maintained its reputation as the ultimate cigar producing country since the days of Columbus. In fact, through the years, the resilient lore of the Cuban cigar has managed to survive catastrophes both natural and manmade, including wars, diseases, and embargoes. Just what is it that makes the legendary cigars from this particular island so unique? It is not the cigar makers or the factories, for I have seen equally skilled workers — many of them exiled Cuban cigar makers themselves — in both the Dominican and Honduras. And I have seen much more modern cigar-making facilities in other parts of the world. Nor is it the weather, for many famous cigar-making countries have identical climates, with an abundance of warm, humid, sunlit days and cool, breezy nights. Besides, you can always train or hire experienced cigar rollers. And the weather can change. But not the soil. And therein lies the main secret of the Cuban mystique. There is no other place that has such an abundance of coarse, rich red earth (although Ecuador, Honduras, and one small valley in the Dominican Republic come extremely close). It is the soil that provides the final ingredient in the magic elixir that gives Cuba the perfect ecosystem for tobacco.

The Four Tobacco Growing Areas Of Cuba

The Pinar del Rio province of Vuelta Abajo produces the best wrapper, binder and filler, and is the only area in Cuba where all three types of tobacco can be grown. The Havana Province in the Partido region only produces wrappers. Santa Clara Province in the Remedios region (which is also called Vuelta Arriba) grows 95% filler and 5% wrapper. In the Oriente Province, only filler is grown, although some of this leaf is classified as binder.

When one speaks of Cuban tobacco the words "Vuelta Abajo" usually give most knowledgeable aficionados a sudden rush of adrenalin. This one area, an abundantly lush valley located on the western end of the island, is world renowned for its shade grown wrapper and filler, the two most taste dominant tobaccos in any cigar. But there are three other well established growing regions in Cuba besides the constantly spotlighted Vuelta Abajo. Moving from west to east along the island, they are: Partido, which also grows filler and a very excellent wrapper (although not as good as that in the Vuelta Abajo); Remedios, in the central part of Cuba, which grows filler and binder; and two sections of Oriente on the easternmost section, both of which also grow filler and binder. However, of these four tobacco producing regions, only the Vuelta Abajo is capable of growing crops for all three ingredients of a cigar: wrapper, filler, and binder. Even if the same Cuban seeds were planted elsewhere on the island, the harvested tobaccos would not be of the quality that this one microclimate is capable of producing. At one time, the topsoil of the Vuelta Abajo, particularly in the Pinar del Rio area, was over two feet deep.

It is a little known fact that in the years just prior to the embargo, most of the Havana leaf that was being exported to the U.S. for stateside cigar making was taken only from the Remedios area. Cuba kept the high-grade Vuelta Abajo tobaccos for their own brands. That helped establish the mystique of the Havana-made cigar, and is the reason why the taste of a good handmade long-leaf Havana has never been duplicated outside of Cuba. (However, it should be pointed out that there are certain machine-made Cuban brands now being manufactured in other countries, such as Germany and Canada, using carefully selected imported Havana tobacco.) It should also be mentioned that, in the past, all Cuban filler, binder and wrapper tobacco was sungrown, but today the wrapper leaf is almost all shade grown. Which is another reason why a Havana cigar made today does not taste anything like the pre-Castro cigars of yesteryear.

But whether grown under sun or shade, today the demand for filler, binder and wrapper leaf grown in the fertile farmlands of the Vuelta Abajo has never been greater. Therefore, on a visit to this legendary area, it was somewhat reassuring to discover that, even with Cuba's faltering economy, when more and more land is — at best — being rotated between tobacco and food crops, this one naturally enhanced section is being preserved for tobacco as much as possible.

Of course, there are other noteworthy areas in the world that are famous for their tobaccos. Ecuador, because of its almost perpetual cloud cover, produces some of the finest natural shade grown wrappers in recent history. The subtle spiciness of Cameroon comes from the foggy, humid regions of west Africa (although Cameroon seed is now also being grown in other countries as well). It makes a thin but very flavorful wrapper, the supply of which, unfortunately, is rapidly becoming almost non-existent due to internal problems within its native country. And of the Cameroon that is grown, less than 7% is suitable for the manufacture of premium cigars. Which brings the focus for a replacement leaf to Indonesia, a nation made up of more than 13,000 islands, of which less than 6,000 of them are populated. Although rice is Indonesia's main agricultural crop, it may soon be overtaken by tobacco if cigars sales continue at their present acceleration. From the fog-carpeted valley floors beneath Mt. Bromo in Java, to Sumatra, a large island in the western part of Indonesia, come delicious wrapper leaves that are now used for both humidified and non-humidified (i.e., Dutch-type) cigars. Another popular region for both "wet" and "dry" cigars is Brazil (mainly in Bahía). Other popular cigar tobaccos come from Jamaica (which grows filler and binder but no wrapper) and the Philippines, with lesser known regions, including India and China, scattered throughout the world.

The largest tobacco growing area in China is near Qujing City, in the Yunnan Province. Although tobacco has been grown in that country before, it was more or less a dormant industry for cigars until recently. China started renewed tobacco planting operations in 1942, but did not start opening up its product to the outside world until 1988. Much of their government controlled tobaccos are flue-cured and used for cigarettes, but, recognizing the growing importance of the worldwide cigar market, the Chinese are now producing a mild and very sweet tasting cigarillo. Whether any of these Chinese cigars will ever become a European or American staple remains to be seen, but it is an interesting trend for international cigar smokers to follow. Wouldn't it be ironic if it took a cigar to finally break down the trade barriers and bring the east and the west together?

No matter where in the world tobacco is grown, everything starts with the seed and the soil. Inasmuch as the world's most popular cigars come from the Dominican Republic, Honduras, and Cuba, let's follow the life of a typical cigar (I realize that's a paradox, as no cigar is really typical) in any of these three countries, from seedling to cedar box.

First, it is important to realize that the tobacco seed determines the size, color, texture and type of plant you will get, while the soil and the climate are what create the taste, aroma, ash color (as we'll discuss in Chapter 4), and burning qualities of the end product. That is why *where* the tobacco is planted is just as important as how it is planted.

Life for a budding cigar begins in September and October, when the pinhead-sized tobacco seeds are first planted in protected, transportable trays or beds. It takes approximately 45 days for the seeds to mature enough to be transplanted in the fields. During this initial growth period, the seedlings are carefully watched over and nurtured by the farmers, much as a nanny guards her youngsters in a nursery. Ironically, cigar smoking is not permitted around the tiny tobacco plants, for fear that a virus could be transmitted to the seedlings by a microscopic residue of ash. Interestingly, there is not as much danger of infection from Maduro cigars, where the extra intense heat of fermentation has most likely killed any potentially harmful organisms in the wrapper. I suppose this could be misconstrued to mean that Maduros are healthier, but I personally have never felt better than when smoking an EMS wrapper.

After about 45 days, the strongest plants are relocated to the tobacco fields, where they are carefully transplanted in rows, at very precise distances from one another. Shade-grown tobacco is planted under a suspended ceiling of cheesecloth or synthetic mesh, to screen out the direct rays of the sun. Sun-grown tobacco, on the other hand, is planted without this artificial cover.

These Piloto Cubano seedlings are 35 days old. Eventually, they will become shade grown tobacco.

(Dominican Republic)

Given enough sun and water, and depending on the texture and density of the soil, the plants mature at a rapid rate, and in roughly another 45 days, they are ready for their first harvesting, or priming, in which certain leaves are stripped off of the main tobacco stalk. These are the leaves that will be ultimately dried, aged, and made into cigars.

There are three basic types of leaves on each tobacco plant. Going from the bottom to the top, they are: Volado — the mildest of the leaves in taste; Seco — a medium flavored leaf, which comprises the largest middle portion of the tobacco plant; and Ligero — the strongest in taste. Thus, the closer you get to the top of the plant, the thicker the leaves become and the heavier the taste. Normally, it takes a blend of all three of these leaves, in varying proportions, to make a cigar. Adding more Ligero produces a stronger tasting cigar; using only Seco and adding Volado lightens the

After 35 to 45 days, the seedlings are planted in fields, at a precise distance apart from one another. Notice the second man from the left, who uses a stick to mark the spot where each seedling is to be planted. A long string, barely visible in this photo, marks the row. Excessive water in this Cibao Valley field was caused by a heavy downpour the day before.
(Dominican Republic)

taste considerably. But a cigar made of only Seco tobacco would probably be too bland and characterless.

Usually, two to four leaves are taken from a plant during each priming. During the course of a tobacco plant's growing season, which can last until January, there will be a total of five to six primings per plant, starting with the bottommost leaves, as they are the first to mature. This permits more strength to go into the upper leaves as time passes. Because they are neither light nor heavy in texture and taste, the center leaves around the Seco classification are among the most versatile for cigar making, while the thicker, heavier Ligero leaves on top are ideal for wrappers. Because the upper leaves are permitted to stay on the plant the

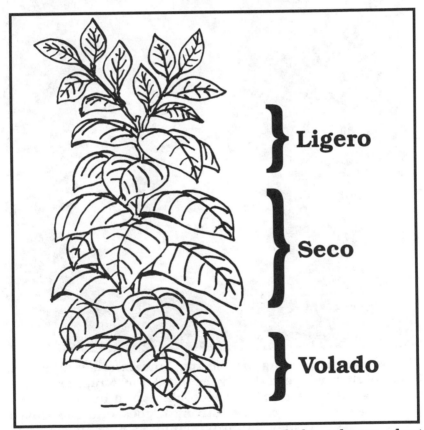

The three basic leaf classifications of the tobacco plant. Volado is the mildest in taste. Seco has the greatest concentration of flavor and aroma. Ligero is the strongest in both texture and taste.

This worker is picking off the top flowers of shade grown tobacco that will eventually be used for wrappers. The flower is never used in a tobacco plant, and by removing it as soon as it appears, more strength goes into the leaves. These plants will spend approximately 85 days in the fields during which time they will grow to a height of 5 ½ to 6 feet tall.

(Cuba)

42

longest, they receive more nutrients, which results in a heavier textured leaf and a stronger tasting tobacco. Most of the leaves used for Maduro wrapper — which requires a much more intense fermentation period (as we shall see later in this chapter) — comes from the upper portions of the plant, which can take the heat, so to speak.

For all its thick, exuberant foliage, each tobacco plant will only yield 14 to 18 leaves of a quality suitable for cigar making. Sometimes, weather permitting, there can be a second planting in December, which increases the harvest season all the way into March and April, thereby providing a much-needed bumper crop of tobacco for the cigar factories. But because Mother Nature is involved, a lot can go wrong with the crop between seed planting and priming.

One of the most universally feared diseases among tobacco farmers is Blue Mold, which can best be described as the AIDS of the tobacco industry. It can appear almost overnight, scarring the tobacco leaf beyond use and completely destroying the plant. Transmitted by microscopic airborne spores, Blue Mold often starts on the underside of a leaf and rapidly spreads from there. There is no problem with Blue Mold as long as the weather remains clear and dry, because in order to thrive, this dreaded enemy needs lots of rain, cold days and very little sun — not your typical Caribbean weather. But once it occurs, the stage is set for disaster. Sudden moisture in the air and a drop in temperature can trigger a Blue Mold epidemic that can spread like a prairie wildfire, destroying a country's entire harvest. Crop dusting and fumigation are the only defenses against this plague, but they are not always effective. In Cuba, for example, they regularly spray every young seedling against this dreaded fungus, but in 1980 Blue Mold still managed to destroy virtually all of that nation's tobacco crop, putting 26,000 workers out of business and resulting in a $100 million loss of revenue, as all exports of cigars were virtually halted. In 1984 this plague attacked the Dominican Republic and in 1985 it hit Central America, in both instances with devastating results. And in 1992-93, after one of the coldest, wettest winters in history, accented by a debilitating shot from Hurricane Andrew, Blue Mold again struck at Cuba's tobacco heartland. Honduras got hit with this plague in 1996. Consequently, in Honduras, where the growing season normally runs from September through March, many farmers now start planting in the off-season — sometimes as early as July — in order to take advantage of unusually good weather and to keep most of the maturing crop away from the potentially cold, wet months of

A healthy Havana leaf from the Vuelta Abajo. This is the start of what could ultimately become a great cigar.

(Cuba)

Tobacco bugs have gotten to this Ligero leaf. The left portion of the leaf will be stripped away, so that the right side can still be used.

(Cuba)

winter. The downside of this practice is the danger of wearing out the soil by too much concentrated planting.

Black Shank is another self-descriptive tobacco disease, which attacks the stem and turns the entire inside of the stalk black, eventually destroying the entire plant. Equally descriptive in name and despised by farmers is the Mosaic Virus, which produces a blue, mottled appearance on tobacco leaves. One of the most effective methods of controlling this scourge is having the workers wash their hands in milk when the seeds are taken from their beds and replanted in the fields. I guess all those ads were right; milk really does make the difference!

And let's not forget the common nemesis of farmers everywhere, bugs. Specifically, aphids and the dreaded tobacco beetle, *Lacioderma*, which many of us have had the misfortune to encounter in our own humidors. These little beasties lay their eggs right in the tobacco leaf. Within 22 days the larva hatches into a worm that gorges itself on the leaf before finally metamorphosing into a pinhead-sized brown beetle and flying off. Of course, by then the tobacco leaf has been destroyed.

Other unseen dangers await the tobacco grower. Back in the early 1960s, when the Honduran cigar industry was just getting started, tobacco fields were cleared and planted right up against the thick, untamed forestland. Nobody realized that within this vegetation dwelt millions of caterpillars, who looked upon the tobacco fields as one fantastic all-night diner. Soon, hordes of these creatures advanced out of the jungle, crawled en masse across the shade cheesecloth, and began to devoir entire tobacco plants, right on down to the stems. These Honduran crawlies had never seen such a succulent feast spread out before them in such a manner. Eventually, the farmers had to clear the jungle well beyond the borders of their cultivated land, and then fumigate the entire area.

With all of this potential devastation, it is a wonder that any tobacco manages to survive at all. But survive it does, thanks to constant surveillance by farmers, plus the use of pesticides, and in some cases, even picking bugs off of the plants one by one, as I have seen them do in Cuba. When each leaf is finally separated from its stalk (primed), the farmer can breath a sigh of relief, for there is less chance of losing the crop once it is literally "in hand," so to speak.

Once the leaves are primed, they are classified by size and texture (not color, because at this point every leaf is green), and carefully braided together with palm strips. These rows of freshly picked tobacco leaves are then taken to curing barns in the

A worker holds leaves that have been stricken with spotted plague, and which have been removed from otherwise healthy plants.

(Cuba)

fields, where they are draped over long poles, called *cujes*, and hung up out of the sun. Here, the leaves are fanned and caressed by the warmth of gentle Caribbean breezes for a period of three to eight weeks (depending on type of tobacco and the weather), during which time they gradually lose their moisture content. During this natural air curing process, the leaves slowly change in color, going from green to patches of yellows and then to brown, which eventually spreads over the entire leaf. If a lighter color is desired, the leaf is removed from the open air drying racks while still partially green and taken to a sealed room where artificial heat is applied. This controls the rate of final coloring and keeps the leaf from becoming too dark. As each leaf dries in the curing barn, it is pushed together to make room for more leaves coming in from the next priming. This procedure goes on until the entire barn is crammed full of air cured leaves, a welcome sight to any cigar maker. Or smoker, for that matter. But the tobacco is still a long ways from becoming a cigar.

When the leaf loses its upward arc and the main vein turns from light green to white, it is an indication that it is ready to be primed.

(Dominican Republic)
photo: Domingo Batista

47

From the curing barns, the leaves are shipped to packing houses, where workers separate and grade them by size, texture, and now, color. This grading and inspecting process will be constantly reoccurring throughout the entire cigar-making procedure, and is one of the reasons we have so many high-grade cigars today, instead of just "cheap smokes." As an example, when buyers come to the packing houses to inspect the tobacco, some of the many factors they check for include color, size, thickness, elasticity, texture, prominence of veins, oiliness, holes, spots or other blemishes, aroma, and taste of the leaf both lit and unlit. It is not unusual to see a buyer take a raw leaf from the bale, roll it up, and smoke it in order to get the pure essence of what he will be paying for. In a way, it is like test driving a car before you purchase it. Broken leaves are set aside, to see if there is still enough area to be used for binder, wrapper, or filler, depending on the type of tobacco. To paraphrase a popular public service slogan, a good plant is a terrible thing to waste. Once graded, each category of leaf is tied together with a strip of palm tree leaf into 20-leaf bundles, called "hands." From here, a most unusual process of fermentation takes place.

At the factories, the hands of tobacco are gathered into huge, free standing piles, called "burros," or bulks, which are square in shape, weigh from 8,000 to 10,000 pounds apiece, and

Raking out the air dried leaves from open wooden shelves in the curing barn. Within a 3 to 7-day period (depending on the weather), the leaves will lose all but 15% to 18% of their moisture. On especially humid days, a gas flame is used to help the drying process.

(Cuba)

48

stand anywhere from three to six feet high. By stacking so many hands of tobacco on top of one other, air is unable to circulate and is trapped inside. As a result, a natural heat slowly builds up within the bulk, releasing moisture, plant saps, and ammonia nitrate from the tobacco leaves. Indeed, upon entering the warm fermentation rooms, the heavy, stinging odor of ammonia is almost overwhelming. This natural fermentation process, which is known as "sweating," physically changes the makeup and characteristics of the tobacco. The color slowly darkens, starches in the leaves gradually turn into sugar (which is why we sometimes taste a subtle sweetness when lighting up a cigar), and the entire leaf gains character and finesse, just as a caterpillar emerges from its cocoon as a delicate butterfly (not those Honduran caterpillars, however). It is imperative that each bulk be made up of exactly the same grades and textures of leaf, or they will not all cure at an identical rate and the bulk will be ruined. Water acts as a catalyst in fermentation, and on those days when it is raining, every bulk in the fermentation rooms dramatically increases in temperature.

After the leaves have been cured in the fields, they are brought to warehouses where they are sorted by hand. Many workers roll their own out of the same product they are sorting, as evidenced by the woman on the right.

(Dominican Republic)

49

To keep track of the fermentation process, a long thermometer is thrust into the bulk and the temperature noted at precise intervals. Rarely is the temperature allowed to rise above 160 degrees Fahrenheit, for the higher the temperature, the darker the tobacco will become and the more strain will be put on the leaf. In Cuba they do not even let the temperature get above 120 degrees for most of their leaf. Normally, in the Dominican Republic and Honduras, the temperature for filler tobacco can go from 120 degrees to 160 degrees, while the temperature for wrapper leaf is monitored to fall within the 90 to 120 degree range. That is because wrapper leaf is generally a lighter and softer tobacco and cannot withstand such a hot and heavy fermentation.

This worker is casing Primero Rosado, a Number 1 cured wrapper that is ready to be worked. Notice how he opens the leaves of the hand for total coverage of the water spray.

(Honduras)

50

Leaves are graded by color, texture, and size.

(Dominican Republic)
photo: General Cigar

The cured leaves are brought to the warehouse for their initial grading.

(Dominican Republic)
photo: General Cigar

The one exception to all of this is Maduro, which must reach a temperature of at least 165 degrees — and usually much higher — in order to darken properly. Thus, a Maduro cigar requires a relatively thick, sturdy leaf, usually from the Ligero portion of the plant. On the other hand, if a Seco leaf can be properly fermented into a Maduro, you will have a noticeably mild tasting cigar. Two of the best leaves for fermenting into Maduro are Connecticut sungrown and Mexican leaf from the San Andrés valley. The longer these tobaccos are fermented, the milder the taste. A long fermentation period also has the effect of darkening the leaf. Thus, the generalization that all Maduro cigars are strong tasting is not true. One has only to light up an otherwise imposing Onyx #750 or an Ashton #60 Aged Maduro to prove this point. Sometimes water is added to Maduro to help raise the temperature, and very often the leaf is put in a pressure cooker to artificially increase the heat and moisture in order to better control the coloring. As an aside, Cuba produces very little Maduro.

No matter what type of tobacco is fermenting, as soon as the heat reaches the desired temperature, the bulk is "turned," or rotated, which is done by taking all the top leaves and placing them on the bottom (in essence, starting a new pile), so that the bottom leaves invariably end up on top. As each hand of tobacco is

Master cigar maker Frank Llaneza inspects newly arrived tobacco leaf in his warehouse.

(Honduras)

During fermentation, the temperature is constantly checked to make sure the bulk is turned at precisely the right moment.

(Cuba)

Arranging tobacco in a bulk for fermentation.

(Dominican Republic)

taken off of the bulk, it is shaken vigorously to dissipate the heat stored within the leaves. Then the fermentation process begins all over again, only with each turning of the bulk, the temperature does not rise as rapidly or as high as it did previously. It can take anywhere from six to ten turns to properly age and color a bulk. This process can go on for twenty to sixty days, depending on whether the leaf is Volado, Seco, or Ligero, with Volado taking the least amount of time and Ligero requiring the most fermentation. In the case of Maduro wrappers, the fermentation process can continue for six months or more, which explains why these cigars are usually more expensive; they simply take longer to make.

Once the fermentation process is completed, each leaf is meticulously separated from the bulk, sorted, inspected and graded. In the case of wrapper leaf, the distinction is made according to the color it received during fermentation (i.e., Claro = a light golden brown; Colorado = medium brown; Maduro = dark brown; Oscuro = brownish black). Each leaf type is packed in bales made of bark from the Royal Palm tree, tied with palm fronds, marked as to the type of tobacco, its origin, and the date of storage, and then put in the cigar factories' warehouses for aging. Here, the tobacco sleeps for anywhere from one to three years, and sometimes even longer. Most factories keep a minimum of eighteen months' worth of tobacco on hand. That way, they are assured of having enough raw material to get through a less than bountiful growing year, or a losing bout with one of the plagues. Naturally, this ties up a tremendous amount of inventory and capital, which cannot be turned into a profit until it is made into cigars and sold. But in order to produce a cigar that remains consistent, year after year, there must be enough available tobacco to blend the old in with the new, much like a fifty-year-old cognac can be a blend of twenty-five and seventy-five-year-old cognacs, so that the taste will average out to fifty. It is the same principle with cigars, for the minute our favorite brand changes taste, we utter the death cry, "It's not the same anymore!" and abandon it forever.

During less demanding years when cigar consumption was languishing, companies like Consolidated Cigar Corporation, General Cigar, and A. Fuente used to have huge stores of tobacco that went as far back as the 1980s. Unfortunately, the overwhelming demand for cigars today has not only depleted this decades-old reserve supply of vintage tobacco, it has raised a very interesting philosophical question for the cigar companies: Do you continuing aging your tobacco as non-profit-producing inventory that ties up precious cash, or do you release it sooner in order to make cigars that will turn into instant revenue due to overwhelming demand? The answer is what separates the good cigars from the bad.

Certain numbers-oriented people have elected to create cigars as quickly as possible, so that their expenditure in leaf is quickly multiplied into profit. But those companies who refuse to age their tobaccos and choose instead to make a quick killing — or rather, a quick cigar — rarely get repeat orders for their green, harsh tasting products, either from tobacconists or their customers. That is why we are starting to see some brands disappear almost as fast as new ones come on the scene. On the other hand, the responsible manufacturer who takes long-term pride in his product puts the emphasis on quality and will opt to wait and let fermentation take its natural course. That is why the three largest firms mentioned above as well as a great number of other manufacturers are experiencing unprecedented demand for their brands.

Given the current cigar craze, warehouses full of eight- and ten-year-old tobacco bales are pretty much a thing of the past. However, responsible cigar manufactures are still holding back production so that their tobacco can properly cure. *That is one of the main reasons for the cigar shortage.* It takes time to adequately age a leaf. But it is time well spent. As justice will have it, cigars that are made with properly aged tobaccos actually reap far more returns on investment, for once a cigar has a reputation of excellence, it gains a steady following that translates into loyal customers and repeat sales.

During this all-important storing/aging process, there is still a very mild form of fermentation going on, but nothing like the dramatic changes that had previously occurred. At the precise time, the aged bales are opened, inspected, and the hands of tobacco are shaken out and rehumidified in a fine mist spray. This is called the "casing" process. Although from a casual glance it appears as uncomplicated as spraying your backyard with a garden hose, the texture of each leaf is different and requires varying amounts of moisture. The wet tobacco is then hung on racks so that the water will gently trickle down the entire body of the leaf. As anyone who has ever over-humidified a cigar knows, tobacco leaves are highly absorbent, and they take to the casing process well. Soon, the stiff, brittle leaf that came in from the aging warehouse is transformed into a thin, pliable membrane that can easily be wrapped around your finger. In a way, the tobacco has been brought back to life after a long sleep.

Once they are moisturized, the leaves that are to be used for binder and wrapper go through the stemming operation, where the central vein in each leaf is completely removed, either by hand or by machine. This separates the leaf into right and left hand sides, which is extremely important in the case of wrappers for handrolled cigars, as there is a definite pattern that must follow the natural form of the leaf. For long leaf filler tobacco, the stemming operation takes place at the warehouses, before fermentation. In this case, only 25% to 75% — depending on the country — of the bottom of the stem is removed, to hold the leaf together during fermentation.

After casing and stemming, the leaves are inspected again, then graded, and finally hand sorted into wrapper, binder and filler tobaccos. These three categories of leaf are then sent to the blender, where they are separated into specific recipes for each type of cigar made at that factory. These recipes are the most closely guarded secrets in the cigar business, and you will have an easier time getting Sharon Stone's unlisted home phone number than you will in getting a blending recipe from any cigar maker.

The creation of a blend is what gives every cigar its character, and most importantly, its taste. Therefore, it is critical that all of the components are brought together in precisely the right proportions for each brand. That means the cigar maker must have an acute knowledge of tobaccos, and what each one can do. For

After fermentation, the leaves are again cased. At General Cigar, a "conditioning wheel" is used to spray moist air into the hands of tobacco so that they will be pliable enough to be worked.

(Dominican Republic)

example, a strong tobacco generally burns slower than a lighter tasting tobacco, so a strong tasting cigar will usually last longer than a mild one of the same shape. In the area of Dominican fillers, as another case in point, Olor and Piloto filler leaf look very similar, but they each produce very distinct differences in taste. To further complicate matters, each of these two-leaf categories have multiple subclassifications within their own leaf type. The cigar maker must know them all, not just by name, but by appearance, how they taste, and how they burn. And then there are wrappers. When specifying Connecticut, for example, it is imperative to differentiate between broadleaf, U.S. shade-grown, Ecuadorian grown, and so on. It is also important to know that a Cameroon wrapper grown in Ecuador (where most of this wrapper comes from today) will have a different taste and burn rate than a Cameroon leaf from Africa, which is distinct from the Mexican grown Cameroon that used to be used on cigars such as

Stripping involves the removal of the center stem, which has the texture of strong twine. Tobacco is stripped by hand or by machine, as in this General Cigar operation. Machine stripping is faster, but some leaves, like Java, must be hand stripped so that they do not tear. It is for this reason that some companies like Consolidated Cigar Corporation employ both methods of stripping.

(Dominican Republic)

In Cuba, all stripping is done by hand. The stems are used in an insecticide called (appropriately enough), "Tabacina." Stemming scraps are also used in short filler cigars for local consumption. Which is another reason you do not want to smoke the "nationalistic" cigars in Havana.

(Cuba)

57

Montecruz. And by that same token, in Cuba a wrapper grown in the Partido region can taste different in a finished cigar than a wrapper that was grown in the Vuelta Abajo.

All of this is simply to show the vast potentials that exist for creating a plethora of cigar brands, each with its own individual characteristics. Within that seemingly endless realm, you have the three components that go into the makeup of every cigar:

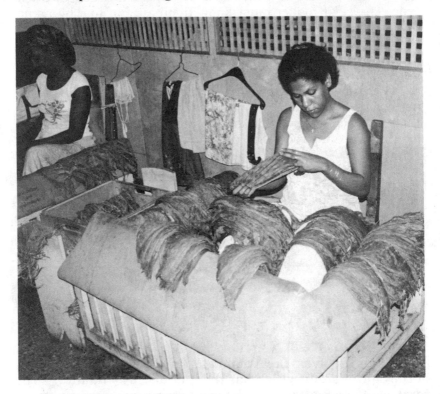

After stemming, the leaves are sorted by color and size. (Note the sorted tobacco leaves placed on the sorter's thighs. It is this practice that gave rise to the legend of Cuban cigars being rolled on a woman's thighs.) In this leaf separation room of Havana's Partagás factory, wrapper leaves are being sorted into their own internal classifications, such as Marevas, Robusto, Chicos, and Piramedes. A Marevas leaf, for example, will be used to make the Montecristo shape, but will also be used for the Bolivar Petite Corona, as these two cigars use the same shape, color and size leaf.

(Cuba)

Filler — This is the "heart" of a cigar. Filler can be made of either long leaf, that is, strips of tobacco that travel the length of the cigar in one piece, or short filler, smaller cut up pieces that are usually used for machine-made cigars. Long leaf filler has the capability of producing a long ash, whereas short filler, by the very nature of its smaller pieces of tobacco, normally cannot form a long ash without crumbling. Long leaf filler is more expensive, and has come to be associated with premium (i.e., high-grade) cigars. However, there are many excellent cigars, such as those produced by the Grave, Topper, and Finck companies in America and Villiger in Switzerland, that use short filler. And some cigars use a unique mixture of both long and short filler, which is sometimes called a Cuban Sandwich (see CigarSpeak in Chapter 10). Then there is "chopped" filler, which is finely cut tobacco, often used in the better grades of Dutch-type dry cigars. "Scrap" filler, on the other hand, is the leftovers of all the above, and is usually found in less expensive cigars and in many counterfeit Havanas. The filler of a premium cigar can be composed of anywhere from two to as many as five different types of long leaf tobacco. It becomes impractical to try to pack any more than that into the relatively limited confines of a cigar's body. Besides, the more varieties of leaf you use, the less total proportion of each there will be. Most blenders use two or three tobaccos quite effectively, although some, like Juan Clemente and Fuente, utilize as many as four different long leaf tobaccos in their filler blends.

Binder — This is the "blanket" that holds the filler in place. It is a specialized leaf, for it must be strong enough to do the job, yet it has to impart a complimentary flavor to the filler and wrapper. One of the many hallmarks of a premium cigar is that it boasts a binder made from a natural tobacco leaf, as opposed to many less expensive mass-market cigars that use homogenized binders, which are made from leaf particles and cellulose. Thus, the phrase, "all-tobacco," has a very real and important meaning when you see it imprinted on a box of cigars.

Wrapper — In many ways, the wrapper is the most important part of a cigar, not just because it provides 30% to 60% of the flavor, but also because it is the embodiment of the cigar's total character. To a smoker's eyes, the wrapper *is* the cigar. The quality of the leaf, the color, the texture, and the aroma all combine to give us a very distinct impression of a cigar even before we light it up, no matter what the binder and filler underneath that wrapper may be. If the wrapper leaf is not appealing to all of our senses, chances are we will not smoke, let alone buy, that cigar. That is one of the reasons why good, well-veined, evenly textured wrapper leaf is so expensive; it literally and figuratively holds everything together.

Using the above three components, a skillful cigar maker can create a masterpiece out of tobacco leaf, just as a talented painter can turn a blank canvas into a work of art. If you consider the filler to be the colors red, blue and yellow, the binder white and the wrapper black, then the cigar maker's cutting board becomes an artist's palate from which he can create an endless number of masterpieces, using every imaginable hue in the rainbow, or in this case, every possible combination of taste, aroma and burn rate. That is one of the greatest beauties and challenges of cigar making. Somewhere out there is a perfect cigar for everyone, and it never has to be the same cigar!

In creating their products, some cigar makers will hit upon a perfect filler-binder-wrapper combination and use it with minor variations for each of the brands within their line. That way they can produce a family of cigars with basically similar characteristics, and very often a smoker who likes one of their brands will also like another. Other factories will create a distinctly different blend for each of their brands, opting for a wider spectrum of tastes among their various cigars, and hoping, therefore, to appeal to a wider spectrum of customers. And still others will create a highly popular blend and use that exact same blend on different cigars, only changing the bands and the boxes in order to appeal to brand loyal smokers. (I therefore find it especially fascinating to note the different ratings many of these exact same cigars often get in independent tastings.) None of the above practices are any better than the other; in fact they are the very reasons we have so many excellent cigar choices today. But because there are so many brands from which to chose, one of the biggest challenges for factories is establishing and maintaining a consistency of appearance, draw, and taste for each of the brands they produce. Consistency is one of the most important characteristics of a good cigar. And that is where the cigar maker comes in.

Basically, there are three different ways to make a cigar, even though the advertising literature of various companies may sometimes give them different labels or use more generic descriptions. They are:

Handmade — The entire cigar is bunched, rolled and trimmed by individual hand labor. It can be one person working alone on a single cigar, or the work can be divided between a buncher and a roller working on the same cigar. The main criteria is that the entire cigar is completely made by hand from start to finish.

Machine bunched/Handrolled — The filler is bunched by machine, and then the filler/binder combination is turned over to a cigar roller, who puts the wrapper on by hand. This technique is often simply referred to as machine bunched.

Machine-made — The filler, binder and wrapper are completely assembled by machine.

Slightly complicating our acceptance of these definitions is a law that states any cigar that is machine bunched can legally be called a handmade cigar because the wrapper is still put on by hand. In fact, if you take a machine-made cigar and only stop the mechanized production long enough to manually put a tobacco cap on the head, in some instances you can still legally refer to it as a handmade product. But legal loopholes and advertising puffery aside, in order to keep things in their proper perspective throughout this book, I shall refer to the above three categories in their purest definitions, just as I have categorized them. Fortunately for the consumer, many people in the cigar industry are now starting to adopt these same definitions.

To my mind, the handmade cigar is a cigar in its purest form. It is the way Cuban cigars were made before there were any Cubans. It is the way the best premium Dominican, Honduran, Jamaican, Filipino, and Mexican cigars are made today. It requires more work and opens itself up to more failures than any of the other two methods (ironically, a machine-made cigar is the most consistent of them all, because everything is regulated and controlled), but it is also the most aesthetically rewarding cigar to smoke.

The handrolled cigar begins with the cigar maker taking a prescribed amount of the filler blend recipe and forming a cylindrical "bunch" of these tobaccos in his hand. This is not as easy as it sounds. The filler is not rolled, but is actually crimped in the hand, so that the different tobaccos fold over one other. In essence, the tobacco leaves are gathered up like an accordion, which has the effect of creating numerous horizontal air canals, which translates into an easy drawing cigar. This method also insures an even distribution of all the leaves used in the blend. That way, when you light your cigar, you are tasting the entire spectrum of tobaccos in the filler.

A poorly made cigar will have its filler "booked." That is, the leaves have been laid one on top of the other and folded over like the pages of a book. This has the effect of concentrating a lot of tobacco on one side (the spine of the book, so to speak), which means you would only be smoking a concentrated portion of the blend. In addition, the more tightly packed tobacco along the spine of the book can cause your cigar to burn unevenly down one side, while the looser "pages" of tobacco create overly wide air channels that can cause you to hyperventilate and your cigar to burn hot. Not a good thing for either of you. Obviously, filler should not be booked; an accordion fold is what you'll find in a good cigar.

The filler is then placed on the binder leaf and rolled, either by hand or utilizing a rubberized rolling guide known as a Leiberman (the fellow who invented it) or a Timsco (the company that sells it). This creates a "bunch," which is simply a cigar without

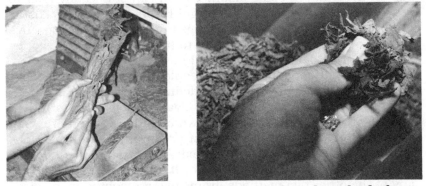

(Left) Long filler tobacco leaves being bunched for a premium cigar. (Right) Quality short filler is made from long filler-leaf tobaccos. In this photo, the short filler contains four grades of Mexican tobacco plus Cuban seed and Olor, with a touch of Brazil for additional flavoring. This pre-blended tobacco will be put into the filler canal of a cigar-making machine.

The components of a long filler cigar (L to R): Four types of filler (this can vary from two to four, depending on the brand), the binder, and the wrapper. A completed cigar is in the foreground. The tobacco was photographed on top of a filled bunch mold.

(Dominican Republic)

In an experimental station at Consolidated Cigar, a worker is taking the various components of a filler blend and separating them by percentages in compartments, in order to achieve more consistent control of the blends that go into each cigar.

(Dominican Republic)

its wrapper. The bunch is placed in a wooden mold shaped to the exact size of the cigar shape the roller is making. Each mold holds approximately ten bunches. When the molds are full, they are stacked in a bunch press, which puts pressure on the molds and squeezes the bunches into shape. The partially completed cigars stay in the bunch presses for 15 to 45 minutes, depending on the size of the bunch and the practice of the factory. At various intervals, the bunches are given a quarter turn within the molds, in order to prevent tobacco ridges forming where the two mold halves come together; these ridges would be visible underneath the wrapper, which is not what you want to see in a well rounded cigar.

Next, the formed bunch is removed from the mold by the cigar roller, who places it on a wrapper leaf that he has expertly and swiftly trimmed to the proper size with a flat, rounded "cuban knife," also known as a *chaveta*. The wrapper has been placed upside down on the cutting board (*la tabla*) so that when it is rolled, the smooth outer surface of the leaf will be showing. Experienced rollers will roll the leaf tip, which contains the mildest concentrations of oils and flavors, into the foot or tuck end of the cigar, while the base of the leaf is formed into the head of the cigar. Thus, the smoke and taste of the tobacco will all work towards

Once the leaves are sorted into filler blends, they are taken to the rollers.

(Dominican Republic)

64

These shade grown seedlings in Honduras are ready for transplanting to the fields.

A field full of future cigars in the Dominican Republic's famed Cibao Valley. Notice the open-air curing barns in the upper left.

photo: Domingo Batista

Open air curing barns are typical of the Dominican Republic. In Cuba, enclosed curing barns are used.

photo: Domingo Batista

Once primed from the plant, the tobacco leaves are tied to poles called *cujes* so they can dry naturally in the warm Caribbean climate.

photo: Domingo Batista

A worker stands on stilts called *zancos* to spread a cheesecloth covering over fields of tobacco seedlings that will one day become Honduran cigars. In the evenings, this covering is raised to let the heat escape so that the plants can cool.

An older curing barn in Cuba. Pre-revolutionary barns were made of thatched palm leaves. As the thatched curing barns succumbed to the elements, they were replaced with tin structures. This transition barn has thatched sides and a tin roof. Cubatabaco's current barns are entirely made of wood and are enclosed. Many of Cuba's curing barns were destroyed during the hurricane of 1992.

Sorting cured leaves as they are brought in from the fields.
photo: Domingo Batista

the fuller flavored part of the wrapper as the cigar is being smoked. Using a thumbnail-sized round piece of tobacco cut from a portion of leftover wrapper leaf trimming (so that the color will match the wrapper), the cap is smoothed down over the head of the cigar and glued in place with a flavorless natural gum from the Tragacanth tree. Some cigar makers, for reasons best known only to themselves, insist on adding a sweetener to this substance, in the mistaken belief that it enhances the flavor of the tobacco. The cigar is then placed in the wooden groove of a "tuck cutter" and deftly trimmed to its proper length.

This entire cigar-making procedure, from rolling the bunch to trimming the tuck, is done with such unbelievable swiftness that it blurs in the camera's lens unless an exceptionally fast shutter speed is used. Therefore, it's not surprising to learn that a skilled cigar maker can roll as many as 700 cigars a day, although factories like Honduras American Tobacco, S.A., makers of such excellent cigars as Punch, Hoyo de Monterrey and Rey del Mundo, purposely hold their best rollers down to no more than 500 cigars a day in order to maintain quality. In the huge Arturo Fuente factory in Santiago, Dominican Republic, some cigar rollers can also turn out up to 500 cigars a day, but the average cigar maker there will only produce from 150 to 200 cigars per a ten-hour workday. And when it comes to special hard-to-do shapes, such as the Hemingway series with its Perfecto tuck, even the most highly skilled worker can only create an average of 75 of these unique cigars daily, which is one of the reasons they end up costing more than an easier-to-roll Fuente 8-5-8 Flor Fina, for example. In Cuba, the average worker turns out approximately 135 of the larger sized cigars per day; smaller cigars get completed at a faster rate.

Which is not to say that smaller cigars are easier to roll. In many ways they are more difficult to make, not only in the physical sense, but also because it takes quite a bit of skill to fit more than one or two leaves into the filler blend (which means the wrapper and binder must augment the slightly reduced taste of the filler). Speaking of taste, because a small ring size burns hotter than a large one, a roller may decide to leave out some of the stronger-tasting Ligero in order to compensate. A smaller ring size also increases the possibility of "plugging" a cigar with a wayward piece of tobacco, thereby interfering with the draw. On the other hand, a large cigar is even more challenging, partly because any defects in workmanship or tobacco leaf can show up more readily. It is also more difficult to construct a large bunch so that all of the different leaves in the filler are equally distrib-

At the Fuente factory, a roller bunches the filler. Notice the
bunching presses in the background.

(Dominican Republic)

At Consolidated Cigar, hand rollers work with hydraulic bunching presses located at each station, thus co-mingling updated innovations with traditional cigar rolling methods. In this way, many companies are preserving their handmade craftsmanship while looking ahead to the 21st Century.

(Dominican Republic)

The Leiberman machine, a rubber mat that is rolled by hand, assures overall consistency in bunching. Notice the bunch, near the cigar roller's hands, starting to pick up the binder leaf.

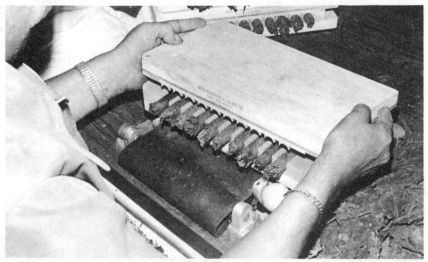

The completed bunches are placed in wooden bunch molds.

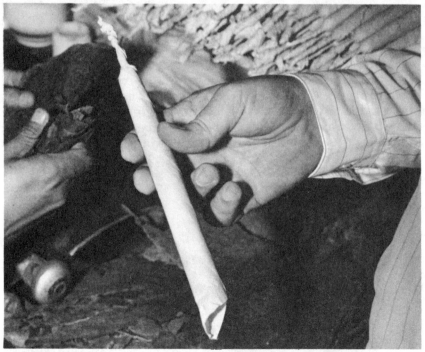

Some wooden molds are not available for special *figurado* shapes. This Avo (7x36/54) Pyramid, for example, is bunched in a paper mold.

(*Dominican Republic*)

uted along the entire length of the cigar, which must be done in order to prevent one particular tobacco from dominating the taste. That is why a cigar roller who has gradually worked his way up into being able to make the larger sizes is paid more than a worker who only makes smaller shapes. Even if his skills are temporarily needed to make Coronas, for example, a worker who has graduated up to making Churchills must still be paid his Churchill rate while making the smaller cigar.

Indeed, there is a form of class system among cigar rollers, and oddly enough, nowhere did I find this to be more in evidence than in Cuba, where the most skilled workers sit closest to the front of the *galera*, while the less experienced are at the back of the room. Cuba has seven categories of cigar makers; the lower the number, the fewer and less complicated the shapes that can be made by each worker in that category. And yes, even in Cuba, a category seven worker will be paid more per cigar than a category five individual. That is one of the reasons a complicated shape such as a Pyramid or a Double Churchill — whether it is made in Cuba, the Dominican Republic, or Honduras — costs more. It simply is more expensive to produce. The other reason, of course, is that it takes more tobacco to make these big-bodied cigars.

Most factories have training programs so that new cigar makers can gradually replace the old ones. Given the increased demand for cigars, these in-house cigar schools have assumed a rigorous new importance as additional rollers are badly needed to boost production. But in some Dominican and Honduran factories, *las tablas* that were formerly reserved for students are now occupied by experienced rollers who each can turn out hundreds of additional cigars per day. In Cuba especially there is a critical shortage of rollers, as more and more people try to leave the island and fewer young Cubans want to enter into such a mundane job. But no matter what the country, apprentices traditionally undergo one to two years of training, after which time the 1 out of 100 who qualifies can usually make up to 150 cigars a day. But not all the shapes. It takes a minimum of six months to learn to make even the most basic of cigars, at least 6 years to become skilled, and a full 20 years or longer for a cigar roller to become a master *torcedor*. Unfortunately, in an effort to increase production, the learning curve has been dramatically accelerated in some countries and, especially in Cuba, many rollers are being given complex shapes to make after only five years' experience. This is why we are now experiencing cigars that are rolled too tightly, packed too loosely, or made under-sized.

Cigar rolling is tedious, monotonous work, and many of the 19th and early 20th century factories had a *lector de tabaqueria* reading out loud to the craftsmen to keep them from rolling their eyes instead of their cigars and mentally slipping off into oblivion. Many times, the choice of literature was the classics, like Homer's *Odyssey* or passages from Shakespeare. As a result, cigar rollers became some of the "best-read" individuals in their neighborhood.

Of course, the radio put an end to the cigar reader in most factories, but in Cuba this nostalgic worker's perk is still being practiced. Except now they listen to the latest news from selected South American publications. Only at the Arturo Fuente factory in the Dominican Republic did I hear music being played to the workers instead of localized versions of radio talk shows. And a surprising number of cigar-making companies elect not to have any audio entertainment at all.

When the bunches are ready, the roller spreads the wrapper leaf on the cutting board and trims it with the sharp *chaveta.*

(Cuba)

70

But whether handmaking cigars to the accompaniment of a reader, the radio, or the human sounds of silence, every worker in every country has one common characteristic: they all genuinely seem to take great pride in their work. In Cuba, for example, no matter which factory I visited, I was greeted by the enthusiastic clatter of *chavetas* being pounded on *las tablas*, which remains this cigar-making nation's traditional and inspiring salute to visitors. Of course, it was pointed out by the lector, I was the only Norte Americano to have visited their factories in quite some time. And the fact that I was writing a book about cigars produced another round of *chaveta* rattling. But even in the other Caribbean countries, every worker smiled when I stopped to take a closer look at their handicraft, and most of the people either blushed or beamed when I photographed the cigars they were making, as if I was taking pictures of their children. Another reason everyone seems so happy, I suspect, is that they all have jobs, no easy feat in a Third World country. Indeed, the cigar industry is a major factor in the employment rate of nations such as the Dominican Republic and Honduras. Those who have the dexterity and talent can have a job for life, and it is not unusual to find a *torcedor* in his 70s who has been with the same cigar-making family or factory for over 50 years.

Once completed by the rollers, the cigars are tied in bunches of fifty, and affixed with a slip of paper giving the cigar maker's name, the name of his supervisor (who has been constantly inspecting the cigars as they were being made) and any other pertinent information the factory may require, such as types of tobacco used, the shape of the cigar, or its brand. This is done as a check; in case any cigar in the bunch fails to measure up to standards, the foreman will know whom to confront. Because each roller is paid by the number of cigars he or she makes, cigars that are rejected are deducted from the worker's pay. The cigar bunches are then weighed to make sure the proper amounts of tobacco have been used, and are passed through a ring gauge to determine that they are the proper diameter for their shape. And once again, they are given a close visual inspection.

Because the tobacco has to be overly moist in order to be worked by the cigar maker, the completed cigar must now be reduced in its moisture content so that it can be smoked. In addition, the various tobaccos within each cigar must "marry," or blend together, much as a chef's special sauce must be allowed to simmer on the stove in order to blend all the spices. Only instead of a stove, the cigars are placed in an aging room. It is here, in these traditional, temperature controlled Spanish cedar cham-

The wrapper is rolled around the bunch.
(Dominican Republic)

Producing the Perfecto-style foot of a Hemingway cigar.
(Dominican Republic)

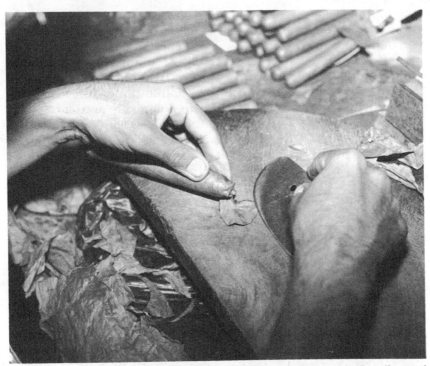

The very skillful process of cutting and shaping the flag of tobacco that will become a "finished head" of a premium cigar. It takes an experienced cigar maker to create this style of head.

(Honduras)

The completed cigar is trimmed to size in the tuck cutter.

(Honduras)

73

bers, that the cigars are allowed to rest for a minimum of three weeks while their humidity levels are evened out and the flavors from the filler, binder and wrapper are permitted the luxury of getting to know one another. Some cigars, many of which fall into the "vintage" category, are aged longer than others. Dunhill Aged Cigars, for example, are aged for a minimum of three months. The Fuente Hemingway and Chateau Fuente are aged for at least six months, as are the Ashton Cabinet Selection Vintage cigars. Fuente's limited edition Don Carlos cigar and the Opus X are aged for a full year, as is the J.R. Ultimate cigar and Cuesta-Rey's Diamond Crown. Davidoff's Dominican cigars are aged in their warehouses in Connecticut, Amsterdam and Rotterdam for as long as one and a half years. And Pléiades opts for an ambitious transcontinental aging program for their cigars, which travel from the Dominican Republic to France (where they are repacked in humidified cedar boxes) and then back again across the Atlantic to the United States, aging all the while.

Cuba used to age their hallmark cigars, such as the Partagás and Montecristo, up to a full year or more in cedar cupboards that date back to the last century. Unfortunately, many Havana cig-

Inspection is an ongoing process in every cigar-making operation.

(Honduras)

74

ars are now aged in those same cupboards for as little as six days, due to an insatiable demand for Cuban cigars and that country's crucial need to turn her tobacco crop into cash as quickly as possible. Thus, they can't really afford to let most of their cigars age any longer, with the exception of a few brands, such as their flagship cigar, Cohiba. This has had the disastrous effect of some smokers buying fresh Havanas and smoking them "green." As an example, when I was in Cuba I purchased a box of Romeo y Julieta No. 4s directly from the factory. Just how directly I was soon to discover. In my excitement to actually have a full box of Havanas in my possession (forget the fact that I was still in Cuba; I was excited), I opened the box and lit one up that evening while sitting by the pool of the Havana Riviera (the former Riviera Hilton). It was a perfect moment. The Cuban moon was full, rising slowly over the skyline and starting to reflect upon

the water. The night air was cool, with just a touch of breeze, and in the background I could hear the surf quietly lapping against the breakwater that lined the scenic Malecón highway. I struck a match. I warmed the foot of the cigar, gently turning it. Then I took a puff. My palate was met with the hollow harshness that comes from a freshly rolled cigar. Correction: a *too* freshly rolled cigar. It had not been aged. Out of desperation, determined to completely smoke my first Havana in Havana, I struggled through the cigar and accomplished my goal, but it was not a pleasant experience. I never reopened that box until back in the States three months later, when I removed the No. 4s from a humidor where I had been storing them. The sight of the cigars instantly brought

A cigar is checked for the correct ring size. The cut-out notch in this Cuban gauge is used for measuring length. Ring gauges can be made of wood, brass, or plastic.

(Cuba)

back pleasant memories of my trip. So, bracing myself for the worst, I went out on the porch and lit one up. To my pleasant surprise, this time the Romeo y Julieta was a much tamer smoke. It had time to mellow in my humidor, and that made all the difference between a barely tolerable cigar and an enjoyable one. A year later I smoked the very last cigar from that box and found it to be rich, creamy and full of flavor. Additional aging had done it. The moral of this story is, when smoking Cuban cigars, chances are it will be much more rewarding if you come across a box that has been allowed to age in a dealer's humidor for at least a few months. Or plan on aging them yourself before firing the first one up. On the other hand, Dominican and Honduran cigars are already well aged and ready to enjoy when they arrive, although in Chapter 4 we'll talk about aging them even further.

After the cigars have been aged in the factory's marrying room, they are again inspected, and then sorted by color. There are approximately sixty different shades of brown, and each cigar must be separated by color before it is boxed. It is a great source of pride for both the cigar maker and the cigar smoker to be able

A Cuban quality control inspector in the La Corona factory randomly selects cigars and forces them open to visually insure that the required leaves in the blends are all there and in the correct proportions, and that the filler tobaccos have not been twisted, which would interfere with the draw.
(Cuba)

to open a box and see the exact same shade of wrapper on every cigar. It doesn't make the cigars smoke any better, but it is an indication of the pride each company takes in its product. Although some Havana brands are not color sorted in the purest sense of the word, they should at least have the darkest cigars on the left hand side, going to the lightest wrappers on the right. And it is a common Cuban practice to put the best cigars on the top row, so if buying a box of Havanas, check the bottom row as well.

Once the cigars are inspected, they are rebundled and weighed, as another check for the proper tobacco contents.
(Dominican Republic)

Carlos Fuente, Jr. inspects the Hemingway Masterpiece in his factory's cedar-lined aging room, that includes electric bug zappers. Another company, Consolidated Cigar, uses a system of electronically induced sexual energy that lures bugs to their amorous deaths. There is no limit to what some companies will do to preserve our cigars!

(Dominican Republic)

Color selection is an exacting art.   *(Dominican Republic)*

Once the cigars have been grouped into the same color categories, they are banded. Each band must be put on (by hand, of course) at exactly the same height on every cigar, so that they will all line up perfectly when the cigars are boxed. Some cigars, like Bances, Hoyo de Monterrey and Punch Premier Grand Cru used to be double banded, which I always thought was an elegant extra touch. However, with rising production costs, these bands have now been redesigned so that they still look like a double

All cigars are banded by hand. A marker on the side of the tray tells the worker exactly how high on the cigar the band should go.

(Dominican Republic)

band, but it is really just a clever printing job. Not to worry; this double banding never affected the taste of the cigar.

Finally, the cigars are carefully slipped into cellophane sleeves to keep them from becoming damaged during transit. Some cigars, like Avo, Davidoff, Santa Damiana, and Juan Clemente (on an optional basis), are shipped in cedar boxes without cellophane, as cello will considerably slow down and even halt the otherwise continuous aging process. Personally, I prefer uncellophaned cigars and make it a practice to remove the cellophane from every cigar the instant I get the handmade box home.

Yes, even the boxes are made by hand, usually by the same factories that make the cigars. There are two types of cigar boxes: 1) a cedar plywood "dress box," in which you rarely see the wood because every available space is covered with a multitude of labels and separate edging designs, and 2) an all-cedar "cabinet box," which utilizes German-made brass hinges and nails so they won't rust while being stored in a dealer's walk-in humidor. Most of the cedar used in making cabinet boxes for Caribbean cigars is Honduran-grown African cedar. Other sources for cedar are Mexico, Nicaragua, and the U.S. Plywood for the dress boxes comes from Taiwan, Korea, and Brazil. Cuba grows her own plywood, but must import the heavier cedar from Honduras. All of Cubatabaco's cigar boxes are made by just one factory in Havana. Some of the most beautiful cigar boxes are made in the DR and Honduras. The fancy routed and shaped boxes for Fuente's Don Carlos and Cuban Corona, for example, could both have a very satisfactory afterlife as jewelry boxes. And the lacquered, prominent cedar boxes that house the Punch Premier Grand Cru Seleccione are classic enough to leave out on a silver serving tray. Equally impressive, General Cigar uses a handsome Jamaican-made mahogany box to appropriately show off their Macanudo Vintage and Partagas 8-9-8 cigars. Elsewhere, smaller companies buy ready-made boxes from the United States, but most firms find it is more efficient to make their own.

Unfortunately, the trickle-down effect of the mammoth U.S. cigar boom has created an unprecedented demand for cigar boxes, which in turn has resulted in an overharvesting of cedar. Some companies are already asking merchants to return their empty boxes so they can be refilled and thus recycled again. Consequently, some manufacturers are now looking towards cedar laminate and other more readily available or less costly woods to replace the gradually diminishing cedar supply. Don't be surprised if mahogany is the next new trend for cigar boxes. Someone may even try plastic, but I will balk at that. Hopefully they are now sufficiently discouraged from even considering it.

Fortunately there are still enough trees to make paper, for cigar companies even produce their own labels. However, rather than continue with expensive four-color printing, many factories are now imprinting individual cigar names and shapes in one color over a multicolored label that has been preprinted by an outside vendor. Cuba, of course, was the first to put a full colored label on a cigar box back in 1837, when cigar maker Ramón Allones decided that his cigars needed some eye appeal. That label remains largely unchanged today. Cubatabaco prints all of their four-color labels in the La Corona and H. Upmann factories. Most of the other large factories, like Consolidated Cigar Corporation, maintain a regular print shop for their labels, and Fuente even has their own silk screening department for attractively decorating certain boxes, such as their Hemingway series.

With the boxes assembled and labeled, the cigars are carefully placed inside, with a colored ribbon or turned up piece of cellophane always present on one of the top layered cigars, in order to facilitate its removal. Prior to cellophaning, some cigars, like the H. Upmann and Padrón, have been pressed together to give them a square shape, a practice that originated to keep the cigars from rolling off of the table. Others, like the Ramón Allones

Most cigars are sleeved in cellophane.

(Honduras)

81

Trumps, have been left in the round, which always struck me as being more natural; let 'em roll! And a few, such as Henry Clay, have purposely been given a rough, out-of-round surface on the wrapper. It's all a matter of each cigar's character, with no effect on how the cigar will smoke. Then the cigars are given one final inspection, and that person will usually put an identifying stamp or tag on the box before it is nailed shut. By hand, of course.

It is difficult to tell a machine-bunched/handrolled cigar from a handmade cigar, except by price. The draw is the same, sometimes even better, because there is less chance for human error in the bunching process. Machine-bunched cigars are usually less expensive, which is why manufacturers first began to utilize this procedure back in the 1950s. Because they are often referred to as "handmade" cigars, little differentiation has ever been made between the two. Up until now, that is. Actually, there is a sizable amount of hand labor that goes into each machine-bunched cigar, and some of the best values can be found in this category. An excellent example of a popular machine-bunched/handrolled cigar is the Dominican-made Primo del Rey. In making this cigar, the pre-blended filler leaf is fed by hand into a machine that automatically bunches it. In the meantime, a worker places a rough-cut binder leaf over a template. A mechanized blade drops down

As a final step, the cigars are once again inspected, re-checked for matching wrapper colors, and boxed.

(Dominican Republic)
photo: General Cigar

and trims the leaf precisely to the template form. The machine then picks up the binder, glues it with clear gum arabic, rolls the filler leaf into the binder and tumbles the finished bunch onto a conveyor belt. From there it is picked up by hand, trimmed, and placed into the cigar molds. From that point on, the machine-bunched cigar is treated exactly like a handmade cigar, going to the hand roller, and following the exact same steps of inspections, color sorting and aging. So these cigars could actually be referred to as semi-handmade, although I think machine-bunched/handrolled is a more accurate description.

The third category, the 100% machine-made cigar, is normally reserved for low-priced, mass market products such as King Edward, Optimo, Dutch Masters, Antonio y Cleopatra, and El Producto. All of these popularly priced cigars are produced by giant mechanized factories located in either America or Puerto Rico. Practically all of them utilize some form of homogenized tobacco leaf (HTL), a process owned by General Cigar Corporation, although there are other variations as well. Basically, homogenized tobacco is an artificially produced product that is composed of tobacco stems and fibers which are mixed with water and other organic liquids to produced a pulp-like material. In fact, the HTL manufacturing process is a lot like making paper, except for the fact that tobacco is used instead of wood. And rather than take the form of a natural tobacco leaf, HTL comes off of a drying belt and is formed into rolls, which are in turn fed into the cigar-making machines. About 90% of all mass market cigars are made with HTL binder and 60% of these cigars use HTL wrapper as well.

In making a mass market, machine-made cigar, short-filler is rolled into the binder. From there, the bunch is force molded by a crimper into the desired shape, which includes forming the head. The shaped bunch is then dropped into a basket, where the wrapper is automatically rolled on. The completed cigar is then mechanically pressed to give it a desired shape. These machines can easily make from 500 to 800 cigars a minute. With this kind of speed, wrappers and binders undergo a tremendous strain, and sturdiness of homogenized tobacco becomes a necessity.

Unlike natural wrapper leaf, which has a definite texture to it, homogenized wrapper appears as a flat matte finish. Homogenized wrapper can be made in any color. Not by fermentation, as with natural tobacco leaf, but simply by adding artificial coloring. Thus, an HTL wrapper can be produced in one continuous sheet of Claro, EMS, Maduro, and even chartreuse, if that is your idea of a good time. Some years ago, an enlightened manufacturer actually printed tobacco leaf veins on his HTL wrapper to give it a more natural look. However, many mass market cigar smokers were not accustomed to seeing real tobacco veins on their wrappers, let alone fake ones, and they began to grow uneasy over these strange lines on their favorite Panetelas. So the practice was discontinued.

A far more palatable option for homogenized tobacco is the addition of flavoring, and cigars that give the smoker a hearty dose of rum, vanilla, apricot or cherry are among the most popular of today's less expensive smokes. I suppose one could even fantasize about having a cigar flavored like a porterhouse steak, for the ultimate experience in smoked meat.

Ironic as it may seem, machine-made cigars are often the most uniform cigars that can be made, because their construction is automatically regulated, with little margin for human error. The use of homogenized tobacco is also a tremendous help in controlling the burning rate as well as the color of ash. In fact, one of the whitest ashes possible is found on a mass-market cigar. Not that a white ash is of particularly great significance, as we shall discover in Chapter 4. Mass-market cigars also provide some of the mildest smokes in the world. That is because the ingredients used in these cigars are actually designed to tone *down* the taste of tobacco. Which is why so many of the people who favor these cigars, the most notable of whom was the late George Burns (see Chapter 8), can light up ten to twenty cigars a day with no ill effects.

There is a very distinct difference between mass-market cigars, which are machine made, and regular machine-made cigars that are not in the mass-market category. Three notable examples are the excellent short filler cigars by F.D. Grave, the Topper Cigar Company, and the Finck Cigar Company. For the cigar connoisseur who prefers the Dutch-type European variety, there are some very worthwhile machine-made cigars, such as the various products from Schimmelpenninck, Ritmeester, Villiger, Agio, Gallaher, and Christian of Denmark, just to name a few. Many of these cigars actually fall into the small cigar and cigarillo categories; some are all-tobacco, while others use homogenized binder in conjunction with the same tobacco filler and wrapper as found in a handmade cigar. Most dry cigars are machine bunched, using short filler. Sometimes this filler is so short, they can put as many as twenty different kinds of tobacco into a single cigar! The bunch is machine wrapped in either homogenized leaf, or, in the case of some of the more expensive cigars, natural leaf. Depending on price and size, the wrapper is put on by

Cedar is cut, marked with the date, and air dried for at least a year. In Honduras, the terrain is so rugged that logs often have to be flown out by helicopter. When ready, they are cut into boards, air dried and then kiln dried.

(Honduras)

The Making Of A Box

Boxes are assembled by hand with nails, glue, or staples, depending on the company and brand of cigar.

(Cuba)

The multi-colored bands of a cedar plywood "dress box" are individually glued on by hand.

(Honduras)

The finished product: cedar "cabinet boxes" waiting to be filled with Hoyo de Monterrey Excalibur No. 1s.

(Honduras)

hand or machine, and can be either natural leaf or homogenized. A thin coating of tobacco powder is often dusted over the wrappers of some cigars in order to give them a more uniform color. A typical factory worker in Europe can turn out 2,000 Dutch-type cigars a day. But keep in mind, these are much smaller than the humidified cigars of Mexico, Central America, and the Caribbean.

Although Habanos S.A. would rather focus attention on their handmade products, machine-made cigars in Cuba are still among the best, as they are produced with all Havana tobacco. Of the thirty Cuban brands currently being exported, twenty-six of them include at least a few machine-made cigars in their line-up, usually in the smaller sizes. Some notable examples are: Quintero Chicos, Partagás Culebras and Petit Bouquet, and H. Upmann Perfectos. All Cuban machine-made cigars are currently being manufactured in the H. Upmann and La Corona factories.

Of course, an obvious question is, if some of the better quality machine-made cigars are so good, then why even bother with the expense of producing handmade cigars? For one thing, it is difficult to get a machine to properly distribute all of the long leaf filler in a bunch. It still takes a human hand to get an even mix throughout the blend. That is why a handmade cigar always has its own distinctive taste. Another factor is the ability of the human

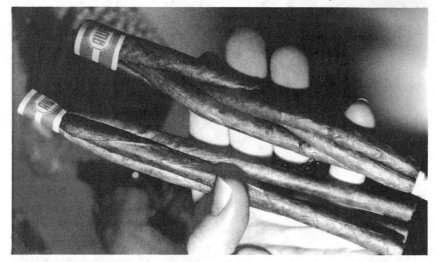

Even machine-made cigars require a significant amount of handcraftsmanship, as evidenced by the before and after twists of Villiger's "AWEG" cigars.

(Switzerland)

A cigar-making machine at the La Corona factory in Havana. The revolving template is for binder leaf, which will be automatically cut and fed into a bunching machine. In the background, an inspector examines the finished product.

(Cuba)

eye to properly gauge and guide the hands through the cigar-making process; each cigar becomes an individual tribute to this craftsmanship. Then there is appearance; a handrolled cigar has its own distinctive look. And taste, for only the very best tobaccos are used. And then, there is that indefinable aura that emanates from every premium cigar, no matter what its size, taste, or nationality, simply because of the fact that it is handmade. Of course, you will pay a little more for all of these extra features, tangible or not, but that has always been the price of hand-craftsmanship.

Even among the various factories that specialize in premium, handmade cigars, there are different methods and philosophies involved. For example, in Cuba, a single skilled worker makes the entire cigar, from beginning to end. This is the traditional method of the historic *torcedores*, a method that is still followed in most non-Cuban factories today. Additionally, in Cuba there are small flags that are posted by the benches of workers who have excelled in their craft. (Interestingly, I've not seen this "reward" system practiced anywhere else.) In the Honduras American Tobacco factory, makers of such excellent cigars as Punch, Hoyo de Monterrey and Rey del Mundo, for example, a separate bunch maker assembles the bunch and then brings it over to the cigar roller. Normally there are two bunch makers per roller, as the rolling operation in this factory is twice as fast as the bunching. This speeds up production while maintaining quality, as the bunchers can devote all of their concentration to this one aspect of the cigar-making process. In the Fuente factory, they prefer to use one buncher per roller, taking care to pair the speed of each team so that they are compatible. This family-owned factory has also established a "Hemingway Hall of Fame," where the top twenty rollers who make the Hemingway cigar ply their craft in a room that contains inspirational articles of Hemingway memorabilia. The fact that a single room has been devoted to the making of one style of cigar is significant, and could only be done by a factory the size of Fuente, the second largest producer of Dominican cigars in the world. In their Santiago factory alone there are 300 *torcedores* in the main *galera*, along with fifteen supervisors and one master supervisor. Plus their own highly efficient Cigar Protection Device: a burly guard packing a semi-automatic Colt Government .45 (I don't know about the cigars, but it made *me* feel safer. After all, these factories are located in Third World countries). And only in the highly efficient Honduras American Tobacco factory did I see some of their most skillful workers making two different cigar shapes at the same time, so that if bunches for one shape were not forthcoming, the roller started on the second shape. This same Honduran company also has a scholarship program for children of the workers. In the DR's Tabacos Dominicanos factory, where Avo, Griffin's, and Davidoff cigars are made, a strict inventory control is practiced, wherein each worker must personally sign for the filler, binder and wrapper leaves that he or she uses each day, and is held accountable for them in relationship to the number of cigars produced. Other factories also use this technique, and it is especially prevalent today in Cuba, in an effort to halt the smuggling of leaf used in off-premise (i.e., counterfeit) cigars.

But perhaps the most innovative of all is Consolidated Cigar Corporation, the largest producer of premium cigars in the world (H. Upmann, Don Diego, Montecruz, Montecristo, Primo del Rey, etc.) Here, in the only factory on the southwestern La Romana side of the island, a number of novel approaches have been implemented in the age-old art of cigar making. The traditional cigar rolling techniques remain intact, but some of the new variations include a mechanical suction test on bunches for the Don Diego and H. Upmann brands to insure that each cigar will get a satisfactory draw (with different calibrations to compensate for each shape. A Lonsdale would require more suction than a Rothschild for example). Only after a bunch passes the suction test is it rolled into the wrapper. And rather than tighten the bunch press by hand, hydraulic presses have been installed at each cigar roller's station. These presses are automatically timed to release the bunch presses at precise intervals. Indeed, it is a bit disconcerting to be walking through this giant factory and hear the self-timed hiss of numerous bunch presses opening up hydraulically. In addition, experimentation is currently going on to test the feasibility of replacing wooden cigar molds with plastic ones, and of doing away with the traditional *chaveta* in favor of a pizza cutter!

For anyone who has visited any of the cigar making countries recently, it is obvious that the current smoker's renaissance is having a dramatic effect on an industry that essentially hasn't changed in over one hundred years. Production is at an all time high, and yet, as we have seen, a cigar is not something that can be rushed. Even so, the unrelenting demand for cigars has resulted in some companies putting the emphasis on quantity rather than quality, with predictable results: underfermented and poorly rolled cigars. Scrap leaf that would never have even been considered for a premium cigar a few years ago is now being eagerly snatched up at inflated prices by newcomers who just want to make cigars, no matter what the end result smokes like. Wrappers, especially larger sized leaves, continue to be an ever-growing (or rather, non-growing!) problem. In the Dominican Republic the prices being paid for top grade filler tobacco has gotten so high that everybody is growing it and there is now a shortage of curing barns. Farmers, who can remember sitting on bales of tobacco hoping that a buyer would someday come along now find that there is a virtual feeding frenzy for their crops, with many firms trying to make up for lost time by dramatically raising prices. As a result, the cost for top quality wrapper leaf has jumped 75% in a single year.

With the cry going out for more tobacco, more land is being cleared for this precious weed, and longer growing seasons are being implemented. New countries are being explored, just as they were during the Cuban revolution and immediately after the embargo. In addition to already established cigar-making meccas in the Caribbean and Honduras, look for increased activity in Jamaica, Costa Rica (which has an untapped wealth of potentially rich tobacco-growing soil just an hour's drive from the capital of San José), Brazil, the Philippines, and Indonesia, where even Connecticut shade wrapper is now being grown (and sometimes referred to as Sumatra, which it is not). Nicaragua, where the government controls 98% of all tobacco, continues to hold the greatest promise, if they can only get their internal problems worked out. The same is true of Cuba, where new land is being cultivated and new strains of seeds, including Connecticut shade, are now being grown in an attempt to increase production. The political turmoil in the West African enclave of Cameroon has resulted in many tobacco recipes switching to other leaf, usually Indonesian. (Today Cameroon wrapper can only be found on a few classic brands, such as Partagas and Hemingway.)

Greed and the twin catalysts of supply and demand are causing other concerns for the end-user cigar smoker as well. One of the most notable attributes of the cigar industry has always been its feeling of family, where manufacturers of competing brands often socialized after hours and where friendships were built up over generations. But now outside entrepreneurs with thick, investor-financed wallets have entered the scene, luring top grade rollers away from their long-time employers by offering dramatic salary increases. It doesn't take a degree in economics to realize that higher wages and the higher cost of tobacco will eventually translate into higher costs for cigars.

The end result of all this will be newer cigars, both good and bad, gradually escalating prices, and — eventually — a less-

Maria Luisa Almanza, Chief of Production for the Partagás factory in Havana, inspects cigars that are being box pressed to give them a square shape.

(Cuba)

ening of shortages. In addition, as cigar smokers become more sophisticated and demanding (especially those who have read this book) and refuse to settle for second rate tobacco in poorly rolled cigars, the survivors in this new era of cigar wars will be those cigars that continue to offer the best quality for the money.

Whether it is made by new methods or old, created by hand, machine, or a combination of both, today's cigars represent one of the modern age's most unique products from the past. In the case of the handmade premium cigar, considering the fact that more than fifty pairs of hands and eyes have guided it down the path to completion, it also represents one of the last great bargains left in a cost-conscious world. But how do we get our money's worth from something that we are about to send up in smoke? That is a question we will answer in the next chapter.

Chapter 3

Finding The "Perfect" Cigar

Like a first date, or a first car, I'll never forget my first cigar. It was a five-pack of Antonio & Cleopatra Grenadiers and it was the summer of my Junior year at Arizona State University. I bought the Grenadiers because they were priced within my meager budget, and in addition to my pipe, I thought they made me look "cool." Besides, they were an easy smoke as I tooled down Camelback Road in my 1954 Austin-Healey four-banger.

Things were a lot simpler back then. I don't recall how many different cigars there were to chose from, but definitely not as many as today. It really didn't matter, because my main criteria was price. For about a year I alternated between the A&Cs and Robert Burns Cigarillos, because those were two brands that I could afford. Then I discovered the Cuesta-Rey #95s. It was the first full box of cigars I ever bought and I went crazy. Not only did you get almost a month's worth of smokes all at once, but afterwards you ended up with a neat cedar box to put things in. From there I went to the newly introduced (at that time) Honduran Hoyo de Monterrey, which was being made with pre-embargo Havana leaf. By this time I was a copywriter at a local advertising agency, and I really wasn't flush with disposable income. But I saved all week so that I could buy the Hoyo to smoke on the weekend. I had begun to form a philosophy that if I was going to smoke a cigar, it would have to be the best that I could afford.

I have long since revised that philosophy to just "smoking the best." For me, price does not always enter into the picture anymore, because very often, some of the best cigars are not the most expensive. When you think about it, and from what we have discovered in the last chapter, it really doesn't cost any more to make an excellent cigar than it does to make a mediocre one. The difference is in how the tobacco was prepared and how the cigar was constructed and aged. So what it really comes down to is knowing what you like and then picking the best cigars in those categories.

Cigar sizes can be confusing if you only think of the name and don't equate it to ring size and length, as the shape names can change from brand to brand. Here are some popular examples (L to R): Flor del Caribe (7 1/4 x 50) Sovereign (really a Churchill); Troya (6 3/8 x 44) Lonsdale; Te Amo (6 3/4 x 44) Double Corona; Don Lino (6 1/2 x 42) Large Corona; El Glorioso Dominicano (6 1/2 x 42) #400 (which is a Corona Grande which is the same size as Don Lino's Large Corona); A. Fuente (5 1/4 x 44) Cuban Corona; Davidoff (6 x 38) No. 2 (which is really a Panetela); New York (5 x 48) La Guardia (actually a Rothschild); Romeo y Julieta (4 1/2 x 54) Rothschild. Sometimes it is simpler to ask for a cigar by shape (i.e., "What have you got in a 7 1/2 x 52 Churchill size with a medium flavor?").

As mentioned in Chapter 1, these really are the golden years for cigar smokers. We have more brands from different countries and types of tobacco than ever before. And in addition to standard shapes such as Churchill, Panetela, and Corona, we are now seeing a resurrection of some of the great old shapes of yesteryear combined with new interpretations, such as the Petite Belicoso, Double Corona, and the newly rediscovered *figurado* shapes such as the Pyramid and super Perfecto (although nobody calls it that; maybe they should). Bigger ring gauges are in, but now I notice a slowly growing interest in small Dutch cigars. There are also conflicting trends that include shorter cigars for quicker smokes and larger ones that are guaranteed to provide at least an hour's worth of relaxation. Indeed, the number of shapes can be overwhelming, especially since most cigar companies have decided to give each new cigar they bring out a shape name of its own. And they've also changed the old tried and true dimensions. In the past, a standard Churchill was 7½ inches long. Today we have "Churchills" that range anywhere from 6¾ to 8 inches in length. It has gotten so that I don't even bother with shape charts anymore. I simply walk into a humidor and pick out the cigar that appeals to me. If I like the way it smokes, I will commit that particular brand's shape to memory, only so that I can order it again by phone or by mail. Or can confidently send my wife in to pick up a box, secure in the knowledge that she won't end up with the wrong size and consequently, the cigars will not end up being Exhibit A in divorce court.

How does one go about picking out a cigar? For starters, never take anyone else's recommendation. I have spent more money on "recommended" cigars I wished I had never smoked than anything else in recent memory. It is like asking someone to order for you in a restaurant. It just doesn't work. About the only person you can possibly go to for advice is your local tobacconist, but only if he is knowledgeable about his product and has an adequately supplied humidor to back up his convictions. That is, the humidor should not just be stocked with cigars that he likes to smoke, but with cigars that he knows to be good. And even then, you have to be specific about what kind of cigar you are looking for. Don't just ask your tobacconist what he thinks is best or what he smokes. His tastes may be entirely different than yours. You've got to tell him what you want. So what do you want?

First, let's talk about the types of cigars that there are in the world today. We already know about mass-market cigars. That leaves the premium and super premium cigars. Premium cigars, by far the most popular category among knowledgeable cigar smokers, can be either machine bunched or handmade. The greatest majority of premium cigars will be completely handmade, and will come from either the Dominican Republic or Honduras. For the money, these are by far the best cigars you can obtain anywhere in the world. Even in Europe, long the Havana stronghold, premium Dominican and Honduran cigars are starting to make inroads, simply because of their consistent quality and tremendous value. You will find all of today's most popular premium cigars pictured throughout this book and, of course, listed in Chapter 9.

Going one step up, one of the newest categories among today's cigar smoking elite is the super premium, which is to cigars what super unleaded is to gasoline. You may not really need them, they will cost more, but very often they will outperform the premium unleaded. Not always, but very often. Some entries in this rarified field include Davidoff, Zino, Punch Grand Cru, Santa Damiana, and Avo. A super premium cigar is normally made with specially selected tobaccos, usually in the filler blend and especially in the wrapper, where it is visually most evident. Super premiums may also come in certain sizes that are not available in the regular line. And very often, the cigars receive extra aging that enhances the flavor.

Another relatively new category is the vintage cigar, which can also be called a super premium, in that it receives special treatment, is made with specially selected tobaccos, and normally (but not always) is aged longer. The vintage cigar's real claim to fame is the fact that it is made with all or part of a tobacco crop that came from an especially good year, much the same as vintage wines. Only with wines, the claim of an excellent vintage is often based on hindsight, as one is never quite certain how the wine has matured until after the bottle has been uncorked. The cigar maker, on the other hand, knows when he has a vintage cigar not only by the way the growing season has turned out, but also by the way the tobacco has matured before it is even made into a cigar. For example, 1986 was such a good year that three years later it was the inspiration for the launching of the Dunhill Aged Cigar series, one of the few vintage cigars (along with Macanudo and a few others) to prominently put the actual vintage year on the box. Likewise, 1990, '91 and '95 were unbelievable vintage years for Dominican tobaccos, and this has manifested itself in even more super premiums joining the "vintage" ranks. Vintage cigars usually have special bands and boxes that set them apart from the rest. They will also be among the most expensive cigars that you can buy. Are vintage cigars worth the money? Some,

In the Dominican Republic, cured tobacco is transported in *serones*, bales made of woven Cana leaves from palm trees.

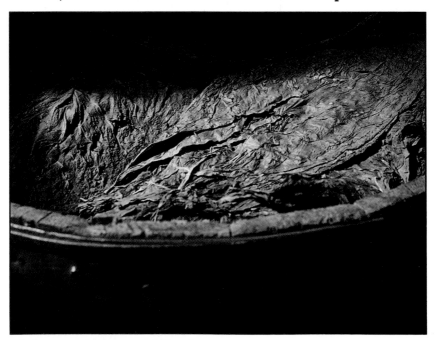

Rich, cured Havana filler leaves from the Vuelta Abajo.

The art of the handmade cigar, showing the traditional *chaveta* and tuck cutter.

Perhaps the epitome of a connoisseur's celebration is realized in this collection of vintage cigars. In the background, the perfect libation for such elegant cigars: a Baccarat decanter of Louis XIII cognac from Rémy Martin.

From the Austria Tabak Museum comes this rare set of brass shape gauges used by Vienna's cigar makers during the late nineteenth century.

A collection of cigar bands from the past make a colorful and historic decor.

Classic turn-of-the-century Havanas, still boxed, are always a collector's prize when they occasionally show up for private sale or at auction.

Named after America's celebrated writer who had an intimate familiarity with both Cuba and cigars, the Fuente Hemingway is one of the most difficult shapes to make — basically a Perfecto with a tapered head for easy clipping and an elongated foot for easy lighting. Truly a connoisseur's cigar. Shown are (top to bottom): the Masterpiece, Classic, the original Signature, and the Short Story. Not shown are the Best Seller and the Prized Edition.

like the Macanudo Vintage, Ashton Cabinet, Romeo y Julieta Vintage, Juan Clemente Club Selection, and Dunhill Aged definitely are. Others are not. And some cigars, like the Fuente Hemingway series (which is aged six months) and their Don Carlos "Reserva Superior Limitada" and Opus X, along with Cuesta-Rey's Diamond Crown (all of which are aged for a full year), plus

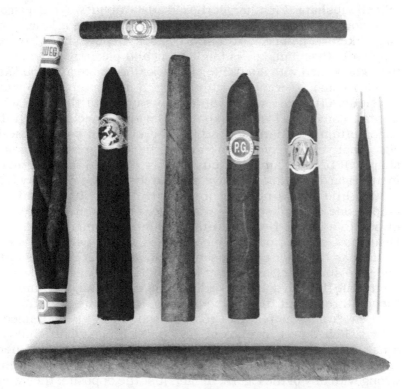

Cigars come in all shapes and sizes, as evidenced by this sampling of classic and *figurado* styles: (L to R) Villiger's original "AWEG," guaranteed to put a new twist into your smoking; La Gloria Cubana Piramides in Maduro; privately handrolled Connecticut shade Pyramid with flat head; PG Belicoso; Avo Belicoso; Austria Tabak Anatol with Sumatra wrapper (the natural reed is withdrawn from the center of the cigar and is used as a wick to light it); (Top) Havana Punch Slim Panetela; (Bottom) a custom rolled 9 ³/₄-inch Torpedo, flaring out to a 50 ring near the foot. This is one of the most difficult cigars to make.

the Punch Grand Cru and the Hoyo de Monterrey Excalibur (both of which offer special shapes and hand selected tobaccos) are not called vintage cigars but certainly could be. As a point of interest, in the pre-embargo years, when Cuba used to age many of their top brand cigars for a year or more, the "vintage" terminology was never used. It is strictly a "new age" appellation for certain Dominican and Honduran super-premiums.

Now that we know what types of cigars are out there, let's talk about shape. First, forget the old adage about buying a cigar to fit your face (i.e., a tall, thin man should smoke a long, thin cigar like a Lonsdale, but a short, stocky fellow should never touch a Rothschild). Life is too fleeting and pleasure too elusive to be concerned with such things. *Smoke the shape that you like.* Don't become preoccupied with trying to match a cigar to your physique, otherwise what would that say about the man who wants to smoke a Pyramid-shaped Davidoff Special T with its wide bottom and narrow head? And even when you do find a cigar that you like, you don't always have to smoke the same shape. Or brand. I am notorious for this. Much to the chagrin of many cigar companies, I have absolutely no brand loyalty, although I do have a number of reoccurring favorites. As an example, one December a few years ago, I went out and treated myself to a box of Honduran-made Punch Premier Grand Cru Diademas, which I promptly christened as the Official Hacker Christmas Cigar for our household (inasmuch as I am the only one who smokes cigars in my household, I figured that was a pretty safe thing to do). That cedar box of cigars and I became fast friends throughout the holiday season, but by the beginning of the New Year I was ready to go on to something else. I immediately switched over to a box of Joya de Nicaragua Churchills in a natural wrapper. Somewhat similar shape, but totally different taste. And in February, I changed brands again. Nothing wrong with any of the cigars. In fact, just the opposite; they were all good enough to warrant buying a full box. But with the weather and the months and the seasons, my tastes change and consequently, so do my cigars. For some reason, I find myself smoking more Macanudos and Ashtons during the summer months, while a box of Fuente Hemingways has always been my traditional way of ushering in the fall; their seven-inch Classics have helped me polish off more than one Thanksgiving turkey. And now I am finding that the Dunhill Aged cigars, Avos, and Juan Clementes are delicious any time of the year. I also enjoy the Davidoff Grand Cru and Thousand Series, as well as various vintage cigars, but prefer to save them for special outings, when I find that it is more prestigious to show off their bands than it is to wear a Rolex watch. As a result of all this brand-hopping, my humidors are overflowing with a plethora of different cigars, and I get great satisfaction from plunging into them as my smoking mood changes during different days of the week or phases of the moon. Years ago I used to favor Lonsdales and Petite Coronas. Today I am a dedicated fan of Churchills, Double Churchills, Rothschilds, and anything else with a big ring gauge. Which is another topic we should get into.

In America, all cigars are measured in inches for the length, and by a unit of measurement called a ring for the diameter of the cigar. One ring is $\frac{1}{64}$ of an inch. Therefore, a cigar that is a 5 x 34 would be five inches long by $\frac{34}{64}$ of an inch (just a little wider than $\frac{1}{2}$ inch) in diameter. However, this ring-and-inches system is not used in Europe. Instead, cigars are measured by millimeters for length, and also by millimeters for the straight across diameter of the cigar's body. Thus, a 5 x 34 cigar in the U.S. would translate to a 127 x 13,5 in Europe.

Ring size and length definitely have an influence on how a cigar will taste. Assuming you are smoking a cigar with the exact same filler-binder-wrapper tobaccos, the bigger the ring gauge, the fuller the taste. The longer the length, the cooler the smoke. As an example, let's take two Macanudos, a 5 x 38 Petite Corona and a 7½ x 49 Prince Philip. Although both cigars use the same Dominican, Jamaican and Mexican filler, Mexican binder, and Connecticut shade wrapper, the Petite Corona will be a milder smoke, while the Prince Philip will have a more full-bodied taste. In a way, it's like turning up the volume on the same CD track. Same song, but different perception of the music at 38 than at 49. And in spite of what I said about brand loyalty, if you find a cigar that you really like, but feel it is a little too intense, try it in a smaller size. Conversely, if you want more of the same taste, increase the ring size. Indeed, to the true connoisseur, the thickness of a cigar is more important than its length, which usually is only an indication of how long the cigar will smoke. But a short cigar does not always mean a short smoke. During the hour and a half ride from Puerto Plata to Santiago one time while visiting the Dominican Republic, Carlos Fuente, Jr. gave me one of his Hemingway Short Story cigars to smoke. It was a strange looking, tapered little cigar, with a ring gauge that went from 43 at the head all the way up to a 46 and then dramatically dropped off to 16 right at the tuck end, with all of this taking place within a 4½ inch body. My first reaction was that this cigar was not going to last me past the next palm tree, and as I lit it, I surreptitiously began looking around the car for something else to smoke. Half an hour later I was still smoking that same cigar. In fact, it almost became a Short Story without end, for it lasted a full 45 minutes. That, of course, was because this little cigar had a lot of tobacco packed into it.

If you want to experiment with just how dramatically shape can influence taste, light up a Davidoff Special R, which is a 5 x 50, and take notes on the flavor as the cigar is smoked. Then, later on, after your palate has had time to clear, do the same thing with the Davidoff Special T, which is a 6-inch Pyramid shape, starting at 32 and flaring out to 50 ring size. Both cigars are filled with the same blend. You'll find that the Robusto starts out full and remains that way throughout the smoke. This is your "control" cigar. On the other hand, the Special T, which starts out with the same ring size as the Robusto, is much milder at the outset (because of its longer length), and tends to get stronger as the smoke is funneled through the narrowing shape as the cigar becomes shorter. By this same token, if you want to taste test a number of different cigars, it is imperative that they each be the same length and ring size, or you will not get a true reading.

As one who likes heavy red wines, rich spicy foods, and full-bodied cigars, I will be the first to admit that taste is subjective. That is why I do not believe in rating systems for cigars. What might be a 10 to me could be a 4 to someone else, especially if they gravitated towards light white wines, delicate vegetable dishes, and mild cigars. Besides, our perception of a cigar's flavor is not just dictated by the tobaccos it is made with. A lot depends upon our mood while smoking, as well as what we have eaten or had to drink before lighting up. If you normally finish a pasta lunch with a cigar, that same cigar will taste differently when you smoke it after a two-hour Sunday buffet. That is why it is always desirable to have different cigars for different occasions. Besides the physical and gastronomic influences upon cigar smoking, our mental attitude has a lot to do with our perception of any given cigar. For many people, a leisurely cigar in the evening is much more memorable than that same cigar smoked during the day at a stressful business conference.

Still, throughout the course of my cigar smoking existence, I keep getting asked how I would rate a certain brand. But now that I have set my philosophies forth, I expect to keep getting asked that question. So I have devised my own system (which we shall use throughout this book from here on), called the Highly Prejudiced HackerScale, or HPH for short. This is not a "better than" rating system. Rather, it is based on a cigar's strength

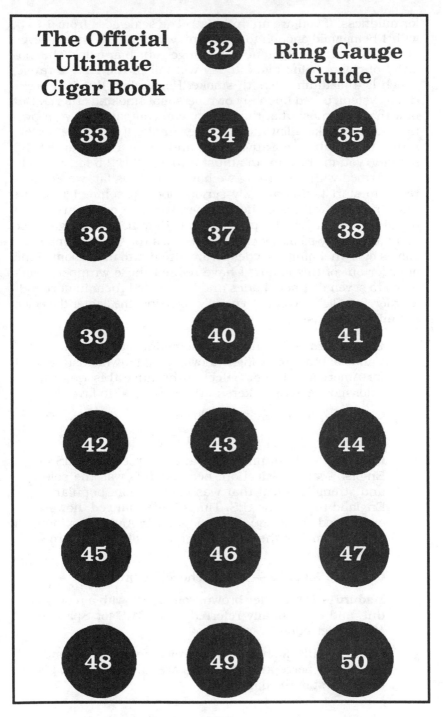

The Official
Ultimate
Cigar Book

32

Ring Gauge
Guide

33 34 35

36 37 38

39 40 41

42 43 44

45 46 47

48 49 50

(or mildness, if you are an optimist). The scale goes from 1 to 3, with 1 being mild enough to make you wonder if the thing is even lit, and 3 having the potency to change your hair color. The majority of cigars being made today will fall in the HPH 2 range, which is a medium strength smoke. Remember, this is a *prejudiced* system, based upon my own personal smoking criteria. But now that you know what that is, you can compare it to your own tastes, and make allowances. For example, if you like Merlots rather than Cabernet Sauvignons, and I give a cigar an HPH 2 reading, you might want to adjust it to an HPH 2.5 for yourself.

Armed with everything we have read thus far, we are now ready to start taking a really serious look at some cigars. The first thing you will see is the wrapper. Wrapper colors are an integral part of the cigar's persona, but they have been given so many names by so many cigar companies that it sometimes becomes overwhelming. In a desperate attempt to make some kind of order out of this chaos, I have refined these wrapper colors down to seven distinct shades and have listed them in chromatic order, from light to dark. Generally speaking, the lighter the color, the milder the taste.

> **Claro Claro** — A light green, sometimes called Jade or Candela, but more widely known as AMS, which stands for American Market Selection because this was the color most cigar smokers in the U.S. used to favor.

> **Claro** — A light, yellowish brown.

> **Colorado Claro** — Light brown

> **Colorado** — Medium brown and often called EMS or English Market Selection, because this was the color and strength of leaf that was always more popular in England than in the U.S. Times have changed, however, and today it is equally as popular in America, which probably makes the AMS designation of Claro Claro a little shaky.

> **Colorado Maduro** — A milk chocolate brown

> **Maduro** — Dark coffee brown, sometimes with a reddish tint, and occasionally referred to as SMS for Spanish Market Selection.

> **Oscuro** — Blackish brown or brownish black, depending on how perceptive your eyes are. In either case, it's the darkest of the dark.

The list goes on and can actually become pretty confusing, with definitions like Colorado Colorado and Double Oscuro, all of which seem like useless attempts to try and reclassify the sixty-plus different shades of brown that the color sorters went through back at the factory. Suffice to say, the simplified definitions listed above should get you through any humidor in the known world.

With wrapper color definition firmly in hand, we next come to the characteristics of each type of tobacco we are likely to find. This is a bit tricky, because we must deal with generalities, being unable to account for the way each tobacco in each brand has been cured and aged. So, realizing that there are exceptions to all of this, here are the basics:

A few of the more popular shades of wrapper, with country of origin (L to R): Maduro (Mexican seed), Colorado Maduro (Ecuadorian-grown Connecticut seed), Colorado (Cameroon), Colorado Claro (Connecticut shade), Colorado Claro (Connecticut shade). Even though the last two cigars both have a Connecticut shade wrapper, there is a 10% difference in color, caused by slight variances in leaf structure and fermentation. This is why color sorting is such exacting work.

Dominican — Generally perceived to be mild, around a 2 on the HPH.

Honduran — Slightly more full bodied or spicier than Dominican. A HPH rating of 2—2.5.

Havana — Medium to full bodied. HPH 2—3. In addition to all-Havana cigars, you will find that Havana is commonly used as part of the filler blend in many European dry cigars (obviously not in any of the cigars and cigarillos that are imported to America, however).

Jamaica — A little lighter in taste than Dominican, but still an HPH 2.

Maduro — Can be sweet and mild or thundering rich and heavy. Generally speaking, if you like espresso, you'll like Maduro. Most Maduro cigars have a deep, chocolatey flavor, while others are like the dust on a country road. There are three different types of Maduro: fermented, fire cured (in which heat is used to control the coloring, much like Candela processing), and Havana pressed, in which pressure creates the fermentation process. Maduros can range anywhere from HPH 2—3.

Nicaragua — Medium sweet, especially the wrappers. HPH 2—2.5.

Ecuador — Mild, flavorful yet subdued. HPH 1.5—2.

Cameroon — Heavier than Dominican. A spicy taste, with a more pungent aroma. HPH of 2—2.5.

Mexico — Not as refined a taste as Dominican or Honduran. Can run the gamut of extremely mild to rough and gravely. An unusually wide range of HPH 1.5—2.5.

Sumatra — Spicy and mild. HPH 1.5—2.

Brazil — More pronounced in flavor; heavy but not disagreeable. An HPH of 2.5.

Philippines — Very light and airy; an HPH 1.5—2.

By combining these tobacco descriptions with their HPH ratings, and factoring in the filler-binder-wrapper combinations that are listed for each brand in Chapter 9, you will be able to get a pretty fair idea of what a particular cigar will smoke like in terms of approximate taste and strength. That in itself should make this book worth more than you paid for it. But there is yet another aspect of selecting a good cigar. It is not enough to simply walk into your tobacconist's humidor, decide on the brand, strength and shape, and snatch up the first cigar in the box. There is the cigar's physical appearance and condition to consider as well.

First, forget about the arcane practice of rolling the end of a cigar next to your ear in order to hear a crackle. All this does is risk damaging the delicate wrapper near the foot of the cigar. If you insist on performing this meaningless ritual, at least have the courtesy to buy the cigar beforehand, so as not to damage it for others. Instead, show your expertise by first taking a close look at the wrapper. A worm hole disqualifies the cigar immediately, but be sure to alert the tobacconist so that he can take precautions to get that cigar box out of there before others are affected. In a premium cigar, the wrapper should be smoothly rolled and evenly colored, with no blotches, although sun spots are okay and won't affect the flavor. The wrapper should also have some grain to it, and you should be able to see the veins of the leaf, which not only give the wrapper character, but flavor as well. These veins will not be as distinct on a Connecticut shade wrapper as they will be on Cameroon, for example, where they are noticeably more pronounced. The veins on a Sumatra wrapper will look like a "t" or a "y." The major veins of any wrapper should run

Sun spots (shown) are not normally found on super premium cigars, but they are harmless and do not affect the taste. On the other hand, blemishes and wrapper discolorations are common on many bundle cigars.

A patch in the wrapper is not something you might want to see, but it does not affect the taste of the cigar. It is simply the cigar maker's way of trying to save an otherwise smokeable leaf.

as parallel as possible to the length of the cigar (within reason, of course; after all they are not drawn on with a ruler. Or at least they shouldn't be). This is an indication that the cigar will burn evenly. It will also tell you that the cigar has been properly rolled. And an oily sheen to the wrapper will tell you that it has been properly cured. If the wrapper is starting to unravel, alert the tobacconist; his humidor is too dry. (This is more of a problem in Europe than America, as some tobacconists on the Continent, specifically those in the smaller towns, have only recently begun equipping their shops with humidification devices.)

These next two inspections can only be done with uncellophaned cigars. Gently feel the cigar, checking for any hard or soft spots that may indicate a poor bunching of the filler which could interfere with the draw. I should warn you that this won't make

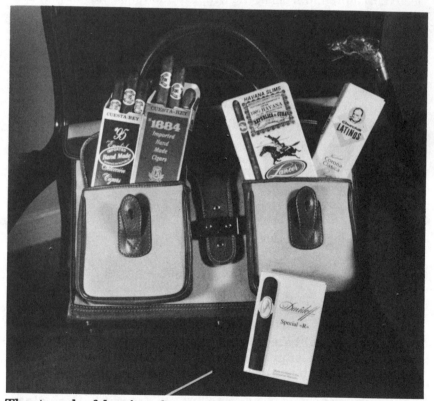

The trend of buying fewer cigars at a time has led many manufacturers to offer their cigars in smaller, easier to carry packages. The leather and sailcloth Saddle Bag Briefcase is from Pusser's, Ltd.

you a friend of the other guy in the humidor who was thinking of buying that same cigar you are now stroking with your sweaty fingers. But so what; it's your money. And your cigar. Now heft it. A loosely packed cigar will feel lighter than a tightly rolled one and may provide an easier draw, although some smokers prefer a more tightly wrapped cigar. That is an individual choice for you to make. If the cigar is packed too loosely, you may take in too much air when puffing and could hyperventilate. That's the light-headed feeling many smokers attribute to the tobacco, but it's possible they were just taking in too much air. Due to the growing lack of experienced rollers and the proliferation of some new and questionable brands, there is a growing concern about getting a cigar that is too tightly packed. Of course, you can always take it back to the tobacconist (with the exception of illegal Havanas, of course), but one way to guard against this frustrating occurrence is to buy a *figurado*, like a Belicoso or a Pyramid. These cigars are more difficult to make and therefore require the skill of an experienced roller, so there is less chance of the draw being too tight.

You can check to make sure that the filler in your cigar wasn't "booked" by examining the tuck end. The filler should appear to flow around in curves, rather than show up as straight lines. If you see some dark centers in the filler, it is probably Ligero, and that thicker leaf will help hold the ash. When you smoke the cigar, you can actually see the Ligero projecting out from the ash, like a glowing peak.

Because of their cost, many smokers of premium cigars buy them singly, but more often they will purchase as many as three or four at a time. This is also a good way to experiment with different brands of cigars or different sizes of the same cigar. Acknowledging this trend, a number of brands are now packaging their cigars in five-packs. Bering has a ten-pack, as does Oscar and Joya de Nicaragua. But by buying cigars by the box, you can often save money, as many tobacconists will give you a price break on a box purchase. Sometimes you can save even more on multiple boxes. Most cigars are packed 20 to 25 per box, and it is a secure feeling in an uncertain world to know that, if nothing else, you've at least got enough cigars to get through the month.

Up until now, we have only been talking about premium and super premium cigars. But there is another category that is worthy of our attention, even though it is sometimes undeservedly frowned upon. That is the classification of "bundle" cigars. The concept of a bundle cigar originated in the 1960s as a way for the consumer to save money by eliminating the manufacturer's cost of color sorting cigars and of putting them in cedar boxes. It proved to be a viable concept and bundle cigars have been popular ever since. Manufacturers were quick to seize upon the idea of using bundles for their "seconds"; that is, cigars that have small imperfections, such as blemishes on an otherwise very smokeable wrapper. Ironically, bundle cigars became so popular that factories began making cigars specifically to be put into bundles. Today, both "firsts" and "seconds" are sold as bundles, and the bundle cigar has become one of the best values for the serious cigar smoker. Even the illustrious firm of Davidoff sells bundle cigars; of course, they are handmade and contain long filler. And for years Cuba made bundle cigars, not only for local consumption, but for high end smokers as well. The Partagás Derby and the H. Upmann Majestic were two Havana bundles of the past that come to mind. There was also a machine-made Cuban bundle cigar from Ramón Allones called Rondos, a 5½ x 43 that

Tubed cigars are like having a mini-humidor in your car or attaché case; most are cedar lined and will keep your cigar fresh for at least three to five days. Some smokers prefer to have their tobacconist clip their tubed cigars at the time of sale, so that they will always be ready to smoke (this is also a good way to check the cigar's construction before you leave the store). The Davidoff Tubos (bottom right) have a unique two-part construction, so that the slit in the side can be opened or closed for letting humidity in or keeping it in. Most tubes are made of aluminum in Italy. Some cigars, like the Hoyo de Monterrey Cafe Royal come in glass tubes. Shown with an engraved silver cigar case and a stamped tin "Seegar" case, both from the late 1800s.

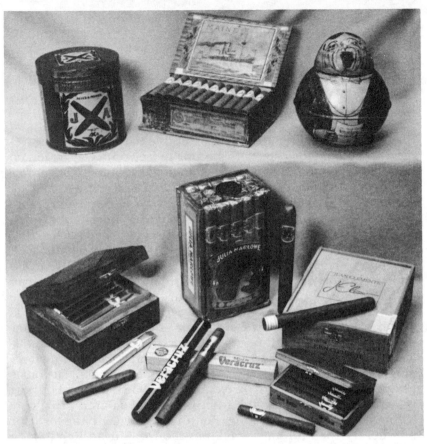

Innovative packaging has always been a part of the cigar
smoker's lure (L to R top row): a 1920s can of J&A Cigars;
an 1898 "Remember The Maine" Spanish American War
patriotic cigar book/box filled with a temporary cargo of
Davidoff Grand Cru No. 5s; and a 1930s "Brownie" singing
cigar smoker tobacco tin. The trend continues today
(Bottom row, clockwise from left): Villiger's Rosewood and
silver inlaid gift box filled with 28 of their Premium No. 7
Sumatra hygrofoil-wrapped cigars; a sensuously topless box
for the Julia Marlowe Sovereign; Juan Clemente's foot-band,
created by noted Parisian designer Gerard Guerre; José
Benitos mini-box of mini-cigars; and the super-humidified
amber glass tubed Veracruz. Other packaging variations
include the cedar-tubed Davidoff Aniversario case that
comes with each cigar, and certain collector's boxes such as
the limited edition Finck Centennial.

109

used a lower grade of tobacco, but sold well due to the bundle cigar's hallmark, lower price.

Of course, there are some drawbacks to bundles. Very often, not only do the cigars not match in color, they don't match in taste. Some are machine made and others use "sandwich" filler, in which the center of the cigar consists of chopped filler that is held together by long leaf tobacco. Because of their nature, many bundle brands are inconsistent, with one batch being great and the next not worthy of lighting up. But due to the growing awareness of value-minded smokers starting to focus more attention on bundle cigars, much of that is changing. Today, major manufacturers like Consolidated, General Cigar, and Villazon are not only crafting the same kind of consistency into their bundle cigars as they have in their boxed brands, but they are manufacturing cigars exclusively for bundles. No more seconds, as such.

The secret in buying a bundle cigar is knowing what to look for. Unfortunately, because of its packaging, it is impossible to examine a bundle cigar as you would a premium. The best you can do is check the package to make sure the cigars around the perimeter haven't been bruised. However, there are a few brands which stand out. Jamaica Gem is one of the most popular bundle cigars in America. It uses long filler and comes in eleven different shapes, including a Grandioso, which measures a whopping 8½ x 60! Too big for conventional bundle packaging, it comes as five 5-packs in a wooden box. Another good Jamaican bundle is Jamaica Bay, which is the same cigar as the Santa Cruz, only without a box or color sorting. For an even bigger bang for your bundle, try the #9 King Cigar from the Dominican Republic, a

Bundle cigars represent one of the best bargains available to the knowledgeable smoker.

hefty 10 x 66. La Unica, which is made by the Fuente factory, is probably one of the most expensive cigars in the bundle category, and features an excellent blend of all long leaf filler. This cigar is not a second, but is a very high quality cigar that is simply packaged without a box. Available in both Natural and Maduro wrappers, it is well worth discovering. Honduran bundles are very much in evidence and are growing in popularity. For example, La Primadora is a Honduran cigar that features all long leaf filler, a choice of Natural or Maduro wrapper, and is available in six sizes, ranging from a 5½ x 42 Petite Cetros all the way up to an 8½ x 50 Emperor. Juan López is an old Cuban brand that is now being made as a long filler, Cuban seed Honduran bundle. Bermejo started out as a Nicaraguan bundle, but is currently being made as a machine-bunched long filler cigar in Honduras — if you like the Bances cigars, you'll like these. And speaking of Nicaraguan bundles, the first brands were brought out in 1992, but I hesitate to mention any of them because their continuous availability is not always assured. These are only a few of the better brands. For more specific information, ask your tobacconist about his best values in bundle cigars. (Just for the record, Cuba no longer makes bundle cigars, although for a while some Havanas, such as the Montecristo, had to be tied in bundles because Cubatabaco did not have enough cedar to make boxes.)

You might also want to ask your tobacconist about his private brands. These are often excellent cigars made by one of the major companies, but they are given a special brand and band for a specific store, tobacco chain, or direct mail tobacconist. They are usually priced well below nationally distributed frontmark cigars made by those same companies and some of them are every bit as comparable in construction and taste as the nationally branded premiums.

And what about Havanas? They remain a proverbial topic of interest, even though American cigar smokers do not have the luxury of being able to taste test and compare these "outlaw cigars," as do our cigar smoking brethren in other parts of the world, most notably Canada, England and Europe. But even in those countries, the opportunity to compare all thirty of the exported Cuban brands is not possible, as no single country has all thirty brands exported to it. Which is one of the reasons that I put as many as possible of Cuba's finest in Chapter 9, so that at least we could know what we have or have not.

Nonetheless, it should be noted that even in the U.S., where Havanas are forbidden, it is estimated that a surprisingly large number of illegal boxes of Cuban cigars, as many as 10 million "sticks" a year — or approximately a sixth of Cuba's annual production — are being smuggled into and smoked within our borders (although if any customs agents are reading this, I'm only kidding!). The penalties for an American citizen buying and possessing post-embargo Havana cigars in the U.S. is $250,000 per offense and up to ten years in the slammer — which some may feel is a little stiff for a 45 minute smoke. For those who do not wish to run afoul of the law, foreign travel provides an excellent opportunity for Americans to taste the forbidden leaf. After all, the more we know about something, the less mysterious it becomes. Besides, there is an understandable tendency for American cigar smokers, when given the opportunity to procure a Havana, to grab whatever is being offered, in the blind belief that if it is Havana, it has to be good. But unfortunately, such is not always the case. A familiarity with the product can at least provide the cigar aficionado with a basis upon which to make a selection. That way, a cigar smoker with a sensitive palate might wisely choose to pass over a Bolivar Coronas Gigante, knowing it possesses a strength that is not for the uninitiated, and instead might wisely opt for a less potent but equally satisfying Rafael Gonzalez.

Which brings us to two myths that must be cleared up. The first is that all Cuban cigars are strong. Anyone who has ever smoked a Juan López or a La Flor de Cano knows the fallacy of that statement. The second belief is that Cuban cigars are better than cigars made in other countries. "Better" is a subjective word; a more appropriate choice would be "different." Different in the way a Beef Wellington is different from a Châteaubriand. They are both gourmet delicacies, but each has its own character and taste. It is the same when trying to compare Havanas with Dominican or Honduran cigars. You can't, as each has a very distinct identity. But of the three, Dominican and Honduran cigars are fairly comparable in price, while Havanas are decidedly more expensive.

There are five major cigar-making factories in Cuba today: La Corona, Partagás, H. Upmann, Romeo y Julieta, and El Laguito (which used to make the Davidoff and Cohiba brands, but today makes only Cohibas). Most of Cuba's cigars use shade-grown wrappers, which is a fairly notable change, as in pre-embargo days all of their wrappers were sungrown. Inasmuch as shade-grown tobacco burns slower than sungrown, a Havana cigar is relatively slow burning and their HPH ratings run the gamut of 2 to 3. Unfortunately, there is a great deal of variation in the quality of today's Cuban cigar. My experience in Chapter 2 is one example. Yet, when I smoked a Punch Monarcas later on that same trip,

I was amazed at the velvety smoothness of the flavor. And the Monarcas is a big cigar. But unfortunately, the Monarcas incident was not an indication that the situation was getting better. While rewriting this very chapter for the second edition, I was examining the dark and oily wrapper of an extremely well made Partagás Lusitania, and, succumbing to temptation, I decided to smoke it. Upon lighting the cigar, I found it to possess that rich, creamy flavor such as only the famed Saint Luis fields of Cuba's Vuelta Abajo could produce. This was indeed the savory excellence for

A collection of Havanas from Casa de Partagas...

...with an equally wide variety from the Casa del Habano.

which Havana cigars have long been famous. Perhaps, I thought, things were changing in Cuba. But then, later on in the week, I smoked a Cuban Partagás 8-9-8 and instantly felt betrayed. It emitted a harsh bite and, although properly humidified, developed an ugly, out-of-control burn running down one side of the wrapper, unusual in an easy-to-light cigar such as an 8-9-8 with its Perfecto tip; it was indicative of a poorly fermented wrapper. So here were two Cuban cigars of the same brand, both presumably made of the same leaf and rolled in the same factory, perhaps even by the same roller. Yet, their smoking qualities were on opposite ends of the pleasure spectrum. But there's more.

On another occasion, while visiting a friend in Europe, I was shown a newly opened box of Havanas he had bought in which some of the wrapper colors were mismatched. Yet in the Havana cigar factories, I saw skilled workers meticulously sorting cigars by color, just as they do in the Dominican Republic and Honduras. I also made it a point to personally inspect randomly selected boxes of cigars in two retail stores in Havana (one is the Casa de Partagás, located in the Partagás factory and the other is at Casa del Habano, in the Havana suburb of Miramar; another reputable factory store, in case you're wondering, is Palacio del Tobacco in the La Corona factory) and in both cases found every box to be beautifully color matched. The conclusion one must draw is obvious: there is a sporadic quality control situation in Cuba that has to be more closely monitored if they are to regain their reputation of consistency. Which, as we know, is the hallmark of a good cigar.

Unlike their exported brands, the cigars smoked by Cubans themselves are of a much lower quality. They are made in factories that are separate from those that make Havanas for export. Two of these factories, located outside the city of Havana, are Villa Santa Clara and Sancti Spiritus. (Their boxes are stamped VSC and SS respectively. Stay away from them.) These local brands, with names like Casadores and Cinco Vegas, are relatively small in size. You won't see any Lonsdales or Churchills being smoked in Cuba, other than by *turistas* and a visiting cigar book author. Which is why some of the locals I befriended referred to me as "el hombre con el puro grande" (the man with the big cigar).

You won't know how well the tobacco has been treated in a Havana cigar until you light it up, but you can give it the same physical examination as discussed earlier in this chapter. I find in that respect, a Havana is no different than any other cigar. But there is a serious problem unique to Havanas that you will not find with their Dominican or Honduran counterparts. And that is the specter of counterfeit Cuban cigars, which was brought to public attention in the first edition of this book. Since that publication, and the resultant increased consumption of cigar smoking, counterfeiting Cuban cigars has become a multi-million dollar business. Americans are especially susceptible to this ruse, as we are not as familiar with the look and taste of genuine Havana leaf as our non-embargoed brethren. Even so, foreign fakes abound. Often made in Brazil, these bogus stogies were initially encountered in Europe, particularly Germany and Switzerland. In the recent past they were not so much in evidence in the U.K., but now that situation has changed (in London I helped dissect a counterfeit short-filler Cohiba!) and I know of instances in Canada as well. The main brands that were faked used to be Davidoff and Cohiba, but now that Davidoff is no longer importing Havanas, most of the attention seems to be focused on Cohiba and Montecristo. But to confuse the issue (and the detection), some of these counterfeit cigars are actually made with Cuban tobacco, scrap leaf that has been smuggled out of the factories by workers seeking to augment their meager wages. Likewise, genuine Cuban bands are winding up on non-genuine "Cuban" cigars. So while the tobacco may be Cuban, it is not top quality leaf, it is not correctly blended, and it is usually rolled by an unskilled person in a cramped apartment, far from the *galeras* of Havana.

In addition, there are now factories in Jamaica and in the Dominican Republic that have been established for the sole pur-

Sometimes a simple cigar band can tell you a lot about a cigar: (L to R) Havana Punch, Honduran Punch, and Honduran Punch double-banded Grand Cru.

But sometimes you have to study each band very carefully to discern the difference. (L to R) Dominican Romeo y Julieta; gold accented Dominican Romeo y Julieta Vintage; Cuban Romeo y Julieta.

Cuban or Dominican — can you tell without reading this caption? (Top tubed cigars): Havana's Montecristo and Dominican's Montecruz (the colors are identical). Boxes: the top is from Havana, the bottom box, using the same artwork, is from the Dominican Republic.

pose of manufacturing phony Cuban cigars made for sale to the American market, using poor quality non-Havana scrap leaf but very often affixing genuine Cuban cigar bands smuggled out of Havana. That's how profitable the American black market has become, thanks to the ongoing embargo that has created an artificially-inflated demand, coupled with our natural inclination to think, "If I can't get it, I gotta have it, at any price!" I should also tell you this is information that I have uncovered at some degree of personal risk, so if you see these facts repeated, at least you'll know the original source.

How can you tell a counterfeit Cuban cigar? One way is to check the bottom of the box. Prior to 1961, all Havana cigar boxes were stamped "Made in Havana - Cuba," surrounded by a double oval line. By the way, these pre-embargo cigars are the only ones that can be legally brought into the United States, as long as they are accompanied by proof that the cigars were made before the revolution. (You might consider carrying a copy of this book with you when you travel overseas in order to help document your purchases.) In 1961 Castro ordered that all boxes be stamped in Spanish and from that year on, only *Hecho en Cuba* has been used. It means, "Made in Cuba." The skeletonized Cubatabaco leaf logo first appeared in 1985 in conjunction with a lettered facto-

The current stamp and seal of authentic Havana cigars from Cubatabaco. Pre-embargo Havana boxes were stamped with a number and letter classification of the cigar (i.e., 10G) and the words, "Made in Havana, Cuba" inside an oval.

117

The current Habanos S.A. stamping on a legitimate box of Cuban cigars.

Although this is a rare glass-topped collector's case of Cohibas, the cigars have not been color sorted. Note the correct Habanos sticker across the upper right hand corner of the case.

ry code. In keeping with the usage of only Spanish on all boxes, in 1989 "*Totalamente a Mano*," which means, "(Made) Totally by Hand," was added to the bottom of all boxes of handmade Havana cigars. Some counterfeits are stamped *Hecho a Mano*, which means, "Made by Hand," or "*Envuelta a Mano*," which means "Packed by Hand," in an attempt to trap the unwary who think all Spanish words look alike. Finally, in 1994 the Cubatabaco box stamp was changed to Habanos S.A. and an Habanos strip was taped across the corner of each box. Currently, the real product will usually be stamped *La Habana, Cuba*, although not all boxes have this stamping. In fact, a bogus box making the rounds is stamped, *La Habana Club*.

There has been much discussion about the letter code that was started by Cubatabaco in 1985 and what it means. Quite simply, it gives the month and year a specific box of cigars was made. But the Cubans, who have usually been very open and honest with me, have balked at revealing the letter-number translation. The main reason for their hesitancy is they feel that once a consumer knows that a box of, say, Bolivar Gigantes, was made in October 1995, that potential purchaser might pass up the cigars and say, "I'd rather have an older box that was made in 1990." But the facts are, given the rarity and desirability of anything Havana, most lovers of the leaf will readily take any bona fide box they can get. And so, to forever unveil the mystery of the Cuban box code, here it is:

There are two sets of capital letters stamped within a square on each box of Cuban cigars. The top set, consisting of two letters, denotes the factory in which the cigars were made. Each factory has two names, a pre-revolutionary name and a post-revolutionary name. For example, the H. Upmann factory is also called José Martí, and uses the initials JM on the box. Here is the complete list, including the box letter code, what the initials stand for, and the actual factory in which those cigars were made:

Box Code	Factory Name	Pre-Revolutionary Factory Name
JM	José Martí	H. Upmann
FPG	Francisco Perez German	Partagás
BM	Briones Montoto	Romeo y Julieta
FR	Fernando Roig	La Corona
HM	Heroes del Moncada	El Rey del Mundo
EL	El Laguito	(none)

The bottom set of four capital letters represent numbers, which translate into the month and the year that particular box was made. Each letter equals a specific number, but there is a code that you must know. To crack this code, think of the word Nivelacuso (or the phrase, "Nothing In View Equals Length And Can Use Some Objectivity," if that makes it easier). There are ten letters in this word. Going from left to right, each letter in the word Nivelacuso goes up the numerical scale and equals a number going from 1 to 9, but then, the last letter in Nivelacuso, an "o," equals zero, instead of the number ten. Thus, "N" equals 1, "I" equals 2, "V" equals 3, and so on. So, a legitimate Cuban box of Juan López cigars that is stamped FR over the letters NISL means that box was made in the La Corona factory (FR=Fernando Rey=La Corona) in the twelfth month (NI = 12, or December) of 1995 (SL = 95).

Of course, now that this is published, Habanos will probably revise the code, just as many of the counterfeiters revised their techniques when we first exposed bogus Cuban cigars in the first edition of this book. But that just leaves another mystery to be solved. After all, trying to head 'em off at the pass is half the fun.

Besides, counterfeit stamps have already been forged, although they often are not used correctly, mismatching the cigars with improper factories or years. For example, if you know how to read the code and translate a box of Cohiba Siglo IVs as having been made *prior* to 1992 (the year they were introduced), you know you don't want to buy that box, no matter what the price. And because the Cuban guarantee label has not changed since 1912, it therefore is no longer a guarantee, as there has been plenty of time to make counterfeit printing plates, although computer technology has made the process even easier and more sophisticated by now.

By putting this information about the growing cancer of counterfeit Havanas in this book to warn you of deception, I also warn the counterfeiters of what we know. There is no way around it. Consequently, none of this is failsafe protection against being stuck with illicite cigars, as almost anything — boxes, bands, labels, stamps — can be copied. I say "almost anything," because the one thing that cannot be duplicated is the physical look and feel and the actual taste of real, properly fermented Havana leaf. Thus, the only foolproof way to detect a fake Havana is to smoke it. Of course, you have to know what a real Havana cigar tastes like in order to be proficient at this method. I was victim of this mixed blessing a few years ago during a trip to Mexico, when I picked up a box of Monte Cristo (sic) Canalejas. Thinking this was a new size that had somehow escaped me, and completely overlooking the fact that Montecristo was erroneously printed as two words instead of one, I got taken. The first puff told me it wasn't a Havana, but by then it was too late. Besides Mexico, Brazil, Jamaica and the Dominican Republic, other non-Cuban *faux*-Havanas are reputedly coming in from Nicaragua and are being stamped "Mexico." Your only defense against the growing number of counterfeits is to buy directly from the duty-free shops when traveling outside of the U.S., or from a reputable dealer when in Europe or England. And because even legitimate Havanas are not all created equal, it is helpful to know the best quality smokes will be found in England, Switzerland, and Spain.

Europeans traveling into the United States may legally transport up to 50 Havana cigars for their own use, although this is somewhat of a grey area within the U.S. Treasury Department. And although counterfeit Cuban cigars are primarily a problem in America, by contrast, European cigar smokers should be aware that many Honduran and Dominican cigars share the same brand name as their Cuban counterparts. For example, Punch and Hoyo de Monterrey are made in both Honduras and Cuba. And Romeo y Julieta, Cohiba, and Montecristo are made in both the Dominican Republic and Havana. Consequently, there has been more than one European tourist visiting the U. S. who was pleasantly surprised to find his favorite "Havana" cigar for sale in American tobacco shops, only to discover that it wasn't a Havana cigar at all. The reason for this sometimes confusing double identity of some cigars is that when Castro nationalized the factories during the revolution, many of the cigar-making families fled Cuba, taking their brand names with them. As recounted in Chapter 1, they eventually began manufacturing their family brand name cigars in other countries, thus creating a dual nationality for many cigars that were formerly only Havanas. Fortunately, there is a trade agreement that forbids Havana and non-Havana cigars of the same name from being sold together. Thus, you will never see a Cuban Hoyo de Monterrey for sale next to a Honduran Hoyo de Monterrey. Instead, the Honduran Hoyo de Monterrey (which is now being imported into Germany, for example) is renamed for the European market and is known as Excalibur.

Whether Cuban, Dominican, or Honduran, there is an all-encompassing, elite category of cigar that I refer to as The Power Smoke. These are cigars that tell the non-smoking world you've made it, or are about to make it. It has absolutely nothing to do with flavor, tobacco, value or the attributes of any brand. It is strictly an image that is presented to the casual, uninformed observer, although every cigar in this classification is definitely high grade. Power Smoke cigars include virtually all of the vintage cigars. In addition, the Ashton Aged Maduro #40, #50 and #60 are Power Smokes, as is the entire Davidoff line. Any Havana smoked in America is a Power Smoke. A Havana smoked in Europe is not, although all of the Cohibas and any of the larger sizes, such as the Partagás Lusitania and especially the Montecristo A, may arguably qualify for this category. Within the Power Smoke league there is also an upper echelon group of cigars that may not necessarily mean anything to the non-smoker, but which definitely will catch the attention of the knowledgeable cigar connoisseur. Cigars in this rarified inner circle include the Opus X, Diamond Crown, Partagas 150th Anniversary, and any cigar that is so new nobody has heard of it yet. But of this latter category, only large sizes qualify. So take a Power Smoke to your next business seminar or dinner. Offer one to your boss. If an associate offers you a Power Smoke, clasp his or her hand heartily and return the favor. You've got a valuable ally.

Another category of cigar, one that is not too widely seen in the U.S. but is immensely popular in Europe, is that of the dry cigar. Commonly referred to as "Dutch-type," these small smokes offer a number of benefits: 1) they require no humidification, as they smoke their best at only 10-12% humidity; 2) most of them come already clipped or pierced, so it is relatively effortless to get one going; 3) they are extremely easy to carry, usually coming in small packs of 5, 10, or 20 cigars; 4) they can be conveniently stored in an attaché case, desk drawer or coat pocket for weeks. I once squirreled away a pack of Dunhill Señoritas in the glove compartment of my car for over a year before I accidentally stumbled upon them one day while looking for my registration. They were a little dry, but they smoked without incident. The highway patrol officer enjoyed them, too. A humidified cigar would have gone to dust.

Dry cigars come in a variety of blends, and can be as mild or as strong as you wish. Basically, there are two types of wrappers: Sumatra, which is light and mild tasting; and Brazil, which is dark and spicy. Tobaccos used within the cigars come from Mexico, Columbia, Java, Cameroon, Italy, Florida, Connecticut and

An assortment of some of the world's most popular non-humidified cigars.

Cuba. Most people select Sumatra over Brazil, simply because it is not so overbearing. But both light and dark wrappers are equally as popular in Germany and Switzerland, with Sumatra being smoked on a regular basis and the darker Brazil often being saved for dinners and special occasions. France remains the largest dry cigar market in the world. As we noted in Chapter 2, some Dutch-type cigars are made with homogenized leaf. In England they do not mind this in a binder, but prefer an all-tobacco wrapper. An all-tobacco dry cigar is still the most popular choice in Germany, France, Belgium, and The Netherlands. The reason these European cigars have not caught on more than they have in the U.S. is that their costs are often compared to a full-sized Dominican or Honduran cigar, which is bigger and has more tobacco. And yet, there are times when you don't want a cigar with a lot of tobacco. Like in between the acts of a play. Or while waiting for a drink to be served. Or the check. Some of the dry cigars, like the Agio Mehari's, Nobel Panetela, Villiger Braniff, Bering #8, or the Dunhill Miniature Cigars are ideal for those moments. Your smoking time and enjoyment can be extended with some of the larger sizes of Corps Diplomatique, Dannemann, or Panter. A Christian of Denmark Corona lasts a full 50 minutes and I have recently taken to enjoying Schimmelpenninck Duets while

Tinned cigars are a convenient smoke when there isn't time for a leisurely full-sized cigar. They may also get you past the censors in a "no cigar smoking" restaurant.

Some of the many made-in-Austria cigars from Austria Tabak, ranging from an HPH 1.5 (Capriole Light) to a 2.5 (Falstaff). Those with Sumatra wrapper fall into the HPH 2 range. Falstaff, Imperiales, and Mozart are cedar-wrapped. Many of these excellent cigars are made with Havana leaf, which disqualifies them for smoking on American shores.

barbecuing and their VSOP Corona de Luxe with a pre- or post-dinner cocktail. These are easy cigars to get used to, are ideal for travel, and provide an enjoyable change of pace smoke that doesn't require a humidor.

Buying a cigar for ourselves can be rewarding, but equally gratifying, I think, is buying a cigar for someone else as a gift. After all, one of the old adages is, "The best cigar is the one you get for free." While any premium cigar can be a welcomed gift, there are a few that stand out, either in terms of packaging or shape. One of the most costly is the Davidoff Aniversario No. 1, an 8⅔ x 48 Giant Double Corona that comes in its own cedar tube. The Royal Jamaica No. 10 Downing St., 10½ x 51 is a hard cigar to forget, as is the Griffin's Don Bernardo 9 x 46 and the 9 x 52 Ashton Cabinet #1. The Montecruz Individuales checks in at 8 x 46 and comes in its own distinctive cedar box with brass hinges. Equally impressive is the Hamilton A, which also comes in its own cedar case and is the same 9¼ x 52 size as the Cuban Montecristo A. An even bigger boxed cigar is the spectacular 18-inch long Cuba Aliados General. The Dunhill Centenas, part of their Dominican-made Aged Cigar series, is a curly-top Belicoso that was introduced in 1993 to celebrate the one hundred-year-anniversary of this prestigious firm. The band bears the 1893-1993 dates and the cigar is available in a five pack as well as boxes of twenty-five (introduced in 1994) for those *really* special friends. Like yourself.

With the increased emphasis on new shapes (or rather, old shapes that have been introduced to new smokers) and vintage or limited edition cigars, a new category of cigar has emerged for the first time. It is the rarified realm of the collectable cigar. Just as *The Ultimate Cigar Book* (first edition) was the first to point out counterfeit Havanas, so do we now focus the spotlight on this latest subtrend of the cigar smoking hobby. To be sure, connoisseurs have been collecting cigars for decades, otherwise, how do you think all those pre-Castro Havanas originally got squirreled away? (These pre-1959 Havanas, by the way, are the only Cuban cigars that can still legally be brought into the United States. I tell you this in case you need a rationale for purchasing a box.) But consciously producing and seeking out special limited edition cigars is a relatively new phenomena. Of course, many cigar smokers are collectors. A simple glance at all the cutters, lighters, cases and humidors that litter my office and den will prove the point. And many of us also like to hoard special cigars. For example, I still have an unopened box of Vencedors, an excellent Canary Islands cigar made by Eufemiando Fuentes in the late 1970s and early '80s, that was sold exclusively by the Tinder Box chain. They are well aged by now and probably past their prime, but I don't care; I like having them around. Likewise, I have put away some of the individually cedar-boxed H. Upmann cigars that were specially stamped and handed out at some of the first Ritz-Carlton Laguna Niguel smokers starting in 1985. I also keep a few of the specially banded Smoke cigars from the premiere party of this high-flying magazine, even though I know the cigars are really Padróns. And on special occasions I will dip into my ever-dwindling supply of 1982-vintage Cohibas that were presented to me by a friend in high places. But these are just little vignettes. The collectable cigar category is much more widespread and intense.

It first came to my attention when readers began telling me they were actively hoarding the first vintage offerings (1986) of the Dunhill Aged cigar. Then, in 1992, Cubatabaco brought out a limited edition of five hundred handcrafted cherrywood humidors filled with Cohiba cigars. Not only the box, but each individual cigar band was numbered. This spectacular offering was obviously to commemorate the 500th anniversary of Columbus' discovery of cigars. At the time of issuance, the price per box was well into the four-digit range. A few years later, at a Dinner of the Century in Paris, a specially rolled box of fifty Cohiba and Trinidad

Whether you shoot par, birdie, or eagle, any of these five-some cigars will help you ace the hole. (Clockwise from left:) Ashton; H. Upmann; Macanudo; Punch Grand Cru; Joya de Nicaragua. The golf balls are by Davidoff.

Torpedoes (shapes that are not normally made for these brands), and signed by Castro, went for $19,500 apiece. That's $390 a cigar! At the Fourth Friar's Club of California Celebrity Smoker, a box of Dominican-made Hamilton cigars signed by George fetched $800. Also in 1996 a farmer in Ireland was offered a million dollars for a cache of 1860 vintage stogies he found hidden in his barn. And contrary to some reports, they weren't even Havanas. Clearly, as Sherlock Holmes once remarked, "The game is afoot!"

Today, limited edition collectables are becoming the new wave of cigar merchandising. For example, in 1995, to celebrate the 150th anniversary of the Partagas brand, General Cigar brought out a one-time run of superlative cigars that were made with eighteen-year old Cameroon wrappers. This rarified leaf was actually discovered by accident, stored and forgotten, in a warehouse in Spain. But the timing of its discovery was perfect, right on the eve of the Partagas anniversary. What a great tribute to a great cigar, one of the very last to still be made with Cameroon

The ultimate gift: a box of premium cigars will earn the gratitude of any recipient, but these manufacturers have gone one step further with special packaging and sizes (L to R): a cedar bookcase filled with 20 Limited Edition Troya Classics. Meticulously aged and selected for this presentation, each box is individually serial numbered; from Dannemann, this handsome campaign-style wooden chest with polished brass fittings contains a connoisseur's selection of their most popular European-style cigars, plus packets of wooden matches. It would be the perfect traveling companion for that midnight train to Budapest; finding one Hemingway Masterpiece by A. Fuente is a rarity, as less than 1 out of 100 wrapper leaves is large enough to fashion into this 9-inch long cigar. Rarer still is the handmade cedar book case filled with ten Masterpieces, making this special order item among the most desirable volumes a Hemingway collector can own.

wrapper. Called the Partagas 150 Signature Series, each cigar was specially banded, tied in canvas bundles of 25 and tagged with the name of the roller, just as they do at the factory, then aged four months and placed in a commemorative box of 25, 50, or 100 cigars. Eight shapes were available and there was even a limited edition within this limited edition. It was the 7 x 52 Don Ramon, which came in a book-shaped humidor that lifted each cigar up as the lid was opened. A copy of a rare original box, only one thousand units were produced. Needless to say, practically every available Partagas 150 Signature Series was immediately snapped up, although I used to see a few of the smaller-ringed 5 x 38 Ds languishing around on dealer's shelves. But not any more. The 4½ x 49 Robustos and the 7½ x 49 AAs were among the first to go, although if you can make friends with someone who still has some in his humidor...

Over in Cuba, the Partagás 150th was celebrated with a special party, speeches, lots of free commemoratively-banded cig-

From the Partagas storage vaults in Havana come these rarities from the pre-Castro past: A 1947 box of Don Joaquin cigars, which included 13 different shapes. On the right is a two-foot long "triple-plus Churchill" that was custom rolled for King Farouk of Egypt, who used to place them straight up in a hookah for smoking with royal guests.

128

Collectable Cigars — (Clockwise from left:) Davidoff's 80th Anniversary Havana; a Dunhill Havana Club Gigante; commemorative 1790-1990 Hunters & Frankau Havanas; a box of 25 Partagas 150th Anniversary "A"; an early 20th century Sherlock Holmes cigar; and a Ritz-Carlton Laguna Niguel commemorative H. Upmann from April 11, 1990.

Women Cigar Smokers — Like their male counterparts, they enjoy a premium cigar for all the right reasons: taste, relaxation, and bonding.

Photo: Scott Wall Photography

Smokeasies — Civilized havens where people can relax with good friends, good conversation, and good cigars, a growing number of these public and private clubs are springing up across the nation and in Europe. The Grand Havana in Beverly Hills, California is one of the hottest, hippest of the smokeasy sanctuaries.

Cigar Clothes — Now you can wear what you smoke. Nicole Miller "Tobacco" (L) and "Stogie" (R) ties are popular limited edition designs. Pop Art cuff links and lapel pins are fashioned from actual cigar bands. In the foreground, a Nat Sherman/Concord Shear jewelry case for carrying it all. Look for a new Nicole Miller "The Ultimate Cigar Book" tie coming soon to a shirt collar near you.

Antique Smoke — Once passed over by collectors as being politically incorrect, these items are now eagerly sought out. (Clockwise from top:) An 1895 silver mounted humidor; a 19th century cigar cutter; one of the earliest known Victorian cigar cases, hallmarked 1855; a patriotic "cigar fan"; a Victorian vesta holder with chain; a tortoise shell and silver cheroot case; and a Dunhill Unique Butane Table lighter from 1954.

Montecristo is the best selling Havana cigar in the world, and accounts for approximately half of Cuba's total production. The No. 2 (fourth from left) is the most popular shape. The Petit Tubos is only available in the U.K. The 9¼ x 48 Monte A (top) is the world's most expensive cigar.

Photo: Hunters & Frankau

This is what bloom looks like: tiny white specks; it can also appear as a light coating of *white* dust that can be easily brushed off (if it's grey-green and fuzzy it is mold!). Notice the rich, oily Cameroon wrappers on these cigars that have been aged for over three years.

ars, and the unveiling of the first of 150 specially built three-drawer humidors, each with a numbered brass plaque, and containing 150 Partagás cigars. One drawer housed fifty Partagás Series Ds, another contained fifty 8-9-8s, and the third drawer was filled with fifty Lusitanias featuring the older-styled *figurado* head rather than the current marble head. This humidor brought $45,000 at auction. Later on, a San Francisco collector paid $85,000 for serial number #150. Other numbers have sold for slightly less.

Collectable cigars always carry a premium price, but many of them are well within reach of the aficionado's wallet. A lot depends on where you find them. And when. For example, I uncovered a cache of Havana Dunhills in, of all places, the Dunhill store on Duke Street in London. I had stopped in for a visit on one of my trips and as a joke (I thought), asked to see the latest Cuban Dunhills, knowing that none had been made since 1989. With a wink their cigar specialist led me to a cabinet full of individually cedar boxed Havana Club Gigantes (a 9¼ x 49, the same size as the Montecristo A), and some graceful Atados (a slender 6⅞ x 28). It seems that, just after Dunhill's pull-out from Cuba, these cigars had been stored in a warehouse on the banks of the Thames and forgotten until April 1995. Fortunately for London and the cigars, during those ensuing years the cigars survived and aged wonderfully. In fact, the unusually warm summer of '95 helped them age even further. "Nobody knows about these, yet," the humidor manager smiled. But now you do. Aren't you glad you bought this book?

But you don't have to travel far to find collectable cigars. Many of them are right in your local tobacconist's humidor. You just have to know what to look for. For example, the Macanudo Vintage Cabinet Selection can still be found in some of the earliest 1979, '84 and '88 years. The reason is that in 1996 General Cigar released all of the remaining inventory they had been holding in order to make room for the new 1993 vintages. And Dunhill Aged cigars are now coming out with shorter runs of each new vintage, which means you will be seeing new years more often, but they won't last as long on dealer's shelves, so if you have a favorite year coming up (such as when your first child is due to be born or when you have finally completed reading every page in this book), best buy a box of those cigars before they are gone. They will not taste any different, because consistency is why different vintage tobaccos are stored in the first place, but there is always a special aura connected to certain years.

Special shapes, certain brands that are no longer being made, and hard to find or limited production cigars like the Diamond Crown are all collectable cigars. For example, whenever I find a box of Ashton Cabinet #2s I grab it because I know they just cannot produce enough of the aged leaf to lay in a large stock. Same with the Hemingway Classic and any really good Maduro. (Should I be telling you all this? What if you buy up all my boxes?) The Fuente Opus X is a good case in point. Actually, the official name is Fuente Fuente Opus X, with the two Fuente names representing Don Carlos and Carlos, Jr., while Opus is a notable piece of music and Opus One is the name of a spectacular limited edition wine created by Robert Mondavi Winery (see Chapter 7). The "X" stands for "Project X," because the growing of the Dominican wrapper that was to make this cigar the first commercially available DR puro was kept a secret for so long, it was dubbed Project X. I know all this because in 1994 I helped Carlito Fuente name the cigar. It is still so well guarded that the Fuente factory has a special aging room just for its limited supply, and of the 1,600 employees, only 32 are considered qualified enough to make this very special "puro." Once while visiting a tobacconist in Georgia, and noticing that he still had a box of Opus X cigars for sale, I was asked about the brand. As usually happens, a small crowd had gathered and this was turning into a mini-smoker. By the time I had finished my story, the box was empty!

One of the problems with cigars that doesn't occur with other collectables is that you can't have your collectable cigar and smoke it, too. More than one aficionado who has somehow managed to latch onto a box full of rare stogies has then had to decide what to do with them now that he's got them. Fire 'em up and enjoy them as they were originally intended? Put them away as an investment? Or resell them to your best buddy for a profit? Personally, I collect every cigar with the thought that eventually I will smoke it. It may only be on a special occasion, but it will someday cease to exist. Another worthwhile use for collectable cigars is giving or trading them to someone else who might not have one. For me, this is one of the most enjoyable benefits of the cigar hobby. I will never forget being in the Havana Studios in Burbank one evening and swapping cigars with the member who had his locker next to mine. Which brings up another point: one of the prerequisites for collecting cigars is that you must have a humidor in which to store them. For some of the high end rarities, you might even want to think about insurance. If you start to amass a sizeable enough collection, putting them on computer and cross indexing them as to country, year acquired, and price paid might not be a bad idea either. To be sure, there are some cigar collectors who have assembled such a valuable inventory of combustionable rarities, they must now grapple with the problem of whether to smoke these collectables or simply keep them in a humidified vault.

All of which brings us to the subject of cost. Just how much should one pay for a really good cigar, collectable or not? There are no retail prices in this book for a reason: ever since the 1970s, cigar prices have been escalating at an unpredictable rate. They also fluctuate dramatically across the country, as each city or state has its own "pleasure tax" that they insist on burdening cigar smokers with. Of course, this is a self-defeating punishment, as the added-on taxes for cigars have forced many to take their purchases out-of-state, either by direct mail or while traveling. Therefore, the municipalities that sought to pick our pockets now find that there are fewer pockets to pick. A far more equitable solution would be to lower the taxes on cigars, thereby increasing volume and hence, revenue. But this probably makes too much common sense for anyone to adopt it.

It is difficult to judge a cigar by its price. For example, in India you can pick up a Rajah, RAF John Hunter, or Picollo for less money than it would take to make a local phone call, but is it worth it? Only you, standing there as the cigar unravels in your mouth, can answer that question. And in England, a Cuban Montecristo A could be substituted for a weekend at Leeds. Which one would be more enjoyable would simply depend on the weather. Price is relevant, and one would assume that a higher price reflected a better grade of tobacco and more care taken with its construction. This is often — but not always — true, and the appearance of super premium and vintage cigars has made more than a few individuals do a double take when they see some cigars costing more than lunch. In many cases, these higher prices simply reflect longer aging times for the tobacco, larger leaves that must be used, extra skill required for making a special shape, or a better grade of packaging to uphold an image. More recently, cigar prices have been escalating because of the demand (you'd think they would be lowering, but that's not how it works). And the price of tobacco is increasing dramatically simply because there is not enough of the best leaves to go around. Moreover, the insatiable demand of the cigar boom has caused a shortage of skilled rollers. As a result, a number of new companies are coming into the cigar industry waving huge amounts of cash at some of the best *torcedores*, who are leaving their long-term employers

131

and going where the money is. Who can blame them? The end result of all these factors is higher prices for cigars, and not all of them are worth it, simply because the manufacturer may have the best rollers but not the best tobacco. It is a successful company that has both and they will invariably have the best cigars.

But with all that said, relatively speaking, most premium cigars are underpriced for the pleasure they give. Therefore, the first criteria should be to find a number of cigars that you like. This in itself can turn into a never ending search and is part of the fun of cigar smoking. Shop around for the best selection. And the best price. Although sometimes paying a few pennies more might be worth it for the feeling of camaraderie you get when visiting a particular tobacco shop. Other times you may just want the best cigars at the lowest cost. Then, when all is done and you have a coterie of cigars whose shape and taste meet your criteria, decide if the price is worth it to you. If it is, you've found your perfect cigar.

Box Fixation — In an effort to attract more customers, many innovative cigar boxes are appearing on dealer's shelves. (Top row, L. to R.) Nat Sherman Hobart; Thomas Hinds Honduran Selection Torpedo; Indian Cigar Arrow (box is designed to fit into a motorcycle saddlebag). (Bottom row, L. to R.) Double Happiness Ecstacy; Nørding Corona Gorda (with see-through window); blue-grey Credo Pythagoras. Also shown is a Toraño Virtuoso nestled in Dunhill's re-issue teardrop ashtray.

132

Chapter 4

The Ritual of Lighting, The Etiquette of Smoking

Anticipation provides more than half the pleasure of the fulfillment. And so it is with cigar smoking. Even before I finish a meal, I am already thinking about the after dinner cigar, and this makes the food even more tantalizing on my palate. In many cases, I am never quite sure what that cigar will be. When out with friends, I have already tried to second guess events by preselecting the cigars I might want, and my cigar case, which holds three, is never filled with the same three. After all, who knows exactly how I will feel or what the evening will bring? If we decide to go for a walk afterwards, perhaps I will want an Hoyo de Monterrey Excalibur No. 1. Or, if coffee is served, I may decide upon a Partagas No. 2. But what if cognac is brought out, and an Avo No. 9 seems more in order? No, one can't be too well prepared when dining away from our supplies in the stockade. On the other hand, when at home, my cigar selection is sometimes much more complicated, as I am faced with a far greater choice to make from my multiple humidors (I have long since discovered that one is not enough). Very often a likely candidate is selected and is poised for the clipping when some inner sense tells me to hold! This is not the perfect subject for tonight's smoke. And back it goes, only to be replaced by Cigar No. 2, which may have been what I subconsciously wanted all along. But whatever the final selection turns out to be, once the chosen cigar is lit, it serves me well and I have never had any regrets. After all, no matter what the cigar or size or country of origin, when picked from my own reserves, they all have one thing in common: I originally thought them worthy enough to bring into the sanctity of my humidor.

There is a certain degree of mental preparedness involved in selecting and smoking a cigar, and much of the enjoyment is simply a matter of perception on the part of the smoker. There is even something about an unopened box of cigars: holding the solid squareness in your hands, tearing off the crisp cellophane, cutting the seal, and unlatching the brass hinge with your thumbnail. And then, opening the lid and unleashing the fresh, pungent aroma of cedar and tobacco for the first time. Finally, lifting out the first cigar and knowing that there are still more pleasures to be had.

One of the cardinal rules of cigar smoking is to always allow enough time to fully enjoy your cigar of choice. When picking out a Corona, for example, you will need at least thirty minutes. A Rothschild may take more time if you are a slow puffer. And any of the Churchill sizes will require forty-five minutes to an hour. That is why many of the smaller cigars are so popular today, because we don't always have sufficient time to enjoy the bigger ring sizes and longer lengths. Smoking a cigar during the day can be quite a different experience than smoking a cigar in the less demanding wee small hours of the morning.

Just when you smoke a cigar is up to you. Your body will usually tell you when it is time to start and when it is time to stop. Or how many you should consume within a given day. One famous French actor segues from one cigar to another by lighting up a new Punch Double Corona with the one he is about to finish. And many enthusiasts glowingly speak of the morning cigar, the before lunch cigar, the after lunch cigar, the mid-afternoon cigar, the before dinner cigar, the after dinner cigar and sometimes even the after cigar cigar. Frankly, those are too many cigars for me. As with everything worth doing, I hold with the philosophy that moderation is the secret to optimum enjoyment. Smoking a megadose of cigars can overload the palate and dull it, which is a bit like chugging an entire decanter of 50-year-old cognac rather than savoring a snifter-full. It is far more rewarding to smoke fewer cigars but to be able to indulge in each one more intensely.

I rarely smoke more than two cigars a day, unless I am on vacation or it is a special event. Normally, I will take a "cigar break" in the middle of the afternoon, just to clear my brain and to take stock of what I have accomplished so far and what else has to be done. The next time I open my humidor, it will be to bask in the luxury of a well earned evening cigar, after dinner and often deep into the night, when all is still and I can slip my mind into neutral and with the help of my cigar, coast through any obstacle course that life has put in my path. After hours is the perfect environment to smoke a cigar, for it is a time when all your senses are freed, and one can concentrate on the sensual feel and taste of handrolled smoke from a distant land.

On the other hand, when at a Gentleman's Smoker, I will enthusiastically and unapologetically succumb to the multiple lures of a Petite Corona with champagne, a Panetela with hors d'oeuvres, a Rothschild after dessert and then a conversational Double Churchill with a snifter of malt whiskey or cognac. After all, a Smoker is a cigar *event!* But then, I may not smoke another cigar for one or two days afterwards in order to allow sufficient time for my taste buds to regroup. While on vacation or during the weekend, I will occasionally fire up a Dutch-type mild cigar at midday, or later on, select something a little more robust to help me watch the sun go down over a shimmering glass of spirits.

But no matter when you smoke, or how often, there is a definite ceremony involved with bringing a cigar to life, so that it may unleash all of the pleasure that it holds. I have a definite prelighting ritual that I go through with every cigar that I smoke. First, I take an exorbitant amount of time to savor the sweet bouquet that emanates from the wrapper. Sometimes my wife shares in this sensual enjoyment, although, as much as she appreciates a good cigar, she is only good for about one or two sniffs. Next, I roll the cigar over in my hand, visually caressing its form, examining the wrapper, and reaffirming my commitment that this is indeed the perfect cigar to smoke at this particular moment in my life. Then, and only then, does the lighting ceremony begin.

The first thing to consider is whether or not to remove the band. In Europe there is no question about the matter, for it is considered good form to defrock a cigar of its band, although I find it somewhat ironic that these bands are then placed prominently in an ashtray or on the table for all to see. If you don't wish to hide the band, then why take it off? I will never forget my shock the very first time I saw anyone tear the band from a cigar. On this particular occasion, it was a rather prominent public offi-

135

cial and I have never forgiven him. Why anyone would want to remove the band escapes me, unless, of course, they are ashamed of the cigar they are smoking. In that case, it is best to choose a different cigar. After all, the band is a sign of your good taste. It tells others that this is the brand you have chosen, and you are proud of it. Unlike the Empress of Russia and gentlemen smokers of the Victorian era, we no longer have to worry about soiling our gloved hands with tobacco stains, but the band still serves as a proud reminder of our cigar's identity. Pride and romanticism aside, there is also a practical reason for not removing the band. Because a portion of the cigar band is often inadvertently glued to the wrapper, you can seriously damage your cigar by trying to peel off the band. Besides, why would you want to undo the handcrafted accomplishment of a skilled worker? But if, for some self-and-cigar defiling reason you still feel a compulsion to remove the band, at least wait until the body of your cigar has had a chance to warm up as it is being smoked. The heat will soften the glue and the band may be easier to slip off without invoking The Curse of the Ripped Wrapper. If you want to avoid the band controversy altogether, you might consider smoking only Punch and Hoyo de Monterrey Rothschilds and Ramón Allones Trumps. These cigars are boxed without bands. The perfect compromise, of course, can be found in the Juan Clemente, which has a band, but it covers the foot of the cigar. In this case, the decision has already been made for you, because the band must be removed if the cigar is to be smoked. In all other instances, I recommend leaving this bit of historical decoration alone.

With the band controversy firmly affixed, we should now expose another arcane practice, that of licking a cigar before lighting it. This unsavory and vile act had its origins in the days of non-humidors, but even then it was a senseless endeavor. To truly re-moisten the cigar you would have to unroll it and lick the filler and binder as well. I will never forget giving an acquaintance an after-dinner cigar at one of the few Beverly Hills restaurants that, at the time, still allowed smoking such things. To my horror and disgust, he immediately started rolling the unlit cigar around in his mouth like an all-day sucker. Before I could grab his throat, the maître d' rushed over and said, "What's the matter, sir, didn't you enjoy the food?" A properly humidified cigar does not have to be licked.

We now turn our attention to clipping the cigar. There are four distinct types of cuts that you can make: 1) the Guillotine cut, in which a straight across slice is taken off of the head; 2) the Punch cut, in which a round sharpened metal tube is rotated into the head and a plug of tobacco is plucked out; 3) the "V" cut, wherein a "v" shaped wedge is cut into the head, and 4) the Pierce, where a hole is punched through the center of the head.

The pierce is one of the older styles of "cuts," although it really isn't a cut at all. The pierce can be effected on any ring sized cigar, but there are some drawbacks to it. The most noticeable is the fact that the single hole very often acts as a collection point for all the rancid acids and tobacco juices. Inasmuch as the smoke (and your tongue) passes over this hole, the taste of the cigar is often adversely affected. Another problem with the pierce is that by boring a hole into the cigar head, there is a risk of crunching the tobacco against the sides and bottom of the hole, which could interfere with the draw, although the machine-made pierce, which is found on many Dutch-type cigars, has eliminated this problem completely. In my collection of tobacciana, I have an elegant gold and alligator skin covered retractable cigar piercer that dates from the 1890s, which shows how well esteemed this type of cut once was. However, for today's knowledgeable cigar smoker, it is totally impractical.

For many years, the V cut was considered best, as it creates an ample, two sided surface to provide adequate draw, and the exposed tobacco — a potential gathering spot for bitter tars — is kept at an angle, away from the tongue. However, there are

The three different types of cuts (L to R): Guillotine; "V"; and Pierce (in this case all three cuts have been machine made on Dutch-type cigars).

some drawbacks to the V cut. For one thing, there are very few clippers capable of making a clean V-type slice without ragging up the edges. Another problem has to do with the larger ring gauges that are finding favor with so many of today's cigar smokers. A standard V-cutter is simply not big enough to accommodate some of the more massive cigars, and anything larger than a 48 ring may only produce a shallow slice instead of a deep cut. The punch cut is the newest innovation and works quite well on most cigars, but unless you use a tool like the Crestmark (see Chapter 6) with a built in plunger, the cutting tool often gets clogged with tobacco. And unless you use a tool like the Davidoff Round Cutter (see Chapters 6 and 7), the hole you make may not be the right size for the ring gauge of your cigar. But the Davidoff doesn't have a plunger and the Crestmark only has one sized hole. Besides, the punch cut doesn't do very well on certain *figurado* cigars like the Belicoso or Pyramid.

Much more practical for virtually all of today's cigars is the guillotine cut, which, like the V, exposes an ample surface for easy draw and full flavor. It is also a much easier cut to execute, assuming the blade is sharp. The only caveat is that some of the pocket-sized guillotine cutters do not provide a large enough guide hole for cigars with big ring sizes. We will cover this topic more thoroughly in Chapter 6. Still, for overall practicality, my recommendation is to go with the guillotine. After all, what was good enough for Marie Antoinette should certainly be good enough for our cigars.

When making a guillotine cut, do not cut too much off the top of the head or you could risk turning your Churchill into a Rothschild. The best guideline is to make the cut slightly above the horizontal line where the cap connects with the wrapper. That way, enough of the cap is left on the cigar to keep it from unraveling. Make the cut quick and definite, unless you are using one of the scissors cutters, in which case you may want to rotate the blades around the wrapper to create an encircling slice that marks the start of a clean cut. Of course, this only works when your cutter is sharp. A dull blade will tear the wrapper and you'll run the risk of walking around with a cigar that looks like a pom-pom.

With our cigar properly clipped, we are ready for the baptism of fire. For this exalted task, only a wooden match or a butane lighter will do. A cardboard match is impregnated with chemicals, and the flame from a lighter fluid-soaked wick leaves a residue; both of these devices will taint the taste of tobacco. Butane, on the other hand, burns clean and odorless, and this, or

The Ritual of Lighting...

First the cigar is clipped just above the line where the cap joins the wrapper.

photos: Ron Mesaros

Using a wooden match or butane lighter, the cigar is slowly rotated as the foot is toasted all the way around. Never let the flame touch the cigar or it will char, producing a harsh taste.

Now gently puff, still rotating the cigar while holding the tip of the flame just under the foot. The fire will actually leap to the cigar and ignite the entire circumference, thus insuring a flavorful first puff. Then relax and sip the smoke as you would a fine cognac. Bon appetit!

some of the extra long cedar smoker's matches, are definitely the flames of choice. After striking a match, be sure to wait until the flare has died down, or your first puff will be a sulphurous one. The flame of a butane lighter is easier to control, although it does burn hotter. But whatever method of fire you select, don't plunge your cigar directly into the flame as if it were a branding iron. This cloddish practice will soot up your wrapper and you may notice the more erudite cigar smokers around you turning their backs, leaving you out of their conversations, and gradually filtering out of the room. Soon you will be left alone, an outcast, without friends, family or hope for the future, all because of this one thoughtless act.

To properly light a cigar, the foot should never be allowed to touch the flame. Instead, it should be held at a 45 degree angle directly over the tip of the flame, which is the hottest part. Then, slowly rotate the cigar, gently toasting the tuck and drying out the filler so that it will be more receptive to the flame. Some people enjoy maintaining this procedure until the end of the cigar is completely charred and bursts into flame of its own accord, with no puffing required. However, this technique, spectacular as it is, also produces a much stronger first few puffs. Rotating and toasting the foot of a cigar is especially practical with big ring gauges, as it enables you to visually insure that the entire circumference of the cigar is being warmed and charred. Some smokers toast their cigars until a thin ring of fire appears around the foot. Then, to help the glow spread, they take the smoldering cigar away from the flame and gently wave it around in the air. This drives the anti-smokers in the room absolutely crazy! A noble gesture, but I prefer to simply toast the cigar and inhale the delicate bouquet that is released from the tobacco, an aroma that we will not be able to smell once we start smoking.

Next, with the foot of the cigar warm and perhaps just starting to give forth with a few wisps of smoke, place the cigar to your lips and hold it directly above the tip of the flame. As you gently puff, rotate the cigar, gradually lighting the entire circumference of the foot. All too often a smoker fails to rotate his cigar while puffing, thus only lighting half the cigar and consequently, only getting half the enjoyment. He then smokes away in pathetic oblivion, like a man who has forgotten to zip up his fly and is wondering what everyone is staring at.

Now sit back and sip the full, rich flavor of the savory smoke, much as you would a fine wine. Cigar smokers never inhale, as the taste of the pure tobacco is sensed only by the taste buds in your mouth, much like a gourmet meal. The tongue is the main gathering spot for all the different flavors of tobacco. Sweetness is sensed on the tip, saltiness on the sides, and bitterness near the back. Exhale the smoke, letting the bellowing clouds drift upward, for smoke is an integral part of the enjoyment of a cigar. (During an experiment in the 1890s, it was conclusively proven that cigar smokers who lit up in a darkened room, and consequently could not see any smoke, did not enjoy their cigars as much as those who smoked in a room in which there was light.) A cigar's taste and aroma are transported by the smoke it creates. Thus, the more smoke, the fuller the taste and the more aroma. Because a bigger ring gauge produces more smoke, it also produces more flavor. But just as a cigar's shape is the embodiment of pleasure, you may not always want a full sized cigar. Sometimes I enjoy smoking two smaller cigars rather than one large one. This, of course, doubles the enjoyment of the lighting ritual. Also, when testing cigars, I often will smoke two similar shapes at once, such as a Dunhill Aged Samanas and a Don Diego Grecos, or will pair up a Henry Clay Breva with an Hoyo de Monterrey Super Hoyo, alternating my puffs and cleansing my palate at intervals with mineral water (carbonated or plain, it doesn't matter) and dry bread, just as you would in a wine tasting. I admit it looks a little strange to the uninitiated to have two cigars going at once, but this is a great way to determine which particular blends you prefer and to compare the tastes of sometimes extremely divergent tobaccos. If you only smoked one cigar at a time, your sense of taste might not be as acute when you finally got to the second cigar. Much better to start out with equal sharpness for both cigars by alternating between the two. Don't forget to jot your observations down in the CigarNotes section of this book; with the multitude of brands that we have today, it will be impossible to recall your reactions to them all.

As you smoke any cigar through the course of its existence, you may find that its flavor will change with its length. (Do not confuse this with the recent phenomena of a cigar not "kicking in" until ten minutes into the smoke; this is the mark of a poorly fermented cigar.) This is definitely true of Pyramids, where the ring gauge changes as the cigar is being smoked, but also is evident with other shapes as well, as the smoke continues to filter through the tobacco and intensifies as the cigar grows shorter. What started out as an HPH 2 could easily end up an HPH 2.5 when you place your cigar in the ashtray for the final time. Because the head of a cigar acts like a filter during the entire length of the smoke, most cigars, no matter what their brand or size, will smoke at their optimum for the first two-thirds of their length and then tend to become harsh, and many connoisseurs prefer to let them go out once they have crossed that threshold. Others will smoke their cigars right on down to their lips, relishing the hotter, stronger taste as their facial hair bursts into flames.

With lessening length comes increasing ash. A long ash on a premium cigar is indicative of a healthy outer wrapper and a well formed long leaf filler bunch. This ash acts as an insulator, and can help cool the foot of the cigar as it is being smoked. However, a soft spot in the bunch of even the best super premium cigar will cause the ash to weaken when it reaches that point and fall off unexpectedly. To avoid this potential problem, I rarely let my cigar ash get more than an inch in length. When it comes time to detach itself from the Mother Ship, I gently touch the tip of the ash to the bottom of an ashtray and let it gracefully depart. But don't attempt to produce a long ash on even the best of the short filler cigars, as their short leaf tobacco physically prevents it from forming.

Perhaps this is a good time to talk about The Fallacy of the White Ash. For years there has been a great misconception of trying to link ash color to cigar quality. About the only thing a white ash signifies is that you're smoking a cigar with a white ash. Ash color has nothing to do with how well a cigar may smoke, although the implied purity of white has undoubtedly caused many cigar makers in the past to unjustifiably strive for this color, thereby perpetuating the myth. All the color of a cigar ash can tell us is the approximate mineral content of the soil in which the to-

A properly rolled long filler cigar should produce a long, firm ash. Also note the thin black ring where the ash meets the wrapper, an indication that the wrapper leaf has been properly cured and aged.

bacco was grown. Obviously, different soils from different areas have different mineral contents and consequently, they produce different ash colors. For example, if there is too little magnesium, the ash is dark. The more magnesium in the soil, the lighter the ash. But too much magnesium will cause the ash of even a long filler cigar to flake off before its time. Normally, the lighter the ash color, the sweeter the tobacco will taste. Consequently, a dark grey ash will be more pronounced in taste that a light grey ash. Nor does ash color have anything to do with the combustion rate of the tobacco. That is determined by the soil's pH (which is why leaf buyers often test the burn rate of a leaf at the warehouses in the fields before purchasing it for cigar making in the factories). Now you probably know more than anyone else in your neighborhood about cigar ash.

Maybe it's the color of the ash, or the patterns it makes, or the natural texture of the wrapper, but I often find myself studying my cigar while I smoke it. Although it is silent, a smoking cigar can tell you many things. For example, that thin, shiny black ring that acts as a fence around the ash and separates it from the unburned wrapper shows that your cigar is well made and the tobacco has been properly cured. On the other hand, if this ring is more like a wide blackened band that is blistered, it is a sign of poor leaf combustion and means that the tobacco wasn't fermented properly. But then, your taste buds probably already told you something was amiss. Which brings up another point.

Occasionally while smoking, you will get a very uncomfortable hollow, almost gaseous feeling in your chest. This is an indication that the tobacco was not properly fermented or aged, and you are getting too much nitrogen and nicotine into your system. The best cure for this malady is to get rid of that cigar and try a different brand. Another disconcerting occurrence is a cigar that starts burning unevenly down one side of the wrapper. Normally, there is nothing you can do to stop this runaway brush fire. I have tried reclipping the cigar and even building a backfire. It never gets better and I am usually left with a smoldering brand that is more dangerous than enjoyable to smoke. Assuming you have lit the cigar properly, this unsettling phenomena can be caused by one of four things: the cigar maker's "booking" of the filler, improper humidification of your cigar, a poorly burning tobacco, or a problem with the actual construction of the leaf that has somehow escaped the watchful eyes of the inspectors at the factory. Normally, the two most frequently encountered culprits are poor humidification and poor leaf construction. Unfortunately, at this junction we cannot do anything about poor leaf construction other than to toss the cigar and take notice of the brand, hoping that it doesn't happen again. But there is something we can do about insuring that our cigars are properly humidified, and that "something" will be discussed in the next chapter.

But, sometimes, no matter how well we've cared for them, we still come across a cigar that just won't draw. These frustrating encounters are usually more prominent with smaller ring gauges, where the bunching is tight. But no cigar is immune, and I have found a hard draw in some well-known premium cigars that were in the 48 and 54 ring categories. No amount of red-faced puffing and re-clipping is going to help. Besides, why ruin your evening by trying to undo what is most assuredly the faulty construction of the cigar itself? The only solution is to take the cigar back to the tobacconist where you got it (assuming it is still relatively unsmoked). Expect a replacement cigar or a credit on your next purchase. Tobacconists are an honorable breed and have, at one time or another, experienced the same thing themselves. They will understand. Or they should.

A counterfeit Cohiba. The short filler does not hold an ash. Note the coarse veins of the wrapper. The uneven burn and the thick black ring are evidence that the wrapper has not been properly cured, as is the rancid taste.

144

Assuming everything goes right, as it most often does, there is no peace like the serene smoke from a good cigar. But occasionally, because there are no artificial ingredients or chemicals in a cigar to make it burn, it will go out before its time. This is especially true if we should be engaged in conversation so stimulating it makes us forget to take the obligatory puff to keep the embers of pleasure lit within the hearth underneath the ash. If that should happen to you, simply warm the end of your cigar over a flame before relighting it. This will release the carbon monoxide and ammonia that has been trapped inside the ash and lessen the shock to your palate when the cigar is reborn, as a relit cigar almost always smokes stronger. There are also times when a cigar that has seemingly died prematurely can be brought back to life simply by exhaling through it very gently. A curl of smoke tells you that there is hope.

Eventually, however, all good things must come to an end and our cigar must be allowed to go out. To try and keep it alive beyond its prime can only taint the otherwise fine memory of that once vibrant smoke, for then it becomes disagreeable and bitter, much like a love affair that has gone bad. When this moment occurs, gently lay the cigar in an ashtray and let it succumb of natural causes. This releases the least amount of odor. Do not crush your cigar as you would a cigarette, as that only spreads the burning ash and increases the total area of noxious fumes. When I smoke my cigars at home, I always dispose of them grandly in the fireplace, or let them quietly go out in a distant ashtray outside, lest anyone complain. It is simply a case of what they can't smell can't hurt you. And thus, the sanctity of my cigar smoking enclave is preserved.

Which brings up a new home improvement innovation spawned by the cigar renaissance, the "cigarden." This is simply a peaceful retreat in the backyard that has been specially landscaped to make cigar smoking more enjoyable. It can be as simple as a shaded lounge chair and an ashtray within easy reach, or as elaborate as a sylvan enclave featuring the gurgling sound of a waterfall and the melodic strains of music through hidden speakers. Of course, other items, such as a bar-b-que, badminton net, or a small gardening plot may also be included as part of the cigarden. In fact, their inclusion may be crucial to the acceptance of the cigarden by others in the household. The main prerequisite, however, is that somewhere in the backyard there be a private sanctuary where one can enjoy a cigar.

But even this precious utopia — one of the few islands of solace left to the modern day cigar smoker — quickly fades once

145

outside the protective environs of our home, the tobacco shop, and the Smoker. Sympathetic understanding ceases to exist on the mean streets of a rabidly fanatical world of anti-smokers. Just as during the Victorian era one hundred years ago, cigar smoking is again being frowned upon in public. Yes, history does have a way of repeating itself, and today, with roving gangs of militant anti-smokers waiting in ambush around every street corner and lurking in every building, the world we live in is no longer considered safe for the likes of us. Our only defense is to band together. We have the clout, if only we would use it. Although there are very few places left where one may smoke a cigar in peace, they must be preserved, either through legislation or by outright acquisition.

Which explains the sudden rise in the number of cigar-friendly private clubs that are springing up all across America. I have christened these bastions of freedom "smokeasies," a gram-

Even in a rabid anti-smoking world, there are some sacred bastions that serve as havens for the cigar smoker. The Duke Street humidor in Alfred Dunhill Ltd. of London is one such place, and bespeaks of gentler times. Soft leather chairs invite one to relax with a Dunhill whiskey, and the cedar cabinets are stocked with a worldly supply of Havanas and Dunhill Aged Cigars from the Dominican Republic.

matical take-off of the speakeasy of Prohibition infamy. A smokeasy is simply a club where cigar smokers can relax in comfortable surroundings and light up in peace. Sometimes there are membership fees, sometimes not. Most smokeasies offer private cigar lockers (or "keeps" as the British call them), as well as deep-cushioned chairs, wide screen television, telephones, refreshments, and other amenities as dictated by the members' wishes and the locale. The Grand Havana in Beverly Hills (and other locations as well) serves gourmet cuisine, features a fully stocked bar, and has become the hot spot for Hollywood's elite, all of whom need a special key to gain access via private elevator. By contrast, Club Macanudo in New York is open to anyone who buys a cigar there (and it doesn't only have to be a Macanudo). In Chicago an upscale men's clothiers has added a cigar lounge so that customers may relax while they shop. Other smokeasies across America may simply be smoke-friendly lounges in cigar stores. In Havana (which ironically has "No Smoking" signs posted in many areas), Cuba's newest (and most comfortable) hotel, Meliá Cohiba, has a special smoking lounge called El Relicario. And in London, which has had smokeasies since Queen Victoria's reign, Monte's, a private club occupying four floors of opulence in fashionable Knightsbridge, is setting the tone for what could very well become a global trend.

But these growing numbers of smoking enclaves aside, there are also subtle ways to win an anti-cigar war fueled by ignorance and prejudice — the two things that cannot be swayed. Rather than pointlessly argue with militant anti-smokers, we must try to win the nonsmokers over to our side. These are the people who are neither anti- or pro-cigars. They are the middle ground and comprise the largest percentage of the American populace. If we can show them that we are more civilized than the radical anti-cigar thugs, we will have made our point. We must convince them with kindness. And courtesy. It does no good to force ourselves upon others, for we only aggravate the situation. As an example, even if I am in a restaurant or bar where cigar smoking is allowed, I will still ask the table next to me if they mind if I smoke, making sure they see my cigar case and know exactly what it is I am referring to. If they don't mind, then all is well. But if they take offense, then I politely thank them for not letting me ruin their evening, and make a big show of putting all of my paraphernalia away. Sometimes the offending party ends up feeling guilty and recants. Or at least apologizes. Usually not. But at least I have shown them that I am a considerate individual and perhaps the next time they read about "rude smokers," they may recall the incident and begin to rethink all this mass media hysteria. In this situation, I have nothing to lose. If I had gone ahead and smoked my cigar, they would have complained, thereby ruining the moment for everyone. So I simply wait for a more hospitable environment (often retiring to the welcoming sanctuary of a nearby smokeasy, or back in the sanctity of my own home), where I can enjoy my cigar with a peace and solitude that they will never know.

Additionally, whenever I encounter a restauranteur who is friendly or at least sympathetic to the cigar smoker's plight, I always make it a point to tell him how much I appreciate his attitude. You can be sure he gets the opposite side of the argument from anti-smokers who are convinced they are being politically correct by dictating other people's lifestyles. And if the maître d' of a restaurant is a cigar smoker (How do you find out? You ask.), it can be mutually beneficial to offer him a cigar *before* he seats you. On occasion I have also sent a cigar to the chef after an especially enjoyable and well-presented meal. It is always reassuring to discover that many of these professional gourmets are cigar smokers.

I have extended my "cigar sensitivity training" to my travel agent, and whenever I plan a trip or a stay in any hotel, one of the questions I always have her ask is if cigar smoking is permitted. If it is not, we find an alternative location. And not surprisingly, it is usually the cigar-friendly hotels and resorts that have the better amenities and a friendlier staff. Loews, Meridian, Wyndam, Hilton, Sheraton, Marriott, Four Seasons and Ritz-Carlton are just a few of the national chains my traveling humidor and I have stayed at and were made to feel welcome. However, just prior to completing this book, I scheduled a cruise with my wife to celebrate the anniversary we never had (because I was writing this book), but immediately canceled it when I found out that the well-known cruise line had adopted a policy of no pipe or cigar smoking on board. Indeed! Piracy is too good a word for that sort of arrogance. Unfortunately, there are very few cruise lines left who acknowledge the fact that the cigar smoker is also a consumer who does more than his share to keep the wheels of commerce turning. Perhaps because of their British registry, the Cunard Lines' QE2 has always permitted cigar smoking on board and even stocks a fairly-priced selection of Havanas. Unfortunately, on all too many other cruise lines, the attitude towards cigar smoking ranges from "tolerant" to "only on the upper decks during a hurricane." So if planning to enjoy a leisurely Lonsdale off the coast of Tortola or a Robusto midst the red rocks of Sedona, be sure to have your travel agent check out whether or not your intended cruise line, resort, or hotel is cigar friendly. Even amongst the chains, some individual properties may not be.

Of course, the airlines have already made their anti-cigar statement, even to the point where the tiniest cigarillo is *verboten*. But there are exceptions, albeit in rarified circles. On one occasion a few years ago, King Carl XVI Gustaf of Sweden was flying first class on Pan American Airlines and asked for a cigar. A

One of the most elegant Smokers in America is hosted by the Ritz-Carlton, Laguna Niguel in Southern California. This annual event is a continuous sellout, in spite of a three-figure cost per person. Attendees include some of the area's most prominent businessmen and entertainment celebrities. The gala black tie affair includes a champagne reception, seven-course gourmet dinner complete with string ensemble entertainment, and afterwards, some of the world's finest cognacs, armagnacs and malt whiskeys served in a wood-paneled library filled with more than three thousand cigars.

photo: Eric Simonson
The Ritz-Carlton, Laguna Niguel, CA

quick thinking flight attendant raced back to the economy section and located a passenger who just happened to have some cigars, even though he was not permitted to smoke them on board (one wonders how he ever managed to get through security with them!). He graciously gave her the smokes and they were brought to the king on a silver platter. "You don't tell the King of Sweden he can't smoke a cigar," a Pan Am spokesperson said later.

In a similar story, an extremely popular actor, who up until this second edition asked me not to publicly mention his name in connection with his beloved cigar smoking pastime, was on a first class flight when he started to light up a favorite Havana. Like a flash the stewardess appeared and read him his rights, basically telling him he could not smoke. Our muscular actor undid his seat belt, rose up to his full height and faced the rest of the passengers. "Anybody mind if I smoke a cigar?" he glowered. Of course, nobody did.

But there are also success stories of the common man. One fellow I met during a cigar smoker's night at a popular Los Angeles eatery really seemed to be enjoying the moment. "Years ago, before cigar smoking became so popular," he related, "the hostess of this restaurant told me I couldn't smoke my cigar in here. Now I come here with a group of guys once a month, we all light up, and that same hostess has to bring us drinks!"

Indeed, cigar smoking victories are where you find them. On one of my daily power walks I routinely encounter a young father puffing on a cigar as he rapidly pushes his newborn son in a baby stroller. With the wheels rumbling and all that smoke, he looks like a freight train but there is always a contented expression on his face. "It's great to get out with your kid and enjoy a good cigar," he once told me. Another dad wrote to me and related how, every Saturday night when the weather is right, he and his boy go out in the back yard. The father has his cigar and a snifter of cognac; his son has a snifter of apple juice and a bubble gum cigar. There is family unity and character-building bonding here that the anti-cigar people simply do not have the capacity to understand.

Whether smoking cigars with others or in the sanctity of our homes, it remains a pleasure that belongs uniquely to us. And by joining together to spread this camaraderie, we are insuring that it remains an ongoing and viable part of everyday life. Gradually, others are starting to accept that fact. Unfortunately, not everyone. But that is a battle we must eventually win. For then and only then, will cigar smoking assume its rightful place as a publicly acknowledged entity of civilized society, and an integral ingredient for quality of life.

The cigarden is a homeward haven. This oasis was designed by the author and brought to life by LandPlan of Los Angeles, CA. It features a trickling waterfall, smoking bench, and wandering paths through thick foliage.

This 19th century painting from the Austria Tabak Museum shows a Victorian gentleman with cigar in hand and properly attired in his smoking jacket. Today, millions of connoisseurs are reviving this great civilized pastime.

Chapter 5

The Secrets of
Successful Cigar Storage

They say that good things can't last forever, but humidification is one method of extending your cigar smoking pleasures indefinitely. It also enables you to save money by purchasing cigars by the box or by stocking up on your favorite brands when they go on sale. Cigars should be stored at 65% to 70% humidity and at a temperature of 70 degrees Fahrenheit. If you have trouble remembering numbers, you can probably get away with a 70-70 mix. A cigar that is too dry will smoke hot, fast, and unevenly; too moist and it will be hard to light and even harder to puff. Either way, you will be deprived of the pleasure you are entitled to.

The best way to store cigars is in a humidor, and we will be discussing the various types available in the next chapter. The most important advice I can give you now is to always use distilled water in your humidifying agent. Tap water tends to cause mold and has additives that can destroy the effectiveness of some humidifiers over a period of time and can even alter the flavor of your cigars. The purpose of a humidor is to recreate the mild humid climate of the Caribbean, where the cigars were made. Which means you wouldn't want to be a humidor salesman in the

Dominican Republic. I always take extra care to check my humidors once a week for moisture level. We all tend to get a bit paranoid about dry cigars, and one of the biggest problems occurring today is overhumidification by aficionados who are just as paranoid as I am. If your cigars start to crinkle up or feel soggy, leave the humidor lid open for a few days or take the humidifying agent out until things settle back down to normal (usually about three days to a week, depending on how waterlogged your stogies have become). Feeling your cigar is the best way to tell if it is properly humidified; those built in hygrometers are usually far from accurate, as we shall discuss in the next chapter.

When checking your cigars, make sure that no greenish blue patches of mold have started to form on them. If this mini-calamity occurs, remove the offending cigars immediately and air out the humidor after cleaning it thoroughly with a dry cloth. A light grey dusting of bloom on the wrapper is permissible, however, and shows that the cigars are aging. You can wipe this bloom off with a soft cloth if you like, or leave it on the wrapper, as one would leave dust on an old bottle of wine. It won't hurt anything and may even enhance the taste.

In many European countries where Dutch-type cigars are all the rage, most notably in Switzerland, France and Germany,

The "ultimate" cigar storage area: the 100-year-old cedar-lined cabinets in Havana's Partagas factory.

154

humidors are not perceived as being necessary, and it has only been since the 1980s that French tobacconists have begun installing humidors in their shops to house the better grades of "wet" cigars. During a recent publicity tour to promote my book in Germany, most of the walk-in humidors that I saw were large, modern, and very well stocked.

If you don't have a humidor, one of the best places to store cigars is in the closet, as this is normally the one room in your house that is dark and has the least amount of temperature fluctuation. If possible, keep your cigars in a cedar box, as cedar enhances the flavor of tobacco over a period of time, much like adding spice to food. If you don't buy your cigars by the box, you can put loose ones in an airtight plastic container. You may want to line the bottom with a few strips of cedar gleaned from an obliging tobacconist to offset any lingering non-tobacco odors. I even know a fellow who stores his bundle cigars in a well scrubbed coffee can with a plastic lid. Of course, your cigars will dry out if you don't have some sort of humidifying agent in there with them. It can be as simple as a moist paper towel or a small sponge placed with your cigars inside a sealed plastic bag. A commercially made humidifying agent, such as EverMoist or Credo, as discussed in the next chapter, is even better as the humidification will be more controlled. Just don't let any water come in direct contact with the wrappers or it will ruin them. Should your cigars dry out completely, they can be rehumidified with no loss of quality as long as the natural oils in the tobaccos haven't evaporated.

The place not to store your cigars is in the refrigerator. I speak from personal experience from many years ago. Most frost free refrigerators have a tendency to suck the moisture right out of things, including your cigars. And because tobacco is highly absorbent, it will tend to take on the flavor of whatever food is nearby. I will never forget those pizza-flavored Perfectos. By the same token, do not store flavored cigars, like the vanilla-scented Arango's Sportsman, in with your non-flavored cigars.

Storing dry cigars presents no special problems, as they remain self-sufficient at relatively low humidity. Ideally, all they need is 12% but I've even kept some in the glove compartment of my car with no ill effects on me or the cigars. Even if you live in a temperate clime, such as in the Southeastern United States, simply keeping these cigars inside, away from the dripping moss, should easily maintain their long-term taste and burning qualities. Just remember to stay away from extremes, such as putting your box of Schimmelpennincks on top of the radiator or on that frosty six pack.

When storing cigars in a humidor, many aficionados recommend rotating your cigars at least monthly so that they will all receive the same degree of humidification (cigars on the bottom of a humidor are definitely not as moist as those inhabiting the upper berths) but this strikes me as being a lot of time consuming work. As most humidors have a moisturizing agent in the top of the lid, my theory has always been that as you smoke the top layer of cigars, the next layer will be humidified in turn. I have yet to have any problems with this practice, although if I were a more responsible person I would probably opt for the rotation procedure. But frankly, I would rather be smoking my cigars than rotating them.

A humidor also comes in handy if you want to age your cigars, as so many serious cigar smokers are starting to do. Actually, cigar aging is not a new trend, as it was very much in vogue with Edwardian smokers early in this century, and every once in a while a forgotten box of pre-Castro (and often pre-Batista) Havanas keep popping up, usually going for unconscionable prices at auction. In 1996 a sheep farmer in Ballymore, Ireland discovered 600 cigars that had been hidden deep in the recesses of his country manor ever since 1860. Thanks to the natural humidity in that area, the cigars were perfectly preserved. It didn't take long for an unidentified American investor to offer a million dollars for the cache. As reporter Kyle Pope of *The Wall Street Journal* pointed out, based on 500 of the cigars still being smokable, that's about $2,000 per cigar or $22 a puff!

Aging cigars is very similar to aging wines or gourmet cheeses. Some cigars can be aged for as long as ten to twenty years, although two to five years is the norm nowadays, as most of us do not wish to tie up our tobacco for too long a period of time without enjoying it. Besides, many of today's cigars will peak at one or two years and then will actually start to deteriorate in quality. And just like wines, some tobaccos will not age at all, while others can have their flavors enhanced immeasurably. The best way to determine which cigars will take to this process is to test smoke an aging cigar every six months. Here is the procedure I use:

In addition to the humidors for storing the cigars I am currently smoking, I have separate humidors in which I keep the cigars that I am aging. I am also fortunate enough to live near a tobacconist who rents out cigar lockers in his walk-in humidor, which increases my aging potential considerably. Firms like Dunhill and Davidoff and a number of other tobacconists — where space permits — also offer this storage service to customers. And most new cigar clubs provide private humidors to their members as part of the reason for joining. But even at home, it is an easy process to tuck a box of cigars away in a special humidor purchased just for aging, or to seal them in an inexpensive and efficient plastic food container with a moisturizer in it. In addition to a 70-70 mix of temperature and humidity, cigars will age best in a cedar box. But remember to remove the cellophane from each cigar as well as the interior tissue from the cedar box, or all your efforts will be for naught. Cellophane inhibits the aging process and the interior paper is a barrier between your cigars and the cedar.

I mark each box that I am aging with the day, month, and year that I first put it down. Before closing the box, I smoke one of the cigars, and note my impression of the aroma of the wrapper and the taste of the tobacco. Approximately six months later I smoke another cigar from the box and refer to my original notes to see if there has been any change in the flavor and wrapper aroma. If there has, then I know I am on a roll. But if there is no noticeable difference, then that box gets "decanted" and smoked immediately. It doesn't mean the cigars are bad; it just means that there is no benefit to keeping them sequestered any longer. You

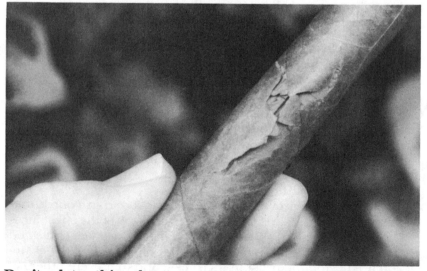

Don't let this happen to you (or your cigars). Overhumidification can split the wrapper. This same effect can be caused by trying to defrost your cigars too quickly.

may want to use the CigarNotes section in the back of this book to keep an aging log for your cigars. And there is nothing to say that you cannot age a number of different cigars in one box, keeping in mind that, being of different tobaccos, if they age, they will most likely age at different rates. And for long term aging, you should have a cedar divider between different brands, so that dissimilar types of tobacco do not come in contact with each other.

You should be warned that there is a specter that can arise as a result of either short term cigar humidification or long term aging, and that is the evil form of *Lacioderma*, the dreaded tobacco worm. The first edition of *The Ultimate Cigar Book* was the first book to bring this plight to the universal attention of the consumer. Even though many cigar makers are now fumigating their warehouses every thirty days, these prolific little creatures sometimes still manage to survive. They do it by laying their eggs deep inside the tobacco leaf. There they go dormant, and that leaf eventually gets made into a cigar. And sometimes a dark humidor that has gotten a little too warm or a little too humid is just what they need to be aroused from their slumber, like some loathsome creature in a microscopic horror movie. Within twenty-two days the larva hatches into a hungry worm that finds itself in an all-night buffet — your cigars! This vile creature, still unseen by human eyes, eats/bores its way through the tobacco leaves, creating a tiny tunnel that leads out to the surface of the cigar. There, bloated and burping hideously after gorging itself on your Double Corona, it metamorphoses into a pinhead-sized brown beetle and, if it doesn't fly out the next time you open your humidor, its body will usually be found in the bottom. Oddly, these tobacco beetles normally confine themselves to a single cigar, but every once in a while they get in a traveling mood. I once opened a box of what used to be twenty-five fully-formed cigars and found nothing but ragged leaves and tobacco dust. A virtual invasion had taken place. Usually the worm will bore straight up and out of a cigar, leaving its telltale hole (which completely ruins the cigar, by the way), but occasionally they will eat a deep trough along the length of the wrapper.

When you discover the deadly *Lacioderma* in your humidor, the first thing to do is take a stiff drink of any of the substances discussed in Chapter 7. Then, return to the scene of the crime and remove the dead cigar. In fact, you must remove all of the cigars if you are to stop the beast in its tracks, and to prevent others of his pack — who may still be lurking in your cigars — from eventually hatching. Actually, only one cigar may have been harboring the larvae, but you can never be sure. There may be others from the same box. For all intents and purposes, all the cigars must be given The Cure: Place them on a light colored paper towel (easier to spot any bugs that way) and scrutinize each cigar for worm holes. If any more are found, throw them out. Then carefully examine your now empty humidor for signs of the beetle's body. Chances are you will find it. What you do with it is up to you. A friend of mine was so enraged at finding the bug still alive he actually drove a letter opener right through its heart — well actually, its whole body — and through the bottom of his humidor as well. A bit rash, but effective. It killed the beetle.

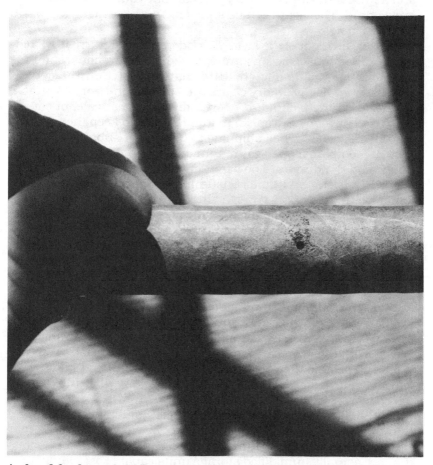

A freshly bored hole of the dreaded *Lacioderma* (tobacco worm). Notice the tobacco dust left around the opening.

Next, put all of the apparently healthy cigars in a plastic ziplock bag, gently force the air out of it, seal it, and place it in the freezer. Leave it there for at least two days. Three is even better. Then, take the bag from the freezer to the refrigerator so that the cigars will thaw out slowly and will not go into shock and split. This is the only time I can recommend putting cigars in the refrigerator. Once the cigars have thawed, remove them from the refrigerator, take them out of the bag and slowly let them return to room temperature. Do not put them in the sunlight to speed up the process or they will split their wrappers. Once again I tell you this from personal experience. In the meantime, completely clean and aerate your humidor. Now you can put your cigars back. The bug is dead. The cigars can be smoked. You have made the world safe. For now.

But the Night of the Living *Lacioderma* may return. It shouldn't, because tobacco crops are sprayed and warehouses are fumigated, but this is one creature that just isn't on the endangered species list. Even dry cigars are not immune from its attack, and the freezing technique — on a much larger scale, of course — is used by many European manufacturers to keep their Dutch-type cigars "clean" when shipping to tropical or subtropical countries. In addition, a few cigar manufacturers in the Dominican Republic and Honduras are now freezing their cigars before shipping, but it is a costly and time consuming process, so not many are following this practice. Thus, a shipment that hasn't been frozen is delayed in customs or sits on a nice warm, humid loading dock in Miami. The bug hatches and the eventual recipient of the infested box of cigars finds he has also inherited some new "pets." But at least you now know The Cure and how to get rid of this beast and save your cigars. Like anything, constant surveillance is the best defense. Check the cigars in your humidor regularly. Not just the top row, but right down to the bottom. Keep your humidor away from heating vents. Given a choice, it is better to keep cigars cool with less humidity rather than overly humid and warm. With these precautions, perhaps someday cigars of all nations will be able to live safely in their humidors and know a life without fear from the wrath of *Lacioderma* — the dreaded tobacco worm.

One final note about cigar storage. Sometimes a table top humidor isn't enough. That's why there are now companies that specialize in making furniture humidors, end tables and armoires that are actually humidified storage units capable of holding hundreds of cigars. But sometimes hundreds of cigars aren't enough. That's why there is now a growing industry of individuals who are

Because they are made and stored in countries that have a naturally high degree of humidity, these cigars do not need any additional humidification to keep from drying out, as they wait, already sorted and bundled, to be boxed.

(Honduras)

Certain cigars, like these 18-inch long Cuba Aliados "Generals," present a unique challenge in finding a humidor — or even a locker — long enough to store them. Their extra length can also inspire some creative smoking practices, as evidenced by these two aficionados at a black tie Smoker; note the double lighting technique, using a mini-blowtorch.

photo: Eric Simonson
The Ritz-Carlton, Laguna Niguel, CA

building private walk-in humidors for cigar connoisseurs in their homes and offices. It isn't as farfetched as it may seem. All you need is a closet or extra bedroom that can be commandeered. Line it with Spanish cedar (standard American "closet cedar" is much too aromatic), weatherproof it, install a portable humidifier with a regulating agent so that it doesn't become too moist and *voila!* You've increased your cigar storage capacity by thousands of cigars. The benefits are many. Now you can take advantage of those great sale prices on boxed cigars. You can stock up on your favorite brands, thereby protecting yourself from future shortages (although you will probably be creating this shortage by stocking up on these brands). You'll always have a variety of cigars to choose from, no matter what size, shape or wrapper leaf you may desire. Many Hollywood celebrities have walk-ins to preserve their privacy when selecting their smokes. A Beverly Hills attorney has his walk-in tucked underneath a staircase in his house. By contrast, a real estate broker is incorporating a huge walk-in as an integral part of his overall house design. With a gleam in his eye, he estimates he'll be able to store more stogies than some third world countries can make in a year.

No, you can never have too many cigars. That's what cigar storage is all about.

Chapter 6

Cigar Accessories:
The Aftermarket of Smoke

Just as you might want to upgrade your stereo with a mega-boosted multi-speaker system, so might you add certain amenities that are designed to make your cigar smoking more enjoyable. They can be novel or luxurious and some accessories are absolutely essential. Like a good cigar cutter.

In most circles, it is not considered *de rigueur* to chomp off the end of a cigar with your teeth and spit it across the room hoping to make a slam dunk in the punch bowl. Nor is the sometimes-condoned technique of trimming a cigar with your thumbnail considered genteel. What is needed is a civilized method of making the four basic types of cuts discussed in Chapter 3. Because the guillotine is the recommended cut of *The Ultimate Cigar Book*, we will deal with this one first.

The most easily encountered and least expensive cutter will be the pocket-sized plastic devices that have a finger loop at one end and are often given away as premiums by some of the cigar companies. If you prefer to have one that is not embossed with a logo, they are one of the most inexpensive items you can buy in a tobacco shop. The blade is basically a razor, and as such, it is not good for a great many close shaves with your cigars. If you use this type of cutter regularly, the average lifespan will be about six months, but most people will lose theirs before they wear them out. Slightly more practical is the Klipit 2000. Not the prettiest cigar cutter in the world, it nonetheless features a stainless steel blade, a positive safety lock and a large enough hole to accommodate a 54 ring cigar. Slightly upscale in design and price is a twin-bladed cutter from Pléiades.

A significant step up in price and appearance is the excellent Donatus guillotine-type cutter from Germany, which sports a Soligen steel blade. It is available in a great number of case styles, including two of the most popular, brushed steel with contrasting gold screws (as pictured in this chapter) and as a briar paneled version from firms such as Savinelli.

By far the most versatile pocket-sized guillotine cutter is the Portable Zino Cigar Cutter by Davidoff. It is one of the few cutters capable of facing up to a 54 ring gauge without shirking its responsibilities. Although it is slightly heavier than some other versions, the Zino has excellent surgically sharp twin blades, so that equal pressure from two sides is automatically applied to the cigar head; the cut is made from the outside perimeters straight through to the center, as opposed to starting from one end and slicing across. This enables the fingers to apply far greater leverage for a faster, surer cut. Because of its unique design, the polished stainless steel blades are self-sharpening, which means that this cutter will probably last indefinitely. Available in black, brown, red, green, grey and white, the Zino, while not inexpensive, is far from being the costliest cutter on the market. Considering its practicality and versatility, it is one of the best values available today.

Now we start getting into the realm of luxury class guillotine cutters, which I find to be surprisingly limited. Perhaps the best variety for a single design can be found with the stainless steel blade vest pocket versions from Dunhill. These British-made works of art are available in a number of finishes, including polished steel, steel and gold, silver plate, sterling silver, gold plate and 18 ct. gold. Elegant enough for formal wear, each cutter comes with a protective leather pouch and a "schackle" for attachment to a watch chain. This is one cutter you definitely won't want to lose!

From France, Dupont makes a distinctive rectangular-shaped pocket cutter in three different finishes: Chinese black lacquer, silver, and gold plate. And Cartier offers their Santos-styled cutter with multiple screws, to match their Santos watch. Definitely not a pocket cutter and more in the line of a desktop accessory is the stainless steel, hand-forged Davidoff Cigar Scissors, which are also available with gold plated handles. Employing the same principle as their Zino cutter, this double-bladed cutter is one of the easiest to use in terms of gauging the size of the cut to the ring size of the cigar. A similar design is also marketed by Michel Perrenoud of Switzerland and other firms as well.

In the punch cut, wherein a round sharpened cylinder is rotated into the cigar head and a hole is plucked out of the cigar, you can run the price gamut from an inexpensive cutter that looks like a .44 magnum bullet (in fact, that is what it is called)

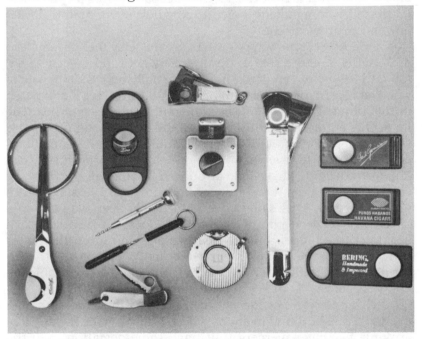

The perfect cut-ups: (Clockwise, L to R) Davidoff stainless steel scissors; Zino Portable Cigar Cutter; Dunhill Sterling Silver Pocket "V" Cutter; Dunhill Sterling Silver Tabletop Cutter; three versions of pocket guillotine cutters, going from a stainless steel Sheffield blade down to premiums from Cubatabaco and Bering; round gold plated Dunhill guillotine; square steel Donatus; two piercers: a Dunhill sterling silver Golf Tee drill, and the Trilogy by Kolpin; a pearl handled vest knife by Spyderco, with serrated blade for frayless slicing.

all the way up to the elegant Davidoff Round Cutter, which comes in gold, silver and gold, or a lacquered finish. This is really one of the best, as it sports three different diameter cutting cylinders so that you can match the proper cut to the ring size of the cigar you are smoking. Otherwise, too small a hole will have the same effect as the pierce: acidic tobacco juices will gradually condense along the cut and eventually ruin the taste of your smoke. Too large a hole is just like making too wide a guillotine cut and you run the risk of taking in too much air and hyperventilating (and you thought that dizzy feeling was due to the tobacco!). But if cost is a factor, the next best choice is the Crestmark Cigar Tool, which has a handy built in plunger that pops out the tobacco plug. It also comes with a rubber cap that keeps the sharp cylindrical cutting edge from making a nice 28 ring hole in your pants pocket or other nearby extremity.

Almost all of the V-type cutters are made by the German firm of Donatus, and are sold under a variety of brands. Their table-top cutter has an elongated handle, usually with side panels of wood, staghorn, or precious material, and features a small notch in the rounded end for removing the nail from the cigar box. The lip of this cutter is used to pry open the lid. Although this style is called a "V" cutter, it also has two guillotine-type slicing holes on either side, with a small hole on one side for European dry cigars, and a slightly larger hole (around a 33 ring) on the opposite side. Unfortunately, I have never found that these side blades work very well. This same style of cutter is also available in a much smaller vest pocket size, which does not have a return spring on the blade, a handy feature only found on the larger version. By far the best of the breed of the "V" cutters are the silver plated hallmarked versions from Dunhill. Both their table top and vest pocket V-cutters are attractively gift boxed.

Cigar piercers, or "drills," are no longer in vogue, although a few can still be found in shops where traditions die hard. There are only two cigar piercers that have some deviation from the norm. One is a sterling silver golf tee that twists like a mechanical pencil to produce a silver drill. It would seem to be the perfect accessory for the duffer who literally wants to make a hole in one. Substantially less expensive is The Trilogy, a small key-ringed metal rod in which the lower part unscrews to reveal a slender drill point. This is designed to be used to pierce three holes, each at a 45 degree angle, in the head of a cigar. Thus, the tars and juices do not condense at a single hole in the center and the smoke is directed away from the tip of the tongue. One thing in the Trilogy's favor: It is the only device than can be used to handle huge cigars like the 66 ring gauge Jeroboam and Half Jeroboam made by Casa Blanca. I will admit to carrying a Trilogy on my key ring in case I forget or lose my guillotine pocket cutter, and it does make a handy (but sharp!) emergency toothpick. There is also a device called the Master-Key Cigar Holder, which is simply a plastic cigar holder with a long hollow tube attached. You twist the tube into the cigar, clamp the holder between your teeth, and light up. It works, but you have to like using a plastic cigar holder.

When selecting a cutter, I opt for the cheaper razor-blade varieties to always keep handy in my coat pocket and the glove compartment of my car. In fact, I literally have one in every coat I own, so that even if I forget my Zino or Dunhill at home, I never suffer the awkwardness of being without a cutter. When these become dull (as they most definitely will) or lost (as they most certainly do), it is a simple matter to get a new one at little or no

Two of the newest cigar cutters: (Left) the Davidoff Round Cutter, made in France. The circular disk swings out from its elegant case, revealing three round steel blades made to fit any diameter-sized cigar. The head of the cigar is twisted on one of the circular blades, which plucks out the center of the "cap" of tobacco, thus creating a clean hole. (Right) Substantially less expensive is the effective twin-bladed guillotine cutter by Pléiades. Shown with two Cuban Montecristo No 2's; note the differences in the heads of these supposedly identical cigars, thus revealing the variations of handrolling.

cost. However, if you smoke quality cigars then you will eventually want a quality cutter. For home use I keep a Zino by my smoking table at all times, and a Michel Perrenoud scissors cutter affixed to the magnet of one of my humidors, so that it is always at hand when I am near my cigars. Likewise, I keep a table top cutter by my chair in the den for emergency use when the Zino is not reachable. When venturing out into society, I carry a gold Dunhill cutter in its leather pouch; it is an impressive way to clip your cigar and that of a friend's. Being a collector of cigar cutters, I will sometimes carry one of my antique clippers on a chain in my vest, although these are mainly for show, as they are not capable of handling the large ring gauges that I usually smoke. Likewise, Winston Churchill always made a great display of wearing a cigar cutter attached to his watch chain, but he rarely used it, preferring to pierce his cigars with a wooden match. Nobody ever took him to task for this; after all, he helped defeat Hitler.

No matter what type of cutter you select, the most important criteria should be the blade. It must be sharp. Otherwise, you won't be slicing the cap of your cigar, you will be crushing it, thereby hampering the draw and negating all of the handiwork the cigar maker put into making the bunch. A sharp penknife is far superior to a dull cigar cutter.

Just as a cutter is the most useful accessory you can buy, acquiring a quality humidor will be the best investment you will ever make for your cigars. A good humidor doesn't have to be overly expensive. But it can be. However, as we discovered in the last chapter, it can be as unpretentious as a tightly sealed plastic container. Or as convenient as the cigar boxes that come with their own humidifying agents, such as Pléiades and Romeo y Julieta Vintage. But what do you do when you and your Significant Other invite a few couples over for dinner and as it happens, cigars are offered at the end of the meal, when everyone retires to the patio or den? Bringing out your Vintage Macanudos on a cookie sheet is not the best way to make a presentation. You might as well light your cigars against the hot exhaust pipe of a Harley Davidson. No, there will come a time when you and your cigars will demand something better.

Whether or not anyone else ever sees it, a humidor reflects what you think about the cigars that you smoke. It embodies pride of ownership and, in many cases, adds a distinctive touch to your home or office decor. Not only does it make a statement that a cigar smoker is there, but it can also say something very personal about what kind of a cigar smoker you are. Some humidors can even turn into heirlooms, passed down through the generations. This is an especially effective rationale for cigar smokers with young children or grandchildren. Or, like some of us, you might decide to take your humidor with you when you go.

There are two basic requirements that any humidor has to meet. It must provide a constant and reliable source of humidity, and it must be airtight. Not all humidors have these traits, which is why many lower end products are losing ground to some of the better grade versions that are constructed more like a fine piece of furniture with a specific purpose, rather than just a box in which you can store cigars.

In addition to its functional ability, a humidor must be able to hold a realistic number of cigars for your smoking requirements. That includes accommodating the shapes you like to smoke. If you prefer 7½ inch long Churchills and a humidor has a storage area that is 6 inches in length, it will not be a good buy for you, no matter what the price. On the other hand, many of the 100 and 150-cigar humidors have movable dividers, which can be adjusted to accept a wide range of cigars, from the 4³⁄₁₆ Partagas Puritos all the way up to the 18" Cuba Aliados General. But beware of some humidors that boast of being able to store 50 cigars. I succumbed to this hype with one well respected brand, but when I got it home I discovered that they must have been referring to 50 Coronas. Try as I might, the best I could store was 25 of my Churchills, and that was only by laying them in horizontally. There is certainly nothing wrong with that. Just be sure you are aware of these limitations and don't take everything you read or hear for granted. It is better to have a humidor that is too big rather than too small. You can always buy more cigars!

Some humidors are lined with cedar, which makes a wonderful spicing agency when stored with tobacco. That is why the aging rooms of all the major cigar factories are lined with cedar. And why cigar boxes are built of cedar. However, there is a school of thought that says because cedar is absorbent, it can interfere with the uniformity of humidity control. Thus, you will find many humidors lined with mahogany or with a finely lacquered and sealed interior. There is no problem with this, for as long as the humidor is airtight and has a proper humidifier, your cigars will be kept fresh and will age according to the ability of their tobacco, but without the cedar flavoring. It is really a matter of personal preference. As for me, I have both types in my home, preferring to keep my cigars for immediate smoking in a 100-unit mahogany humidor without cedar lining, while keeping my aged cigars in a 150-unit with cedar lining. However, my personal preference is for cedar; I like that extra hint of spice in my smoking.

In a classic example of cause and effect, the ongoing cigar renaissance has created an unbelievable plethora of humidor manufacturers, both old and new. Clearly this is the one perceived accessory that everyone deems to be in the most demand. And maybe they're right. After all, once you graduate from buying two or three cigars at a time and start acquiring boxfuls, where are you going to store all those stogies? Virtually every style of humidor is available, from glass jars to unfinished wooden models to elegantly lacquered veneer to reconstructed humidors made out of antique jewelry boxes and writing desks. Indeed, on a recent trip to Europe, every antique dealer I spoke with bemoaned the growing scarcity of 19th century "laptop" writing desks due to the fact that entrepreneurs were converting them all into humidors which were eagerly purchased "by you crazy Amer-

Humidors that fit a budget and a space (clockwise L to R): Rosewood with cedar lining plus hygrometer and detachable humidifier, from France, by Hollco-Rohr; a Punch Grand Cru box easily converted to hold cigars such as the Tabacaleras Corona Largas or Bances Cazadores; Savinelli Bordeaux Series, filled with a variety of cigars.

ican cigar smokers!" But no matter what the style, good humidors don't come cheap.

One of the best values for an above average humidor today is imported by Savinelli. Available in 75 and 150-cigar sizes (or 25 to 50 of the larger shapes), they are cedar lined and come with adjustable interior panels, a hygrometer and an adjustable sponge-type humidifier. Available in bordeaux, black, and burlwood paneling, they offer matching ashtrays and lighters as optional accessories.

You might also want to check out the Italian-made humidors imported by Club Imports, which are fairly priced, and come in 25 and 50-cigar sizes (slightly more or less, depending on the actual size of your cigars) plus a 100-cigar Conference Room Humidor with briar burl veneer, inner serving tray, brass handles, and a lock and key for keeping out those sticky fingered mail

Elegance in humidification (clockwise from L): Michel Perrenoud 100-cigar size in mahogany with brass inlays, detachable humidifier, and optional magnetically held cigar scissors; D. Marshall custom made burlwood with lift-out cedar tray, gold plated humidification tubes plus Credo system; Davidoff No. 3 burlwood with cedar lining and lid-mounted magnet for cutting tool; Zino acrylic humidor with two humidifying agents, and sufficient room to store cigars singly or by the box. Shown with a cigar dealer's show mat from the 1920s.

171

room trainees. In addition to adjustable dividers and a choice of finishes on most of these cedar lined humidors, the Club Imports humidors utilize a specially treated circular sponge with adjustable moisture control openings, but as an extra cost option, you can have the excellent Credo humidity regulator, which we'll discuss later on in this section.

Stepping up into a much more elegant arena, Michel Perrenoud of Switzerland produces a finely handcrafted series of humidors that is more like a piece of furniture than a cigar accessory. I have one of their gold-hinged, brass inlaid mahogany humidors which boasts of a humidifier so efficient, it only has to be re-moisturized once every two months. The only fault that I can find with their excellent craftsmanship is that they use finished hardwood for their interiors and only line their humidors with cedar on special order.

Also made in Switzerland are the legendary humidors of Davidoff — all cedar lined, many with lock and key, and all with Davidoff's exclusive self regulator that maintains a constant humidity level of 70 to 72 degrees fahrenheit. A wide variety of fancy grained wood finishes is offered. Davidoff humidors range in sizes from 40 to 200 cigars, plus a smaller series of travel humidors that can hold from 6 to 18 cigars. In addition, their Zino line, which is made in France, includes a beautiful tobacco leaf model (with an actual tobacco leaf embodied in the lid), and two sizes of humidors constructed of both clear and smoked acrylic with gold plated accents, for those who like to look at their cigars even when they are not smoking them. The larger acrylic model, which holds up to 90 cigars, features two of Davidoff's self regulating humidifiers, one on each side — a highly effective arrangement.

The elegance of custom handcrafted humidors is the hallmark of Dunhill, which offers two distinct ranges, both of which are handmade. The most widely encountered are in a 25-cigar size, with 22 ct. gold plated hinges, mahogany lining and available in three satin matte veneers: walnut, mahogany, and Australian silky oak. The second range is only available in Dunhill stores, and features a larger 50 and 100-cigar format, mahogany lining, a choice of high gloss thuya, maccasser or walnut veneer with inlaid "antique" marquetry lid, and lock and key. A less expensive semi-gloss green, blue or maroon variation of this efficient humidor is also available. The Dunhill humidors in both ranges utilize their revolutionary Humidity Control System, which is a glycerin-based regulator that is charged with water and lasts for approximately four weeks, after which time it must be re-moisturized. But the real benefit of this system is the fact that it can be removed from the humidor and handheld to reveal a sliding scale that gives an extremely precise humidity level reading. The system itself is inexpensive, and must be replaced every eighteen months or so. Perhaps this is finally the answer to most factory equipped hygrometers, which I find to be less than accurate.

In addition to these two humidor ranges, both of which were introduced in 1993, Dunhill has inaugurated their Bespoke Box Service, which simply means you can get any type of custom humidor you want, designed to your exact specifications. That means a concert pianist can have a humidor shaped like a piano. Or a major league hitter can have a humidor shaped like a bat. The list is endless, should one feel inspired to engage in this bit of cigar creativity. Even the prewar ivory Dunhill label could be replicated, although today I am afraid that you might have to settle for pseudo-ivory polymer. And if you're in the market for a very high end humidor that can double as an exquisitely inlaid ar-

From Fernández de Córdoba comes solid craftsmanship made from 19th century wood. The Palos travel humidor on the left was fashioned from the weathered wood of an old barn. The 225 cigar Granada on the right uses mahogany from an old railroad car. Note the special UV treated antique glass lid.

chitectural model, check out Dunhill's limited edition offerings by Viscount David Lindley.

D. Marshall is a craftsman who is also very much concerned with customizing his well-known humidors for customers. For the most part, he prefers to sell direct, rather than through retail shops, although you have seen many of his humidors at some of the best tobacconists throughout the world. Made in a variety of exotic wood finishes, and in sizes ranging from 50 to 500 cigars (and larger, on request) each D. Marshall humidor takes approximately four months to construct, and features his "One Thousand Coat" deep glass-like exterior finish. Inside, his humidors are lined with Spanish Cedar and all hinges are gold plated and mortised into the walls of the humidor. A very exacting Credo humidification unit keeps cigars stored in his multilevel humidors in a constant state of readiness. In addition to optional lock and key, personalized name plates are available. Although hardly inexpensive, these are some of the best humidors on the market; D. Marshall humidors are so tightly constructed that I only have to replenish the moisture in the humidifying agent once every two months.

But realizing that economy is a fact of life, Daniel Marshall has brought out his Ambiente (which means "environment" in Italian) series, which features the same exacting construction of his higher priced models, but instead of expensive wood grain finishes, this series is surfaced in a matte lacquer finish. Colors are black, green and burgundy and 65 cigar and 125 cigar sizes are offered. Not to be overlooked is D.Marshall's stylish leather covered travel humidor. As an extra touch, all D. Marshall humidors come with a selection of D. Marshall specially banded cigars.

Another unique and finely crafted humidor series that deserves mention is by Fernández de Córdoba, solid old world designs that are constructed of weathered antique woods taken from various barns and buildings from around the country. For serious cigar smokers, this is the ultimate in recycled elegance! Not counting the ⅞ inch thick, naturally textured antique wood exterior (milled down from one inch planks), the interior of each humidor is made of ⅜ inch thick Spanish cedar, features handles and hardware cast from antique designs, and offers an optional glass lid that is specially treated so that ultraviolet light doesn't affect the color of your cigars while still permitting you to see them. Besides being innovative in design, each humidor is built like a fortress. They are all signed and numbered and a special limited edition is made from mahogany planks taken from old railroad cars. A variety of designs are available, from a 12 cigar travel size to a 500 cigar chest. My personal favorite is the 225 cigar Granada model with a sliding drawer for accessories.

Cigars for cars (clockwise from L): All leather twin compartment cigar case from Arango; D. Marshall Italian leather-covered travel humidor with its own humidification system; Nat Sherman's leather and canvas cigar folio.

Indeed, such exquisite humidors are more than just a place to store your cigars; they become a statement about your lifestyle. Which makes me wonder about the lock and key that is prevalent on so many humidors today. About the only reason I can see to have one boarded up in this fashion is to keep your man servant from pinching a smoke while you are out in the back forty shooting grouse. But then, any thief worthy of a good cigar would probably just cart off the entire humidor. Still, I suppose a lock does keep visiting cousins from pawing your aged Dominicans.

One of the best humidor buys that I know of was made by actor-producer-sun tan king George Hamilton, and occurred on the night of June 7, 1996. We were sitting at a table together during a charity auction at The Friars Club of California Celebrity Smoker IV. A humidor came up for bid that had been donated by comedy legend Milton Berle; on it was a brass plaque that had the

Mobile humidification: The all-cedar Humidif with detachable humidifier comes in a variety of sizes for all cigars. This model, the No. 12, can easily accommodate a Don Diego Lonsdale, Bering Hispano (shown in Maduro), and Pléiades Sirius. Also shown: the Davidoff leather-covered, cedar-lined traveling humidor, filled with Davidoff 3000s. In lower left is a cased Victorian amber and silver engraved cigar holder.

Friar's Club name and the date engraved on it. As an added enticement, Berle offered to autograph the humidor to the lucky bidder. George got it for $3,000 and Milton signed the inside of the lid with an inscription similar to the one that was on the humidor he had given to John F. Kennedy when he was president. That humidor had fetched $574,500 at the Sotheby's auction in April of that same year.

"George," I said as he proudly brought the humidor back to our table, "the last humidor that Berle gave to anyone brought $574,500. You just saved yourself $571,500!"

After the smoker, and noticing that the sun had not yet come up, we all went over to Hamilton's Wine Bar in Beverly Hills for a final cigar. There the humidor was placed on a table and George told anyone who would listen how he had saved over $500,000 that evening.

While on the subject of humidors, this might be a good time to discuss humidifiers. In the distant past, the old brass and clay moisturizer that Dunhill used was one of the best, as were some of the blotting paper devices that were sandwiched in between a perforated metal holder that was affixed to the inside top of the lid. It was a simple concept: soak some water into an absorbent material and let it permeate the inside of a closed box, checking it every few days to see that it had not dried out. That same basic principle applies today, only now we use everything from organic sponges to sophisticated looking devices that have been patented by some of our most respected firms. The Davidoff internal self-regulator is not available separately, but the Dunhill Humidity Control System is.

There is another humidifying device that I consider to be one of the best. It is the Credo Precision 70, so named because it maintains the moisture inside a humidor at a constant 70%, as long as the device is properly charged with distilled water. The Precision 70 can easily humidify 75 — 100 cigars, while the smaller Rondo can accommodate 25 — 50 cigars. There is even a thinner size for travel humidors but these require filling every week or so. The Credo system is what many of the top custom humidor makers use, and it is also the system selected by many cigar makers who put humidifiers in their cigar boxes. The Credo is available in black or gold, and comes with a magnetic mount for the inside of your humidor. It only needs to be rehumidified once a month, and its modest cost is a small price to pay for keeping your cigars healthy and fresh. No matter what type of humidifying device you use, only fill it with *distilled* water. Tap water has a tendency to cause mold. We may think it's okay to drink, but you certainly don't want to expose your cigars to the stuff.

If your humidor is cedar lined, it is always a good idea to pre-humidify it for a couple of days before you place your cigars in it. The reason is that cedar, being absorbent, will compete with your cigars for the humidity unless it is already moist. In addition, moist cedar acts as a mini-humidifier itself, releasing a greater amount of its aroma into the air surrounding your cigars. Of course, there is no reason to pre-humidify non-cedar humidors like those from Michel Perrenoud and Dunhill, as the interiors are hand lacquered to a hard, nonabsorbent finish. Speaking of finishes, make sure your humidor stays out of the sunlight, as those fancy veneers can fade. The warmth of the sun isn't exactly good for your cigars either.

Because tobacco leaves are so highly absorbent and sensitive to moisture, the more cigars you put into your humidor, the more moisture will be required, and you will have to replenish the water in your humidifier more often. The best way to tell if your cigars are not drying out is to feel them. Unfortunately, the hygrometers that come with most humidors are rarely factory set for anything resembling accuracy. To correct this almost universal oversight, take your hygrometer out of the humidor and wrap it in a damp washcloth for an hour. Then take a look. If it is not registering 100 per cent humidity, adjust the spring loaded needle on the back with a pencil so that is pointing at the 100 mark. The best bet, of course, is to invest in a digital hygrometer, such as the excellent model made by Western Humidor.

I make every effort to check my humidors once a week, but find that the D. Marshall, Davidoff, Zino, Elie Bleu (some of the most attractively inlaid humidors on the market), Dunhill, and Michel Perrenoud products only need replenishing about once every six to eight weeks. With this new wave of humidors, it seems as though you really do get what you pay for. On the other hand, if you should come across an antique humidor that you wish to put back into service (make sure it's not warped before you buy it), you may want to replace the older moisturizing unit with a Credo, or simply put a shot glass of distilled water in with the cigars. But be careful; if the humidity level reaches 85%, mold will start to form, especially on those cigars nearest the humidifying unit. And before putting cigars into any antique humidor, clean every inch of its interior with alcohol and let it air out for a few days. Who knows who kept what in there before you bought it!

And finally, there is a pocket humidor that can accommodate any of today's popular cigar sizes, ranging from four Macanudo Ascots all the way up to three Primo del Rey Aristocrats. It is called the Humidif and is made in Europe. What makes this pocket case so unique is not only the fact that it is made entirely of Spanish cedar, but that it has its own replenishable moisturizer built right into the lid. There are fifteen different sizes of the Humidif, enough to insure that at least three of your favorite cigars will always be fresh, wherever you go.

Lighters are another viable commodity that no cigar smoker should be without. Some of the most novel lighters are those that incorporate both a cigar clipper and a butane lighter in one slim

From wide bodied jets to wide bodied jet flames, these lighters will accommodate the largest ring sizes. (L.to R.) Corona gold and red lacquer with 45 degree angle flame; Dunhill Unique in gold and silver barleycorn finish; Colibri Quantum "flameless" Cigar Lighter; Prometheus Neptune with double flame and gas jet ignition.

179

design. Versions of these are made by Colibri and Rowenta, both with electro-quartz ignition and a stainless steel blade. Colibri also makes a Quantum waterproof all-weather lighter that uses no flame — just an adjustable mini-blast of blue-hot heat. I have lit cigars in a rainstorm with this lighter, as well as on the bow of a ship, as wind doesn't seem to affect it either. Personally, I prefer the 90 degree pipe lighters such as the Quantum Pipe and the Pipette, as this angle enables me to "paint" the end of my cigar

Women's cigar accessories still have a long ways to go, but these items are in the forefront. (L. To R.) Prometheus gold and silver Moritz; Colibri angle flame Elite in jade and gold; Prometheus Renoma dual-flame in satin silver. Shown with a briarwood cutter by Savinelli and surrounded by a cigar band necklace from Pop Art.

180

with the glowing heat without burning my fingers. These are some of the most surefire cigar lighters on the market. The Colibri Elite has a 45 degree flame that works equally as well. But one of the most innovative developments is the advent of the wide flame lighter, which utilizes a twin burner to create a broad flame for firing up the biggest ringed Robusto. Dunhill, Colibri, Prometheus,

The lighter touch: (clockwise, starting at 7 o'clock) Dunhill Unique, a 1930s design updated for butane and available in gold or silver; Colibri Quantum all-weather electro-quartz with water resistant housing; Corona 1876 Series with briarwood panels; Colibri 190 Cigar Cutter-Lighter; Dunhill extra long Smokers Matches; and Davidoff's sterling silver matchbox holder with cedar matches. All surrounding a 1930s unopened box of La Palina Pals cigarillos, made by the Congress Cigar Company in Philadelphia.

and Savinelli are just a few of the better brands. Like Colibri, Prometheus also has a "flameless" model for cigar smokers.

Not as advanced in technology, but using the principle of electricity all the same is the Heritage Lighter by Pioneer Manufacturing. Back around the turn of the century, electric lighters became all the rage once people found out that Edison's invention wasn't going to make them go blind. Of course, just as quickly

An early American lighter for some early American cigars: This 1906 Heritage electric cigar lighter is being reproduced by Pioneer Manufacturing, Inc. of Battle Lake, Minnesota. The original was made for the Klein Cigar Company in New York, back in the days when electricity was still a novelty. It was intended for futuristic-thinking homeowners and upscale cigar stores. This replica duplicates the oak and brass original but is now powered by four C-cells. Like the original, the swing-out wick only works with lighter fluid, so that is the concession you will have to make if you want to amaze your friends with this sparking accessory. Ask your tobacconist to order one of these unique antiques for an old-fashioned smoke. The Judge's Cave and Muniemaker cigars by F.D. Grave and the centennial boxed Travis Club Senators by Finck Cigar Company have changed very little since they first made their appearances over 100 years ago. These cigars are still being made by the founding families.

A classic case of the Old West. Custom made to the author's specifications, this antiqued leather cigar case by Wild Bill Cleaver of Vason, Washington, easily holds three 7 1/2 x 50 cigars, or even larger Pyramids if you place them in the case upside down. If more room is needed, the interior compartment is removable. And if the loop-levered Winchester 1892 carbine, serial #756277 looks familiar, it is because this photo was taken at the ranch of Chuck Connors (TV's "The Rifleman").

as they came in these lighters went out, when the growing advantages of lighter fluid and the convenience of paper safety matches were discovered. Gone but not forgotten. One of the most obscure and rarest electric lighters, the Heritage is again being made in America of solid walnut with brass plated antiqued parts. It is an exact duplicate of the 1906 original and even though it uses lighter fluid, it is guaranteed to be a conversation starter as well as a cigar starter at your next Smoker.

While on the hot topic of lighters, we must not forget the basic match, or more specifically, the cigar match, such as those put out by Dunhill, Davidoff, Pléiades, Arango, Bering, and a sulphurless match by Club Imports. Their extra length allows plenty of burning time and flame to properly toast even the largest ringed cigar without toasting your fingers. The cedar wood that is traditionally used for these specialized matches produces a faint hint of flavor during the initial few puffs, as an added bonus.

One of the biggest challenges for cigar smokers has always been finding a way to safely carry our smokes. But stuffing them in boots, belts, bullet loops and pockets has never been able to supplant the cigar case. In the past, the most popular cases were those made of leather, metal and wood. Just like cigar making, not much has changed through the years, because today the most popular cigar cases still are those made of leather, metal and wood. Savinelli has two distinct styles of Italian-made leather cases that come in fluted and unfluted designs and are available

A case for cigars: (L to R) Dunhill black leather "two finger"; Dunhill Sterling Silver Barley-pattern Cigar Tube; Davidoff Bright Wood Cigar Tube; Davidoff Golden Diacut Twin Cigar Tube; and Savinelli's Firenza Leather Cigar Case.

in natural or bordeaux. Of special interest is a case that they make especially for Rothschilds. Dunhill offers a classic black box calf leather series of cases accented with rust colored stitching. It is available in two, three, four and five-cigar sizes. They also produce a sterling silver Barley-designed single and double cigar case, for the ultimate in luxury and the perfect presentation piece of a special cigar for a special individual. The twin cigar case even has an area reserved for engraving one's initials. Not to be outdone, Davidoff catalogs black or claret dyed leather cigarillo cases,

Newest leather cases on the scene include (L. to R.): black with insert tubes, from Hollco-Rohr; two-finger soft case from Spain and a hard Italian tortoise shell finish, both by Club Imports; four-finger Burgundy by Savinelli.

Elegance in Ashtrays: (L) The lead crystal ashtray is from
Switzerland by Michel Perrenoud. (R) Galleria Collection
wood and brass cigar ashtray is from Savinelli. Shown with
an 1880s silver vesta "cigar bundle" holder.

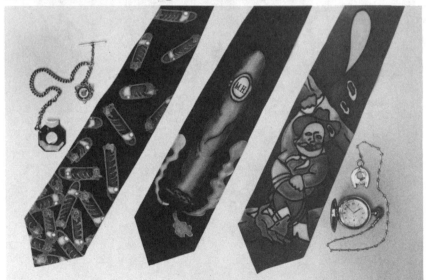

Tie one on: Photographer and cigar lover Marc Hauser has
created a series of ties so that we can show our preference
while sitting in no-smoking areas. A tortoise-shelled Eloy
cigar clipper and an Elgin 1928 pocketwatch with antique
gold horseshoe cigar cutter are the perfect accessories.

black kid leather open ended cigar cases with metal trim, and a complete range of silver, gold and lacquered wood single and double cigar tubes. They also have hand lacquered wooden cigarillo cases designed to match the veneer finishes on some of their humidors. Wood is also the material of choice for the Italian pipemaking firm of Mastro de Paja, which produces a briar cigar case with a cedar insert. And Nat Sherman and Arango both make handsome and handy leather cigar travel cases that easily fit in your car console or attaché case. For roughing it, there are now canvas cases with Velcro closures.

When buying a cigar case, it is always better to get one that is larger, rather than smaller. That way you are not limited by the size of the cigars you can put in it. It is a lot easier to slip a small cigar in a big case rather than the other way around. I always look for a sturdy case that will protect my cigars and will hold at least a 50 ring size. Admittedly, these are sometimes dif-

Whether it's sporting clays, trap, skeet, or upland hunting, shotgunners can take a tip from the Olympic team and decorate the stock of their scattergun with their favorite cigar band. Note the smoke rising from the ash and drifting into the pistol grip. This is the talented work of Jessie D'Angelo, one of Hollywood's hottest artists. For more information, contact Pachmayr Shooting Park in El Monte, CA.

ficult to find. Some cases, like the museum quality "old west" cigar case custom made for me by Wild Bill Cleaver, have a separate insert that slides out, so that even bigger cigars may be accommodated. Very often a cigar case will cost as much or substantially more than a box of cigars, but even when carried in your coat pocket, it is an accessory that is eventually going to be seen. But more important than image or presentation, if you only save one cracked wrapper a week because you carried your cigars in a case instead of unprotected in your pocket, the expense and lack of aggravation will be worth it.

Cigar clothes are also among the "hot" new trends fired up by the cigar revolution. Smoking jackets have been around since Victorian times, thanks to firms such as Sulka and Turnbull & Asser, but now people are starting to take them seriously. Also in vogue are cigar band cuff links, money clips and necklaces by Pop Art, and an entire range of hats, shirts, jackets and caps from General Cigar featuring their Macanudo and Partagas logos. And the ultra-hip design firm of Nicole Miller has created a limited edition *The Ultimate Cigar Book* tie based upon the dust jacket of this very book!

You may find some of these accessories more applicable to your lifestyle than others, but they all have their place. Indeed, Man does not live by his cigars alone. Which, by coincidence, just happens to be the theme of the next chapter.

Chapter 7

Spirits & Smoke

Since their inception, wines and cigars have had their similarities ardently compared by connoisseurs. It is only natural. Both started coming into their own around the mid-19th century, when the 1855 World's Fair gave France an opportunity to unveil her now-classic grapes just as Cuba was gaining enthusiastic acceptance for her Havanas. And just as a Bordeaux is a blend of different grapes, so are cigars composed of different tobaccos. Moreover, cigars are fermented and aged, just like wine, and each has a point at which they will peak. Even the fairly recent trend of vintage cigars was inspired by the classic designations of vintage wines, right on down to putting the year on the label of the bottle or box.

But why stop at wines?

When it comes to pleasures of the palate, cigars can be teamed up with any number of potables. In fact, for over one hundred years this has been the basic premise for Gentlemen's Smokers in Europe, England and the United States, a tradition that has been gaining a dramatically renewed impetus in recent years. Today, many of these gatherings are no longer just limited to men, but women as well, and not only are cigars brought out in the company of fine wines, brandies, cognacs, and ports, but also armagnacs, bourbons, malt whiskeys, and even beer as viable and popular alternatives. Indeed, there is a very definite cedar aroma in a glass of 6-year-old Sempé V.S.O.P. Armagnac that can be matched up with a number of cigars, and the hefty undertaste from a snifter of Blanton's single-barrel bourbon or Glenmorangie 10-year-old highland malt whiskey can be just the complement to any Dominican, Honduran or Cuban cigar that rates a 2.0 or better on the HPH. And the lightness of Japan's Sapporo beer is a perfect match for some of the HPH 1.5—2 Brazilian or Philippine cigars.

As with many full-course cigar night dinners, let's start with the wine and cigar pairings first, although I must warn you that, just like my preferences for cigars, the examples I am about to give are favorites from my own lifelong taste tests. After reading these recommendations, you may wish to venture out on your own and blaze a different path through the gourmet's world of spirits and smoke.

Champagne usually signals the beginning of a celebration, getting us off to an effervescent start. The 1985 Piper Heidsieck Rare, which comes in a replica of a 1785 bottle that was presented to Marie Antoinette, is light and spicy and can be paired with cigars like the Santa Damiana Seleccion No. 100 or either of the Davidoff Aniversarios. The distinctive handpainted bottle of Perrier-Jouet Fleur de Champagne (with its re-creation of a 1911 design that was brought back in 1989), holds a taste that is medium in body, but also distinctively spicy. An Ashton Cordial, Corona or Panetela would go well here, as would some of the Corps Diplomatique, a Villiger-Kiel, or other similar-strength Dutch-type cigars. The year 1985 was not an especially good one for vintage champagne, but the Mumm Grand Cordon (made of 50% Pinot Noir and 50% Chardonnay) is one that could be tried for its light and airy taste that goes well with any of the HPH 1.5—2 cigars from the Philippines or the DR. For a decidedly heftier flavor created by a better year, try the 1988 Bollinger Grande Annee Brut; its blend of 70% Pinot Noir and 30% Chardonnay produces a strong fruity flavor that complements cigars like Licenciados or the Dunhill Aged. Moving one step up in staying power, the Krug 1982 is mellow yet full-bodied and now starts to get into the realm of the spicier Dominicans like the Vueltabajo and a few of the milder Hondurans like the Thomas Hinds; they won't overpower the champagne, which in this case should dominate.

I am not a white wine drinker, but in order to give a passing nod to those who are, I have picked out a Cuvaison 1990 Chardonnay, the same wine that was served at the Moscow Summit. It is tangy, fruity, and characteristically dry. If anything, I found it crisply stimulating, and perfect for the Pléiades Orion or the slightly fuller Juan Clemente Corona or Grand Corona. You might also want to compare it with the excellent chardonays from Grgich Hills Cellars in Rutherford, California, a winery that is known for the consistency of its whites.

Being a fan of heavy California reds, I must admit to putting much of my wine and cigar tasting efforts into this category. So staying with Cuvaison for a moment longer, readers of the first edition of this book no doubt got turned on to the 1989 Cuvaison Merlot and if you put some down for aging, you've got a real treasure. But there is still hope, because Matanza Creek, well known for their Merlots, also has good potential for aging with their 1993 vintage.

Working our way up the intensity ladder and skipping over the Pinot Noir, we next come to Zinfandels, of which the 1994 Mondavi was one of the first ones considered. The Robert Mondavi Winery was started in 1966 by Robert and his son Michael, who is a cigar smoker. That in itself would rate a special look at his family's fantastic wines. One of the most modern wineries in the world, Mondavi (along with Chateau Mouton-Rothschild) produced the classic Opus One, an exceptionally heavy velvety red that is as difficult to find as the Opus X! Although I found their '94 a bit light for a Zin, it has plenty of undercurrents of berries and plum and holds great potential for aging. But if you're one of those people who cannot wait and must drink it now, try it with some of the HPH 2 Dominicans, such as The Griffin's or Match Play or a Macanudo in the larger ring sizes. Also worth noting is the '94 Zinfandel from Beaulieu Vineyards, their first.

And now we get to the top rung category of my favorite wine, Cabernet Sauvignon. Some of the best California vintages from the past that might still be available include the 1987 and the 1990 through 1992 bottlings. But it is with the current offerings that some of the best potentials for short-term aging are present and it is here that we found the Robert Mondavi 1994 Cabernet Sauvignon just waiting to be drunk with any HPH 2 — 2.5 cigar. The wine has an undertaste of berries laced with velvet, but it still begs to be put down for about five to six years, after which it should be able to tackle anything from a Nicaraguan Padrón to a Cuban Bolivar.

Next we come to the offerings of BV. Started in 1900 by George de Latour, Beaulieu Vineyard produces some of the finest reds in Napa Valley. Winston Churchill was a frequent visitor to the winery and was a big fan of their Cabernet Sauvignon. Today's cigar smokers would do well to follow in his steps. Especially when they lead to the 1992 Georges de Latour Private Reserve Cabernet. This is the one to seek out at all costs and lay down. It will last for decades. Or drink it now and you'll get every dollar's worth. A bottle will cost you as much as two Cohiba Esplendidos, but it will be worth it. It is definitely a special occasion wine for those special occasion heavy duty HPH 2.5 cigars (so it should come as no surprise to learn that BV's winemaker Joel Aiken is a cigar smoker). Rich, thick tasting and meaty, it grabs your taste buds and doesn't let go for a long, long time. Try it with roast boar or a thick Porterhouse steak; pasta or chicken simply won't do for this one. For something a little less intense, try BV's 1992 Reserve Tapestry (a Bordeaux varietal blend).

For many years, Cuvaison, located in California's Napa Valley, has been well known for the character of their wonderful

What more fitting complement for a warm summer's day than the medium dryness of a 1991 Cuvaison Chardonnay from California's Napa Valley, offset by a pasta salad. And for dessert? Take your pick, depending on how long you can afford to linger: (L to R) Peter Stokkebye Santa Maria No. 1; Dunhill Aged Valverdes; for fuller taste in wrapper or ring gauge, a Royal Jamaica Corona in Maduro; Don Tomás Supremo; Primo del Rey Churchill; or a milder Tresado No. 100. We didn't have the pasta salad for this photo, but our luncheon party thoroughly enjoyed the wines and cigars.

full-bodied reds. I had the pleasure of experiencing a glass of their 1977 Cabernet Sauvignon library issue (which I have always interpreted to mean that you can no longer get it unless you find a bottle hidden in the library). It was one of the most superb, velvety heavy California reds that I have tasted. Likewise, the 1989 and '91 Cabernets discussed in the first edition of this book were well worth laying down. But equally interesting and more readily available is their 1993 Cabernet Sauvignon, which has more tannin and hence, is more intense than the '92 and holds great potential for aging. I would easily pair this Napa Valley wine up with a Joya de Nicaragua Maduro, Fuente Hemingway or a Dominican-made Montecristo. And just as 1995 was a

Leaves & Grapes — Some perfect wine and cigar pairings: (L. to R.) a Cuban Montecristo Petit Tubos (a size only available in the U.K.); in the Davidoff crystal "Rayon du Soleil" ashtray: Vueltabajo; Diamond Crown; Match Play; Creston; Santiago Cabana; in tube: Dunhill Aged Cabreras. The wines: (L. to R.) Jekel 1992 Malbec; Caymus 1992 Cabernet Sauvignon; Mantanzas Creek '93 Merlot; Mondavi '94 Zinfandel; BV Georges de Latour 1992 Cabernet Sauvignon; Cuvaison '94 Merlot; Groth '93 Cabernet Sauvignon; and Wyndam Estate '93 Bin 444 Cabernet.

good vintage year for Dominican and Cuban tobacco, so does it promise to be a good year for California reds.

Speaking of California reds, one of the more unique wineries is Jekel, located away from the well-trodden trails of Napa-Sonoma and a little farther south, in the Salinas Valley, near Monterrey. Founded in 1972 by film animater Bill Jekel but now under new management by Brown-Forman World Wide Wines Group, this winery has only recently come into its own, with a unique method of pesticide-free vineyard management (i.e., good bugs eat the bad bugs and earthworms break the soil down into nutrients) and careful spacing of new and old growth vines. All of their reds are worth trying, but especially interesting is their Petit Verdot and Malbec. Jekel's Petit Verdot comes in at an HPH 2—2.5, slightly velvety and laced with berries. It is just made for a Honduran like the El Rey del Mundo, Thomas Hinds, or Zino. The '92 Malbec is only slightly lighter in taste, but rich and creamy and exceptionally mellow. Try this one with a Diana, Griffin's, Dunhill Aged or Match Play.

In an effort to keep the Cabernet section even more geographically diverse, I have selected a few offerings from Australia, which is an up and comer as far as reds are concerned. These are not "big" reds in the California sense, but are eminently drinkable. First on my list is Wyndam Estate Bin 444, 1992 vintage, which I found to be an HPH 2 but on the full side of medium. It also had a slightly salty undertaste, which makes this wine fare better with heavier cigars rather than lighter ones. Like the Avo or the Habanica. Or try Penfold's Bin 707 or any of the Cabernets from Whitehall Lane. Taylor's and McWilliams are two other Aussie labels to watch for in Cabernets.

I decided to broaden the scope of my wine and cigar offerings even more by inviting Emmanuel Kemiji, Master Sommelier at the Ritz-Carlton, San Francisco, to give his recommendations. I first met Emmanuel at one of the Ritz Carlton Smokers at Laguna Niguel, and in addition to his extensive wine expertise, Emmanuel is a fellow cigar aficionado. I had been particularly impressed with his wine tasting ability during an after-hours' wagering session, wherein he had been able to guess the country of origin of an unmarked bottle of Indian champagne simply by taking a few sips and ruling out what countries the champagne was *not* from. Besides, Emmanuel was duly taken with the cigars that I had brought to smoke, which proved to me more than anything else that he was a true gourmet. Offering a selection of medium-light to medium-tasting cigars for lunch (Dunhill

Aged, Macanudo and Julia Marlowe), Emmanuel responded with his recommendations for the accompanying wines.

"With these cigars, which I consider the perfect choice," he said, "I would recommend an assertive yet light wine, such as the Hermitage Blanc from the Rhone Valley. It has long staying power that lingers on, with good depth and penetration."

I could say the same thing about the cigars.

For the afternoon cigar, the recommendation was a Manzanilla sherry by Hidalgo, served cold. It has a hazelnut, salty tang, yet is crisp and light. But we found out that it doesn't travel well, so it must be fresh. The cigars would include the Griffin's No. 400, the Oscar 400, and as alternatives, a small Oscarito or the Dannemann Espada with Sumatra wrapper.

The obligatory evening cigar brought forth Emmanuel's suggestion of a Mortlach 27-year-old single malt or my own choice of The Macallan 18 or 25-year-old, of which we'll be hearing more about later, along with my recommended cigars.

We are now ready to enter the lair of the higher proofs, which normally dwell in wood paneled rooms with deep leather chairs and softly crackling fireplaces. But here one must be careful, for very often a heavy cognac or malt whiskey can numb the palate to a point where the flavor of your cigar will be lost. Also, because of the wide divergence of spirit strengths in these after-hours drinks, you may not always want to team up a strong cigar with a strong whiskey, and may find it more rewarding to vary the tastes, matching a medium-tasting HPH 2 cigar with a stronger cognac, for example, or smoking a hefty 2.5 cigar with a lighter libation so that the tobacco remains in control. I realize this is not the accepted practice, but I find it is sometimes better to let the cigar command the palate, especially after a medium to heavily textured dinner. On the other hand, when the night is dark and stormy and the wind blows cold, I find there is nothing better than meeting nature head-on with a potent snifter of 107 proof bourbon and a full-bodied cigar that is equal to the task.

At this point in the book you should have a firm grasp on the intricacies of the various cigars in the world. But what about their casked counterparts? It sometimes helps to review the nature of these drinks so that we may have a better understanding of why one goes so much better than another with a specific cigar.

Cognac is no doubt the first thought that comes to the minds of most when the agreeable suggestion of an after dinner drink and a cigar is mentioned. In fact, so entrenched in tradition is this combination that in 1993 Dunhill created an entire image campaign around this dynamic duo, with other firms such as Fuente following suit. Cognac, of course, is distilled and aged from brandy, but it cannot be called cognac unless it is made in that specific southwestern region of France. The limestone soil and the slow-method distillation in alembic stills (which are stills that are peaked like an onion and made of copper) plus the aging in white oak barrels that must come from the Limousin forests, all join together to produce this highly revered after dinner drink. For our Spirits & Smoke parings, I opted for the superb varieties of cognac from Rémy Martin, which has the largest reserves of vintage cognac in the world and is the only blending house to use grapes that are harvested from the two best growing regions of France — the Grande Champagne and the Petite Champagne. You might say that these two areas are the Vuelta Abajo of the cognac producing vineyards.

There are five different classifications (and price ranges) of Rémy Martin Cognacs. They are: V.S.O.P. (which stands for Very Special Old Pale — now you know), aged for 8 years; Napoleon, named after Napoleon III — not Bonaparte — and aged for 15 years; XO Special (the XO standing for "Extra Old"), aged for 25 years; Extra Perfection, aged in special barrels for 35 years; and

A special evening demands special cigars and special cognacs: (L) Rémy Martin Extra Perfection and (R) Rémy Martin XO Special. In the front row (L to R) Macanudo Vintage No 1; Dunhill Aged Peravias; Davidoff Special T; Romeo y Julieta Vintage, and a box of Cohiba Coronas Especiales that have been aging since 1981.

finally, Louis XIII, which is an aged blend of 50 years and comes in a registered Baccarat Crystal decanter, such as the bottling pictured with the vintage cigars in one of the color photos. The greater age of each cognac also coincides with a greater percentage of Grande Champagne grapes, with the V.S.O.P. starting out with 51% and the Louis XIII ending up with 100%. This combination of greater aging with a higher percentage of Champagne Grande ends up creating a series of tastes that have increasingly more depth. Do not confuse "depth" with strength, because the longer a cognac ages, the less alcohol it retains. Cognac is really a blend of agings from various casks in order to create an average age of the bottling. Thus, an 8-year-old V.S.O.P. could actually be an equal blend of 6 and 10-year-old cognacs; by law, all cognacs must be at least 4½ years old.

A close cousin of cognac — but up until recently noticeably less well known — is armagnac, which also comes from a distinct region in southwestern France, one that is approximately 100 miles south of cognac, but produces a product that is decidedly different. Armagnac was first distilled in 1411 — two hundred years before cognac — but up until the early part of the 20th century most armagnacs were only used in the blending of cognac. But now armagnac is being discovered on its own merits, somewhat like malt whiskeys have been embraced on their own without having to blend them into scotch. Although there are those who may disagree, I find that armagnac has a lighter taste and aroma than the thicker and heavier bouquet of cognac, and thus, it is a somewhat more delicate alternative, better suited to Dominican cigars, in some cases, than Honduran or Cuban.

Unlike cognac, which is distilled twice, armagnac is only distilled once. It, too, is aged in casks of Limousin oak, where it can mature anywhere from one to twenty years. And, like cognac, it is blended to produce a specific age and quality of taste. With armagnacs, the designations are as follows: VS (for Very Special); V.S.O.P.; and Reserve, all of which indicate that the youngest brandy distilled into armagnac is at least four years old. Then there is Extra; Napoleon; EX; and Vielle Reserve, all of which have blends wherein the youngest armagnac is a minimum of five years old; some substantially older. Some armagnacs are vintage, and are labeled with the year that specific armagnac was put into the cask for aging.

With a criteria towards quality and total variety of product, I have selected Sempé Armagnacs for our cigars. Sempé is family-owned, and has vintages going all the way back to the early 1900s. They also produce substantially more obtainable and affordable varieties, including: V.S.O.P., which is aged a minimum of 6 years (this became one of my late night libations when finishing this book, as it was not so overwhelming that it prevented me from going back to work after a glass and an HPH 2 cigar); 15-Year-Old, which is only slightly fuller in taste; Grande Reserve, a 50-year-old blend that is noticeably rich and smooth to the point of overpowering a cigar with a 2.0 HPH rating and easily qualifying for a Cuba Aliados or Los Cabrillos from Honduras, or a Partagas or Hoyo de Monterrey from either Honduras or Cuba. In addition, Sempé produces a Baccarat Crown lead crystal decanter that is filled with their excellent 20-year-old blend. Plus, they offer a series of collectable Limoges porcelain crowns decorated in 24 ct. gold and containing a variety of their well-aged armagnacs. Most armagnacs have a slightly fruity, almost woodsy bouquet. You'll find them mellow and easy to control. Well, at least I did, or this book would never have gotten written.

For a late night read, a copy of *My Lady Nicotine* (or better yet, *The Ultimate Cigar Book*), and then pick a pair from this quartet: the Ramon Allones Trumps (the middle cigar is always wrapped in tissue — like a "trump cigar") or a box of Santa Damiana Cabinet Selection No. 300. For a pourable accompaniment, try a snifter of Rémy Martin VSOP cognac, or for a slightly lighter touch, the Sempé VSOP armagnac.

Now we get into the headier brews, my favorites. First on our list are the single malt whiskies (whisky is spelled without the "e" for the Scottish product only). Distilled from barley malt and fermented with yeast, they are classic examples of how soil and climate can affect the taste, much like cigars. Before distillation, the malt is dried over a peat fire, which is the smokey "peatiness" we read about and sometimes taste in Scottish malts; Irish malt whiskey is dried without peat and thus, has no smokiness. Different regions of Scotland and Ireland produce distinctly different tasting whiskies. Single malts are not blends, and are produced in their own individual distillery, each of which is fiercely loyal and competitive, proclaiming theirs to be the best. There are only two Irish single malt whiskeys, of which Bushmills is the undisputed world leader, but there are over 100 different Scottish malt whiskies, not all of which are readily available. Some, like Cragganmore and Laphroaig, are too light for my tastes (with the exception of Laphroig 15 Years Old, which is a powerhouse). My preferences lean toward heavier, peatier products, such as The Glenlivit 18-year-old and the wonderful full-bodied warmth of 16- Year-Old Lagavulin, both of which go well with a heady Joya de Nicaragua Maduro, a MiCubano, or a Montecristo from either of the two countries in which they are made.

Two other favorites are Glenmorangie 10-year-old and the more intense 18-year-old from the Highland region of Scotland. Even more complex, although not as intense, is Glenmorangie's 12-year-old Port Wood, aged in American bourbon oak casks for a minimum of ten years and then "finished" for the last two years in wood barrels that were formerly used for port. The result is a light, complex, copper-colored whisky that demands meditation with the most flavorful cigars in the HPH 2—2.5 range. Also worth uncorking is Glenmorangie's 12 year-old-Madeira Wood and 12-year-old Sherry Wood bottlings. But perhaps one of the all-time high marks should be given to The Macallan, from the Speyside district of the Scottish Highlands, which is available in a 12, 18, and 25-year-old spread, each one having more depth in taste and increasing proportionally in price and availability. I find the 18-year-old to be the best of the three, having substantially more character than the 12-year-old, but none of the roughness of the 25-year-old, which, over the years, has saved me hundreds of dollars in the differences in price. The Macallan is double distilled and aged in sherry casks, and that sweet undercurrent of flavor is distinctly evident in every sip. Another Speyside single malt that is definitely worth investigating is Aberlour, a surprisingly affordable 10-year-old with more depth and character than some whiskies that are much older. Aberlour single malts are aged in both bourbon and sherry casks, and then blended together (although this is not a blend, it is the same single malt) for finishing, much as completed cigars are allowed to marry their tobacco flavors in the aging room. The result is a medium strength, smooth, flowery experience. Although Aberlour, Glenmorangie and The Macallan malt whiskies are each distinctively different, they all can easily bridge the gaps between cigars that range from an HPH 2 all the way up to HPH 3. Any of these combinations would be a perfect way to celebrate the Scottish rite of Hogmanay on December 31st, when a person with a gift of *uisge beatha* — the water of life — is guaranteed a New Year of good fortune. And those fortunes would no doubt be realized if that person was also bearing a box of cigars.

Although mainly thought of as an autumn and winter drink, I consider any season an opportune time to enjoy that distinctly American invention, bourbon. The gradual reclaiming by bour-

Fireside friends: (L to R front row) Ashton Cabinet No. 2; Havana Montecristo No. 1 (or try the more readily available Dominican of that same name); H. Upmann Corona Brevas. Any of these cigars will compliment the three malt whiskeys in the back row: (L to R) Glenmorangie 10-Year-Old; 10-year-old Bushmill's; The Macallan 18-year-old.

bon of its rightful crown of appreciation has been a vindication of my beliefs, for this is the one libation to which I have remained fiercely loyal through my brief span thus far on this planet. I collect bourbons as one would collect cigars, although I find that, unlike cigars, I have definite loyalties to certain brands.

Bourbon is made from a corn-rye-barley mixture that is ground into a fine meal and cooked with crystal pure limestone water that flows from the unique underground springs of Kentucky and Tennessee. The result is a thick, liquid "mash." Some distillers add a small percentage of mash from prior fermentations (a few of which go back for generations) to help link taste and aroma from batch to batch; this addition of "sour mash" adds a distinct subtlety and taste to the bourbon. All bourbons must be aged in new charred white oak casks, and it is this char that gives bourbon its rich amber color. Likewise, bourbon's distinctive caramel and vanilla tastes are derived, respectively, from the char and the oak. Unlike the aging process for scotch whisky, where a damp, cold climate causes the proof to decrease over the years, the hot summer temperatures of Kentucky and Tennessee actually cause

The Playboy Cigar by Don Diego is versatile enough to accompany any of these after hour libations: (L. to R.) Glenmorangie Port Wood single malt; "For the Lover of Fine Cigars" double distilled brandy by Germain-Robin; a 1985 vintage port by Sandeman.

a bourbon's proof to increase. Thus, in the aging process, knowing when to quit becomes more than just a figure of speech.

Among my favorites for a late night repast with a Hoyo de Monterrey Excalibur No. 1 or an Ashton Cabinet No. 2, are two of the "small batch bourbons" from Jim Beam. The first is Knob Creek, a 100-proof elixir that is aged for nine years in the deepest char possible. The second is the 107-proof Baker's, named after Jim Beam's grandnephew Baker Beam, who is also the master distiller, and who uses a strain of jug yeast handed down from his granduncle's time. Both of these full power drinks are rich, heavy with flavor, yet unbelievably mellow. They are also extremely potent, and care must be exercised in their use, lest you send your senses into warp drive with multiple snifters at a single sitting. Also not to be missed is Wild Turkey Rare Breed, a barrel proof blending of 6, 8, and 12 year old stocks. For true elegance in a limited bottling, try Wild Turkey 12 Years Old (if you can find it), in which some of the very best bourbons in the distillery are selected by Master distiller Jimmy Russell and allowed to age for a

A fellow cigar connoisseur and one of the great master distillers of single barrel bourbons, Booker Noe (L) samples his namesake product with the author. Booker's is the only bourbon on the market that is both uncut and unfiltered, with proofs that range from 121 to 127. If that Fuente Hemingway gets too close to the glass, it might light itself!

full 12 years. This, and a box of Butera Bravo Cortos got me through an especially frantic Christmas a few years back.

I am also a fan of certain single barrel bourbons, in which all of the bottlings are taken from just one barrel. Blanton's, Rock Hill Farms, and Booker's (from the private reserve of Booker Noe, grandson of Jim Beam) are three favorites that offer a wide enough divergence of proofs to go with any cigar. And don't miss Wild Turkey Kentucky Spirit, a full-bodied potable that comes in a distinctive "flared feather" decanter.

Slightly tamer, but no less flavorful, is the double distilled smoothness of Maker's Mark 90 proof, or, when you can find it in, the much-preferred limited edition 101 proof with its distinctive gold wax over the cork. Also worth settling down to is Gentleman Jack, a more refined relative of the ubiquitous Jack Daniel's. Made in Tennessee, this 80 proof cousin refers to itself

Late night entertainment: Shown with a 1904 vintage Edison cylinder player are these melodic full-bodied parings: (front row L to R:) La Reserva No. 2; Honduran Punch Premier Grand Cru Britanias Deluxe, Fuente Hemingway Classic; Honduran Hoyo de Monterrey Excalibur No. 1. Potent potables in the back row (L to R) Blanton's single barrel bourbon, Baker's 107 proof; Knob Creek 100 proof; Gentleman Jack 80 proof; Maker's Mark 90 proof.

as a whiskey, rather than a bourbon, as it, like Jack Daniel's, is drip filtered through a 10-foot layer of maple charcoal before being put into barrels. But Gentleman Jack is unique in that it has its own patented formula, and is actually drip filtered through charcoal a second time, immediately after aging and just before it is bottled. A slow and delicate process (it takes from 10 to 12 hours for a single drop of this whiskey to trickle completely through the vat, and too much filtering can strip the precious liquid of both color and taste), the result is a much smoother flavor that invites a meeting with some of the richer Dominicans, such as the Romeo y Julieta Vintage or a Davidoff Grand Cru.

Not all spirits have to be high octane to go well with cigars. A carefully selected ale, porter or beer — or a diverse pairing of multiple brands — can accent the taste of almost any premium cigar. For example, the bitter-yeast flavor of a Boddington's Pub Pale Ale (in which a specially designed nitrogen cartridge within the can mixes air with the pale gold ale to produce a "hand pulled"

Full bodied cigars for a full bodied flock of Wild Turkeys. The smokes: (L. to R.) Fuente Fuente Opus X; MiCubano; a box of Savinelli ELRs; a Bolivar belicoso. The bourbons: (L. to R.) Wild Turkey 12 Year Old; Kentucky Spirit; Rare Breed.

204

taste and thick frothy head) works well with a Dominican H. Upmann or a Partagas Limited Reserve (especially the larger ring sized Robusto). The medium-spiciness of an Italian Moretti compliments the flavors of a Licenciados or a Peterson. And there is something reassuring about having a Mexican beer like Pacifico or Corona with a Mexican cigar like Cruz Real or a maduro Te-Amo.

Although many of our adventures with spirits and smoke will occur at dinners or Smokers, it does not always have to be in a formal setting. Far from it. And even far from home. In Havana I found it could be as simple as enjoying a Quintero or El Rey del Mundo cigar along with a can of Bucanero or Hatuey beer. Or sipping a glass of rare 25-year-old, 80 proof Montecristo rum, which is made in Havana but bottled in Spain, while smoking a

Late night rare repasts: (L. to R. back row) Lagavulin 16 Year Old; Aberlour 10 Year Old; last of the rare old pot still bourbons, A.H. Hirsch 20 year old; super premium and mellow Johnnie Walker Gold Label. In the front row: (L. to R.) Davidoff Round Cutter; Avo, a hallmarked pewter combination cigar case/whiskey flask by Baekgaard; the Hamilton A (same size as the Montecristo A); similar sized MiCubano; leather and metal traveling case by Cigar Classics loaded with a Camórra San Remo.

favored Montecristo No. 2 Pyramid in a back room of the Partagás factory. And the Dominican Republic is the only setting in which one can enjoy a snifter of Burmuda Aniversario rum. Potent, pungent, with a heavy aftertaste that coats the nose, it is not exported. Fortunately, the Partagas and Fuente cigars that I had with it are more readily available. Also more obtainable is the pairing of a prepackaged Davidoff Cognac (made by Hennessy) with a Davidoff cigar. For European unity, try an old French burgundy, with its mushroomy, oaken scent, with a French-boxed Pléiades. And a Villiger Export has been seen in the company of more than one vodka martini. To further compliment certain drinks, try chocolate — the traditional mate to many cigars, such as the chocolaty-tasting Maduro wrapper of a Honduran Punch.

And finally, when all is done, there is the small but potent cup of *café Cubana* — Cuban coffee. Strong, black like the rich-

Suds and cigars can combine a variety of North American and British beers. In case you're wondering what the "Australian" Foster's is doing in this group, this can was actually brewed in Canada.

est Oscuro leaf, and thickly sweetened with coarse brown sugar. This is the drink they serve in the cigar-making *galeras* of Havana, Honduras, and Santiago de los Caballeros, as the dusty sunlight of late afternoon filters in through the windows and basks the rich brown leaves in sultry warmth. It is a drink that is used to help cleanse the palates of the leaf buyers, who smoke the raw, green tobacco before committing to a price and a purchase. Raw tobacco can smoke sweet. It is not often that it does, but it is an indication of a particularly good grade.

And so it is with our selections of wines, whiskeys, bourbons, and beer, intertwining their meticulously produced tastes with the handblended flavors of the world's best cigars. A soothing influence that settles the stomach after an evening of gastronomic debauchery, or just a relaxing way to ease out of the day. This is the pleasure of spirits and smoke.

There is a worldwide variety of beer to match up with a variety of cigar blends. That's the Klipit 2000 in the foreground.

Chapter 8

Celebrity Cigar Smokers

It is an old cliché, but if it is true that "we are known by the company we keep," then cigar smokers have a very enviable reputation. Indeed, some of the most intelligent, perceptive, handsome, beautiful, talented, creative and illustrious people in the world are cigar smokers.

Almost every prominent man (and even some women) were cigar smokers in the early years of American history. Their ranks included many people who forged the social and economic structures of our great nation. In government it was Henry Clay (who subsequently had a cigar named after him), John Quincy Adams, Daniel Webster (who also had his own cigar), and numerous presidents, including James Madison and Abraham Lincoln. Big top showman P. T. Barnum was a cigar smoker, as was humorist/author Mark Twain, who used to pay $4 a barrel for his cigars and was once asked by a reporter if he was smoking too much.

"Only when I smoke two at a time," was his reply.

Robert Louis Stevenson, H. L. Mencken, and Rudyard Kipling were cigar smokers. In fact, it was Kipling, who in 1886 penned the oft-quoted line from *The Betrothed*, "A woman is only a woman, but a good cigar is a Smoke." Unfortunately, those words have come back to haunt him, as it is believed that 1% to 5% of today's cigar smokers are women and that percentage is rising. We know for a fact that Whoopi Goldberg smokes cigars, as does Bette Midler and Madonna. And so do Demi Moore, Tia Carrere, Ellen Barken, Linda Evangelista (who also collects humidors), and actress/model/talk show host Lauren Hutton. Academy Award nominee and Golden Globe winner Sharon Stone, who holds the title of Chevalier dans l'Ordre des Arts et des Lettres from the French Minister of Culture, has a star on the Hollywood Walk of Fame, received the Independent Spirit Award in 1996 and is a voracious reader of books (including this one), smokes cigars. But perhaps the beautiful and talented Joan Collins said it best when she stated at Hamilton's Wine Bar one night, "Only fine cigars are worth smoking and only men who smoke fine cigars are worth kissing."

Lucille Ball smoked cigarillos, Marlene Dietrich preferred Panetelas, and Amadine Aurore Lucie Dupin, better known as George Sand, even has a woman's cigar smoking club named after her in Santa Monica, California. "Little Miss Sure Shot" Annie Oakley liked to puff on a cheroot to calm her nerves both before and after her amazing trick shooting exhibitions. And Amy Lowell, one of early 20th century America's most celebrated poets, started stocking up with more than 10,000 cigars around 1915 out of fear that the impending "war to end all wars" would disrupt her supply. She was right, of course.

Some of the world's greatest military strategists were cigar smokers, including Sam Houston and his nemesis, General Santa Ana. Ulysses S. Grant smoked as many as 25 cigars a day, no doubt due to the pressures of The Great Rebellion. One of the world's greatest consulting detectives and literary cigar smokers was Sherlock Holmes, who followed the unorthodox practice of keeping his cigars in a coal scuttle but made up for it in *A Study In Scarlet* by properly identifying the dark, flaky ash of a Trichinopoly cigar (as vile tasting as they come, I can attest) and penning a monograph on 140 different ashes that does justice to our own dissertation on ashes in Chapter 4.

In more recent times, Ira Gershwin, Albert Einstein, Sigmund Freud, Orson Welles and the Duke of Windsor were cigar smokers, as was one of the most recognized cigar men in the world, Sir Winston Churchill, who was said to have smoked over 300,000 cigars in his lifetime. Considering the fact that he lived to be 90, that's not quite 3,334 a year, or about 9 cigars a day, assuming he started smoking when he was a baby. Churchill kept over 3,000 cigars stored at his Chartwell estate in a humidified room with three shelves labeled, "Wrapped," "Large," and "Naked." Of course, "naked" means uncellophaned but still, one can speculate. One of the most famous wartime photos of Sir Winston shows him scowling, and without a cigar. In fact, that was the reason he was scowling. Famous portrait photographer

CBS "Late Show" superstar David Letterman made cigar smoking and entertainment history in December 1992 when he and his Romeo y Julieta Churchill were photographed at a news conference announcing his major television network move. A devoted cigar lover, Letterman prefers easy-to-spot Havana Churchills for news conferences and usually has a Punch Punch waiting for him after the taping of every show.

Like so many entertainers who started in vaudeville, George Burns began smoking cigars on stage because it gave him time to puff and pause while waiting for a laugh, or while thinking of a better line that would get an even bigger laugh. This technique must have worked, for George became one of the most legendary comedians in show business and the only celebrity to literally put his cigar print in Mann's Chinese Theater on Hollywood Boulevard. The Cigar Smoker of the Century, we will miss him.

"Mr. Television," Milton Berle began smoking cigars at age 14 and has endured throughout the generations because of his quick wit, forthright charm, and some might say, his ever-present cigar. In addition to his thousands of guest appearances and countless TV shows over the years, Milton is often a featured star at many of the nation's high profile Smokers.

Yousul Karsh yanked the cigar from Churchill's mouth the instant before he clicked the shutter. And thus he captured that menacing bulldog glare that ended up inspiring millions of Britons on to victory.

Cigars have also inspired authors such as Ernest Hemingway (who, like Clay and Webster, has a cigar named after him) and Somerset Maugham, who, in his book, *Summing Up*, wrote:

...I promised myself that if ever I had some money that I would savor a cigar each day after lunch and dinner. This is the

At the Ritz-Carlton Laguna Niguel Smoker, the author tells a cigar joke to Oscar nominee Randy Quaid, an enthusiastic cigar smoker who has appeared in numerous motion pictures, including *The Last Picture Show*, *The Last Detail*, *LBJ: The Early Years*, the blockbuster hit *Independence Day*, and Turner Network Television's critically acclaimed *Frankenstein*. In the TNT movie, the talented actor played the part of the monster, but without a cigar.

photo: Eric Simonson
The Ritz-Carlton, Laguna Niguel, CA

214

Sydney Pollack is a multi-talented actor-director who has appeared before the cameras in films such as *Tootsie, Husbands and Wives, The Player,* and *Death Becomes Her.* But his behind-the-camera directorial skills are equally impressive, crafting such memorable films as *Tootsie, Jeremiah Johnson, Three Days of the Condor, The Way We Were, Out of Africa,* and *The Firm.* With such impressive Hollywood credentials, it is not surprising that Sydney often casts cigars for starring roles in his private life.

only resolution of my youth that I have kept, and the only realized ambition which has not brought disillusion."

In the excellent book, *The Marx Bros. Scrapbook* (Harpers & Row, 1989), comedian Groucho Marx revealed why he started smoking cigars:

"...It gave you time to think. You could tell a joke and if the audience didn't laugh you could take some puffs on the cigar..."

Motion picture writer-director John Milius has written some of the most memorable lines for moviegoers, including those who saw *Apocalypse Now* (he wrote it) and *Dirty Harry* (he wrote and directed it). John also directed such cult classics as *Conan the Barbarian*, *Magnum Force*, *The Wind and the Lion*, *Red Dawn*, and *Flight of the Intruder*. He started smoking Havana cigars with John Huston, but has since branched out to include Dominicans and Hondurans. Today John insists on having "issue cigars," on the set of any movie that he makes.

216

Motion picture actor Jim Belushi is an avid fan of Cuban Bolivars, Cohibas, and Partagás for evening smokes, but prefers Por Larrañaga and the Dominican Davidoffs and Fuente Hemingways during the day. The star of movies such as *Red Heat, Salvador, About Last Night, K-9, Taking Care of Business,* and *Mr. Destiny* (the latter two being the only past motion pictures in which he smokes cigars), fans have seen him in such recent releases as *Jingle All The Way, The Peril of Being Walter Wood,* and *Retroactive.*

Photo: Richard Reinsdorf

And if the joke wasn't funny?

"Then we used a different cigar!"

Legendary comedian George Burns used this technique for practically all of his almost one hundred years in show business. He smoked his first cigar at age fourteen. During his lifetime, he smoked an average of ten cigars a day, with no certain time or ritual. Just when he felt like lighting one up. Or when he was on stage. Although not widely known, he used his cigars for timing his act. In the years just after Gracie passed away, with no one to help him with his jokes, he marked the wrappers of his cigars so that he would know when he had been on stage long enough. His favorite brand was El Producto Queens, and the company

Believing that one self-drawn portrait is worth a thousand cigars, three-time Pulitzer Prize winner Jeff MacNelly poses with his syndicated creation, Shoe. MacNelly and Shoe are both relaxing with dueling Ashton #50s, which Jeff's wife Sue refers to as "solid fuel rocket boosters." Among MacNelly's Shoe books is, *A Cigar Means Never Having To Say You're Sorry*.

proudly delivered two boxes to his home every two weeks. On January 20, 1996, George's 100th birthday, I happened to be in England and made it a point to drive by the London Palladium, where he was originally scheduled to celebrate his centenary but had to cancel due to the flu. There, I gently deposited an ash from my Punch Double Corona on the curb in front of the theater in his honor. Sadly, the Cigar Smoker of the Century passed away on March 9th of that same year. On the day of his funeral, hundreds of friends and fans gathered in front of his house and an unidentified individual solemnly handed out glass tubed El Producto Queens. Bright and articulate right up to his final years, George always had a one-liner for every occasion. One of my favorites, which he told me many years ago and which has often been repeated, was that when he first heard that Milton Berle had paid ten dollars for a cigar, George quipped, "If I paid ten dollars for a cigar, first I'd make love to it, then I'd smoke it."

In a true display of camaraderie, actor James Coburn presents one of his cigars to a pleasantly surprised author.

photo: Eric Simonson
The Ritz-Carlton, Laguna Niguel, CA

219

Today, a cigar is still the mark of success for numerous Hollywood celebrities, such as Tom Cruise, Jack Nicholson, Roger Moore, Mel Gibson, Bill Cosby, Paul Sorvino, and Dean Stockwell, who always appeared with a Zino Honduran as the cigar smoking hologram on "Quantum Leap," and starred with fellow cigar smokers Rob Lowe and Jim Belushi in the motion picture, *The Perils of Being Walter Wood.* Pierce Brosnan smokes cigars, as does Bruce Willis, John Travolta, Jason Priestly, Brad Pitt, Matt Dillon, Jerry Seinfeld, Tom Selleck, Joe Pesci, Danny DeVito, Chevy Chase, Tom Arnold (who asked me to autograph his first edition of this book even after he perused the Celebrity Cigar Smokers chapter and didn't find his name in it), Robert Duvall, and Robert de Niro, who prefers extra large Havanas. Other Havana fans include British interviewer David Frost, a devotee of the Romeo y Julieta No. 2 and Ted Danson, who used a box of Havanas to sign off on the historic last episode of "Cheers." But you won't find

Rick Dees, internationally syndicated Top 40 disk jockey and a devoted cigar fan, proudly displays his highly collectable box of commemorative Cohibas. The special box and 1994-dated bands were produced to celebrate the formation of Habanos S.A.

220

George Hamilton, shown relaxing in his condominium over-looking the Los Angeles cigar scene, is the ultimate urban cigar smoker. A talented stage and screen actor, he has played roles as diverse as Hank Williams in *Your Cheatin' Heart*, a lawyer in *Godfather III*, title roles in *Evil Knievel*, and *Zorro The Gay Blade*, and a vampire in *Love At First Bite*. He both starred in and produced the latter three motion pictures. Active in skiing, tennis and a fitness regimen of daily work-outs, he is also a big fan of the sun and has his own line of skin care products. Proprietor of Hamilton's wine and cigar bar in Beverly Hills, a trendy hangout for some of Hollywood's hippest cigar smokers, it was only natural that he would eventually have his own cigar. Appropriately enough, it is called the Hamilton (see Chapter 9 for more information). He is shown here holding one of the first boxes produced and smoking one of its contents.

many of Castro's products in the humidor of Rush Limbaugh, America's conservative talk radio host who probably has done more to publicize cigar smoking than anyone; he prefers the American-friendly Dominican and Honduran varieties. Every one of the individuals in this chapter is proud of what they smoke and have no compulsion about being seen in public with their favorites brands. But this type of commendable honesty is not always the case, as I have had a few celebrities who covet their cigars both on screen and off personally ask me not to mention their names in this book. And of course, as a matter of courtesy, I feel I must honor those requests, even though you know who many of them are. Perhaps a letter from each of you would convince them

Robert Davi (L), memorable in hits such as *Die Hard*, *License to Kill*, and *Showgirls*, enjoys a cigar with fellow actor Joe Mantegna (R), an award-winning stage and screen talent who has been seen in films such as *The Money Pit*, *Three Amigos*, *Godfather III*, *Forget Paris*, and *Up Close and Personal*. You've also heard his voice on Mercedes-Benz commercials and "The Simpsons."

222

Beautiful and talented singer/actress Leslie Easterbrook may be best remembered for her TV role as Rhonda Lee in "Laverne and Shirley" and as Captain Callahan in the highly successful *Police Academy* movies, but she is a gifted singer and stage actress as well. Her millions of fans have seen her in motion pictures on three continents, and she has appeared in numerous television series. Not surprisingly, Leslie is an avid cigar aficionado.

photo: Eric Simonson
The Ritz-Carlton, Laguna Niguel, CA

Widely known for his box office breaking and set-smashing su-
percop "Shaft" roles, Richard Roundtree has since emerged
as one of Hollywood's most versatile talents, having appeared
in motion pictures such as *City Heat* with fellow cigar smoker
Clint Eastwood, the smash hit thriller *Seven*, and *Original
Gangsters*. Television audiences have seen him in "Roots,"
NBC's remake of "Bonanza," "Christmas in Connecticut" (directed by another cigar smoker, Arnold Schwarzenegger) and
numerous guest appearances on some of TV's top rated shows.
Premium cigars, carried in his distinctive brown leather cigar
case with gold nameplate, are Richard's favorite co-stars.

photo: Craig Sjodin
Touchstone Television

224

The author shares a cigar with superstar Arnold Schwarzenegger at the Friar's Club of California Celebrity Smoker. The talented actor has come a long way from his early bodybuilding days, emerging as one of the world's truly great personalities. Equally adept at both action and lighthearted roles, his blockbuster motion pictures include *Terminator, Total Recall, Kindergarten Cop, Twins, Eraser,* and *Jingle All The Way.* He is also chairman of the Inner-City Games Foundation, which sponsors numerous sports activities for well over 100,000 inner-city children across the nation. A well-respected connoisseur of cigars, it is not surprising to learn that Arnold and his equally talented wife, Maria Shriver, own one of the most cigar-friendly restaurants in Southern California, Schatzi On Main in Santa Monica.

Photo: Ken Levine
Friar's Club of Southern California

that there is more to be gained from joining their fans than hiding from them.

But whether rich or poor, famous or unknown, a good cigar never differentiates, and makes each and every one of us feel like a superstar.

Stan Schuster (L) of Grand Havana Room in Beverly Hills, enjoys a smoke with co-owner and actor Joe Pantoliano, not only a great talent but perhaps the most enthusiastic cigar smoker in Hollywood and unforgettable in motion pictures such as *The Idolmaker, La Bamba, Used People, The Fugitive, Bad Boys, Congo, Steal Big Steal Little,* and *Bound,* just to name a few.

This Cigar is really smokin'! Riding in the patriotic red, white and blue silks of owner Allen Paulson, jockey Jerry Baily has ridden this champion racehorse to fifteen consecutive wins, making Cigar a contender to break Citation's 16 consecutive win record of 1948-50. An official U.S. Horse of the Year and an unofficial Horse of the World, Cigar has won more than $8 million as of 1996. No horse in the history of thoroughbred racing has ever earned more. This is one champion who truly lives up to his name.

Photo: Benoit & Associates
Courtesy Del Mar Racetrack; Del Mar, CA

228

Chapter 9

International Compendium
Of Cigar Brands

At last, here it is. For the very first time, the chapter that you and I wished we'd had when we first started smoking cigars. Correction: you now have this chapter. I didn't. But I wished I did. Which is why I am writing it now. It is an almost-complete listing of practically every current cigar brand of which information was obtainable. I say "almost-complete" because it is the nature of the cigar industry for new brands to appear almost overnight, in the hope that we will accept them into our hearts and humidors, while others mysteriously evaporate like a cloud of smoke in the breeze, because we did not feel they were worth putting a match to. So as long as there is a single *torcedor* rolling a new cigar, this listing can never be complete. And I hope it never is.

Believe it or not, this was one of the most difficult chapters to write. Not only because of the virtual plethora of cigar brands that are currently in existence, but because many of the companies, for reasons best known to themselves, simply refused to supply information. This, in spite of numerous letters, telephone calls, faxes, and personal pleas. On the other hand, much of the information that I managed to uncover was the direct result of total and absolute cooperation from those companies listed. Even when information was not forthcoming, I ventured out into the far regions of the Caribbean, Central America, and Europe to unearth whatever treasures I could dig up and bring back, either on paper, on audio tape, on film, or in my head. But unfortunately, I kept encountering a few brick walls. Still, this is the first time in the history of cigar smoking that such an exhaustive *detailed* reference section of brands has been compiled and made available to the aficionado. If you don't see a particular cigar chronicled within these pages, it is because the information was not provided or simply did not exist. Conversely, the amount of information you now have before you is directly proportional to the amount of information I was able to obtain, either from the companies themselves or from my own exhaustive research. That is why some brands are covered more fully than others.

It is my hope that any brands not listed, no matter how obscure, will subsequently come forth into the spotlight, to be included in any future edition of *The Ultimate Cigar Book* that is published.

So, here then, for your reading and smoking pleasure, is the world's first International Compendium of Cigar Brands, which I have assembled in the sincere belief that the more we know about those things that bring us pleasure, the more we are able to appreciate them.

Absolute — (Dominican Republic) A cigar closely tied in with the world famous vodka. A few silver banded "experimental" cigars were made in 1992, then taken off the market for further refinement. Nonetheless, I thought I'd put them in as someday this brand may become readily accessible.

Adipati — (Jakarta) Relatively thin, non-humidified (i.e., European style) cigars, very mild, made of Sumatra and Java tobaccos.

Agio — (Holland) This world famous brand includes an extensive array of cigarillos and cigars, all of which are the "dry" European variety, and offered in either Sumatra (light) or Brazil (dark) wrappers. Agio began with a tipped cigar, which soon became a best seller on the Continent. Today their Mehari's is one of Agio's most popular cigars worldwide, but especially in Belgium and Germany. Other well-known brands include Mini Mehari's, Panter, and Red Label small cigars. Of excel-

230

lent quality, they are all machine made with Java, Sumatra, and Cameroon tobaccos.

Al Capone — (Germany) For the gangster in you. A nice, mild short smoke when on the lam with your moll.

Alton — (Great Britain) This company has the distinction of being the only handmade cigar company left in England. Located in Nottingham, they use Havana wrappers and binders and Jamaican filler. Their Corvanna sub-brand cigars range mostly in the medium-sized category.

Andujar — (Dominican Republic) Wasn't that the name of a movie with Robin Williams where all the animals in an ancient board game come to life? No, it's really a mild flavored new cigar brought out in 1994 by Oscar Rodriguez, who also makes the Oscar cigar. This cigar is named after Captain Rodrigo de Andujar who, some say, was appointed by Columbus to present the first hand rolled leaves of tobacco to Queen Isabella. Each of the six Andujar shapes, such as the Romana, Azua and Santiago, are named after provinces in the Dominican Republic. These uncello'd cigars contain a Dominican filler and binder with a Connecticut shade wrapper and are blended to an HPH 1.5—2. Although it has no relationship to the cigar, Andujar is also the name of a limited edition armagnac sold only in France.

Antonio & Cleopatra — (Puerto Rico) A longtime favorite, this mass-market cigar began life in 1888 as a popular Cuban brand. Today it is made with natural Candela or Indonesian wrapper (a change from the original and now scarce Cameroon), homogenized binder and Cuban seed short filler. Over 110 million of these machine made smokes are produced a year.

Arango Sportsman — (Tampa) One of the newest flavored cigars to hit the market in recent times, as an answer to those people who constantly complain about your cigar smoke. This short-filler cigar is machine-made with tobaccos from Honduras, Dominican, and Ecuador and is heavily laced with vanilla flavoring. Which means you should not store the Arango Sportsman anywhere near your other cigars, or it will start to smell as if someone is baking cookies inside your humidor. To be sure, smoking this mild-tasting cigar ac-

231

tually permeates the air with a very pleasant aroma. Of course, if there happens to be an anti-smoker in the crowd who also hates cookies...

Arango Statesman — (Honduras) A vanilla-flavored, all-tobacco long leaf filler cigar that is machine bunched and hand rolled.

Aromas de San Andrés — (Mexico) Originally called simply "Aromas," this is one of the oldest brands in all of Mexico. Today, it is also one of the most elegantly wrapped. Each cigar comes encased in an amber glass tube and is cushioned with a pillow of foam against a rubber cap which keeps the cigar secure and humidified for a minimum of six months. But that's not all. Each tube is then wrapped in gold foil and slipped into a gold box which is capped off with a red ribbon. For years it was only available as a 6⅛ x 40, but recently four new sizes have been added to the line. Although expensive for a Mexican cigar (due, in part, to all that fancy packaging), the Aromas de San Andrés makes a relatively inexpensive and impressive gift, either for your host or for yourself. As far as smokability is concerned, it is quite mild yet stimulating, and rates a 2 on the Highly Prejudiced HackerScale. Up until the early 1990s these distinctive cigars were only available via the national Tinder Box chain, but now they can be found at tobacconists throughout the United States, Canada, and Australia, although not always in the same packaging.

Arturo Fuente — (Dominican Republic) Headquartered in Santiago, in the heart of the richest tobacco-growing regions of the DR, this is one of the few family-owned cigar-making companies still in existence. It is also the largest cigar factory in Santiago and one of the leading premium cigar manufacturers in the world. Tracing the history of this respected cigar-making family is like following the history of the cigar industry itself. Having roots in both Spain and then Cuba, Don Arturo Fuente left Havana in the late 1800s to bring his cigar-making skills to various factories in the United States. Finally, in 1912, he decided to produce clear Havana cigars in Tampa under his own name. His son, Carlos, soon joined him in the family operations. And now, Carlos, Jr. and his sister Cynthia have joined with their father to continue their grandfather's tradition. At various times since the Cuban embargo, the Fuente family has had factories in the United States, Puerto Rico, Nicaragua, and Honduras. All too often they ended up losing their factories and all of their personal possessions due to the volatile nature of some of these countries. Finally, in 1980, they settled in the Dominican Republic, and opened a small factory that employed a total of seven people; they made their first Dominican cigar on September 4th of that year. Today, the Arturo Fuente operations employ more than 680 people in their rambling, 80,000 sq. ft. factory in Santiago, and another 150 cigar makers in the small town of Moca, where the Fuente family opened a second factory (which has since expanded) in 1990 in order to keep up with worldwide demand for their cigars. Two more new factories opened in the Santiago area since 1995, now bringing the total number of Fuentes' workers to more than 1,600. In addition, the Fuente family still operates a factory in Tampa, where they manufacture a separate line of machine-bunched handrolled cigars (in contrast to their Dominican cigars, which are 100% handmade). It is interesting to note that of their original seven Dominican employees, six are still with the company. Arturo Fuente is one of the very few cigar manufacturers who use as many as four different types of tobacco in their various filler blends. Moreover, each style of cigar has a different recipe, thus assuring an unusually wide spectrum of tastes and aromas throughout the entire line. Their broad range of tobaccos for wrappers, binders and fillers include the highest grade leaf from Connecticut, Mexico, Brazil, Cameroon, Nicaragua, and, of course the various Dominican tobaccos. Under the A. Fuente brand, they make more than twenty different styles of long filler, handmade cigars, including such outstanding examples as the rich cedar-wrapped Rothschild-style Chateau Fuente, the mild and historic Flor Fina 8-5-8, which was a favorite of Don Arturo (the 8-5-8 numbers pay tribute to his age when he passed away; it reads the same forwards or backwards), and the eminently full, sophisticated flavor of their celebrated Hemingway series, one of the few cigars left that still uses rare Cameroon wrappers. All of their cigars are aged a minimum of 21 days. Some, like the Chateau Fuente, Hemingway, and

Don Carlos are aged even longer (see Chapter 4). And of course, there is the legendary Opus X, which created a mild hysteria when it was introduced on the east coast first and Californians were catching flights to New York to buy a few (true story!). In addition to making their own brands, the Fuente's main Santiago factory also makes the Ashton and Julia Marlowe cigars, while their Moca operations are kept busy turning out all of the hand-made, long filler cigars for Cuesta-Rey (including their best-selling La Unica bundled cigar) and the Fuente's Montesino brand. The Fuente family also produces various private brands for selected merchants and mail order firms in the United States. In all, the four facto-ries produce over 28 million cigars a year (that's a jump of an additional 10 million cigars since 1993, making them the second largest cigar producer in the DR), with the majority of them exported to the United States. The rest are shipped to Europe, where the Panetela and Corona are the most popular sizes, although neither cigar is the shape that they make for the U.S. and the flavor is a much heavier blend. Still, none of the Fuente cigars, either in the U.S. or in Europe, are overpower-ing. If there is one thing that every Arturo Fuente cigar possesses, no matter what the shape or where or when it is smoked, it is character.

Ashton — (Dominican Republic) One of the most elegant and richest tasting cigars of the "new breed." First in-troduced in 1985, the Ashton name originated with William Ashton Taylor, a celebrated high-grade pipe maker from England. Because his name was so closely associated with the quality workmanship of his Ashton pipes, it was decided to retain that aura with the intro-duction of a long filler, handmade premium cigar. Avail-able in eight elegant shapes, these cigars are produced by the most skilled handrollers in the Arturo Fuente factory. Ashton cigars feature a Connecticut wrapper and Cuban seed Dominican binder and filler, blended to give a medium flavor that is deepened by four to six months of aging. Also well worth trying is the very mel-low Ashton Aged Maduro, which was brought out in 1990. Only the darkest of the Connecticut broadleaf wrappers are selected for this cigar, which rates a mild 2 — 2.5 (depending on size) on the Highly Prejudiced

HackerScale. It is one of the sweetest, mildest maduros I have ever smoked. Also not to be missed is the Ashton Cabinet Selection Vintage Limited Edition, which has the distinction of having the longest nomenclature of any vintage cigar in this book. This gourmet delight was brought out in 1988, and is among the very best of the vintage cigars. Featuring specially selected Connecticut shade wrapper and aged for a full year, these choice cigars have a slightly heavier blend than the rest of the line, which adds more character to the smoke. All of the Cabinet Selection offerings are shaped cigars; most of the sizes feature a rounded head and a Perfecto-style foot. A semi-Belicoso shape and a 5½ inch Pyramid are also included among the Cabinet Selection. Ashton cigars, especially their Cabinet and Maduro ranges, have a tendency to linger on the palate and provide what wine connoisseurs refer to as "a long finish." Ashton cigars are sold in the U.S., England, Germany, France, Belgium, Switzerland, Luxembourg and Japan.

Astral — (Honduras) Introduced in 1995, this somewhat dry-tasting HPH 2 cigar has a Honduran-grown Connecticut shade wrapper, a Honduran binder and a Honduran and Nicaraguan filler, giving it a slightly sweet, coated sensation on the palate and making it taste more like a Dominican cigar than the Honduran it actually is.

Avanti — (United States) If you like licorice, you'll love this dry cigar, which is cured with anisette. Warning: don't keep a box of these babies in your car on a hot summer day or your vehicle will smell like a candy store.

Avo — (Dominican Republic) This excellent cigar was started in 1986 by Avo Uvezian, a multi-talented entrepreneur who also wrote the classic hit song, "Strangers in the Night," even though he's not credited on most releases (it's a long story). Handmade by the same Tabadom factory that also produces the superb Davidoff, the excellently crafted Avo features a Connecticut shade wrapper, Dominican binder, and four different types of long leaf Dominican filler. Previously only imported to the United States until 1997, when it finally began appearing in tobacco shops in Europe. In addition to its excellent blends, one thing that makes an Avo unique is that it is aged for six to eight months before being shipped to tobacconists. The Avo's tastes run slightly to the rich side

235

of medium with a strength of HPH 2.5. Four new sizes were introduced in 1995 under the Quartetto baton as part of the XO line. Like its namesake, an Avo Uvezian cigar is a perfect companion with food or drink, especially if there happens to be a piano nearby.

Baccarat — (Honduras) This brand had its beginning in 1871 with Carl Upmann, brother of the more renowned Herman, whose name is immortalized by the well-known H. Upmann cigars. It seems that Carl was also a cigar maker, having started in New York and then moving to Tampa sometime around the turn of the century. By the late 1960s, the U.S. branch of the Upmann cigar-making family had relocated their operations to Honduras with the intent of creating a C. Upmann cigar for the growing North American market. Meanwhile, the H. Upmann brand was well established, as it had been continuously made in Cuba since 1844. Moreover, the giant Consolidated Cigar Corporation was already importing their excellent Dominican-made H. Upmann cigars into the United States, the same market that was now being targeted by the C. Upmann side of the family tree. Consequently, a lawsuit erupted. When the smoke cleared, Consolidated retained the right to continue marketing the H. Upmann brand and the Upmann family was not permitted to use their name on any cigar that they made. So, in 1978, the Honduran cigar that was to be C. Upmann underwent a name change to Baccarat. Through the years this cigar has only had moderate success and from 1986 to 1988 it seemed to disappear completely. But since 1990, it has been slowly making a comeback, due in part to its affordable pricing in the premium line and a more aggressive approach to marketing. Baccarat cigars feature Havana seed Honduran-grown filler, Mexican binder, and Connecticut shade wrapper. They have also entered the rarified air of the vintage cigar with their La Fontana brand.

Backwoods — (United States) Machine made in Macadoo, Pennsylvania, this small, mass-market cigarillo was introduced in the early 1980s. It has a "wild" filler (ragged on the ends), no binder and a broadleaf wrapper.

Bahia — (Costa Rica) A medium, slightly rough flavored cigar introduced in 1995.

Bances — (Canada) Most cigar aficionados are not aware that a Havana-leaf Bances still exists, but exist it does. It is machine-made in Toronto by The House of Horvath exclusively for the Canadian market. Utilizing a short filler and homogenized binder, this tubed Corona de Luxe provides a very mild and pleasant tasting smoke, producing an HPH 1.5-2.0.

Bances — (Tampa/Honduras) A true dual-nationality cigar, with some of the smaller, machine-bunched sizes being made in Tampa, while the larger shapes, such as the Brevas, Cazadores, Corona Inmensas, Corona Especial, Presidents, and the No. 1 are completely hand-made in Honduras. This best-selling cigar started out life in 1840, where it was originally made in Cuba by Francisco G. Bances. By 1886 it was being made by the Bances y Lopez Company. Not especially popular in Havana circles, it eventually faded into obscurity. However, in 1959 it was resurrected in Tampa as a U.S.-made clear Havana cigar. (As a sidenote, Bances was also the first cigar to feature a double band.) In an effort to keep the cigar alive, the manufacturer began buying up all of the Havana leaf that they could find. Then the embargo hit. Suddenly, Bances became one of the few all-Havana cigars that could still be legally purchased in the United States. It was also the first post-embargo cigar to be produced in the U.S. using all Havana tobacco. These prestigious selling points gave Bances an unprecedented marketing edge over all the non-Havana cigars, and Bances soared in both popularity and sales. But as the supply of Havana leaf eventually was consumed, the manufacturers began to look elsewhere for their premium tobacco. They eventually settled on the fertile soil of Honduras. Today, Bances remains a top handmade cigar which still retains its historic Cuban seed flavor.

Bandi — (Canada) An inexpensive, medium-mild machine-made cigar for the Canadian market.

Bauzá — (Dominican Republic) Originally an old Cuban family name and a very popular Havana cigar that was started in 1868. Since 1993 it has been made by the Fuente factory and can be found in the United States and a few other countries, including Venezuela (where it is a completely different cigar that is hand made by another firm). But the Fuente-made Dominican version is handmade with Dominican and Nicaraguan long filler, a Mexican binder and Cameroon wrapper, all of which are very rich and heavily blended. A spicy HPH 2.5.

Beldina — (Portugal) A flagship cigar from the Azores Islands, and handmade by the Fabrica de Tobacco Estrela. The filler is a blend of Brazil, Havana, Java, and Dominican tobaccos, with a Dominican binder and a choice of Java or Nicaraguan wrappers. Heavy tasting (HPH 2.5), available in eleven sizes and moderately priced.

Bering — (Honduras) This popular cigar has been around since 1905, when it was first made in a small wooden frame factory in Tampa's famed Ybor City. Today the Bering brand is owned by the giant cigar conglomerate Swisher International, which has taken noteworthy steps to upgrade this popular cigar's appearance and taste, in order to better acclimate it to the growing premium market. In the late 1990s the entire Bering cigar-making operation was transferred to Honduras, where the all natural, long leaf filler cigars are now completely handmade in the famous Honduras American Tobacco factory. To complement their already popular Natural and Candela wrappers, an excellent Maduro cigar was introduced in 1992. And in '93 Bering came out with a premium high-grade cigar. Worthy of searching out is their new 8½ x 52 Grande, which comes in a 15-cigar hinged cedar box. The taste is an HPH 2—2.5 medium-heavy flavor. Up until a few years ago the red-banded Berings were those shapes that were often sold in packs and in non-tobacco stores, while the brown bands, the ones most of us were familiar with, were the high grades that were sold through various smokeshops throughout the country. But now all the bands have been consolidated into one bright red design with gold lettering, so that should lessen the confusion. As to their quality, all I can say is that on my father-in-law's 80th birthday I asked him what he wanted and he said, "A box of Berings!" He got it.

Bolívar — (Cuba) Named after South American hero Simón Bolívar, who hailed from the central highlands of La Gran Colombia (in what later became Venezuela) and led the revolt against Spain. However, this cigar's early history was not as dramatic as its namesake. Started in 1901 by the Rocha family, a lack of marketing kept it from achieving any noteworthy prominence until the 1950s, when it was acquired by Ramon and Rafael Cifuentes. Then things began to change for the better. Today, the Bolivar has become one of the all-time great Havanas, but one that is definitely not for the uninitiated. The smaller, machine-made shapes do not seem to have the taste-fulfilling high octane flavor that this cigar is capable of giving, and that is found in the larger, handmade Bolivars, which are so eagerly sought out by true cigar connoisseurs who revel in their ultra rich, robust taste. A firm and solid 3 on the HPH and worth every puff. A superb late night, après-banquet smoke. If unsure about your affinity for this heavy a cigar, start out with the 4½ x 26 Panetela and work your way up, slowly.

Butera Royal Vintage — (Dominican Republic) Introduced in 1993, these handmade cigars were inspired by Mike Butera, a talented and award-winning high-grade pipe carver who also has a deep appreciation for premium cigars. The filler tobaccos are expertly blended of Cuban Seed Dominican and Olor. A special aged Java binder adds a bit of seasoning to the taste, and the wrapper is a specially selected dark Connecticut shade leaf. The cigars go through four "sweats" or fermentation processes, which rids the raw leaf of all ammonia and enables it to be smoked down almost to the band without producing a rancid taste or odor. They have an elegant meaty flavor — like prime rib rather than porterhouse — and age exceptionally well. The cigars are available in six shapes ranging from the 6½ x 44 Cedro Fino to the hefty 6 x 52 Dorado 652. Butera Royal Vintage Cigars are sold in the United States, Europe and Japan.

Calixto López — (Philippines) Named after a Spanish General, this was originally a lesser known Cuban brand that began in 1881. It is now being handmade in the Philippines of long leaf filler that produces a very satisfying medium-tasting blend. Their "twisted bunch" Culebras and the 8 x 45 Czar are worth checking out.

Calle Ocho — (United States) Made in Miami. Available in eleven sizes.

Camacho — (Honduras) An excellent, full flavored HPH 2.5 cigar that was named after Simón Camacho, a Nicaraguan patriot. Filler and binder are Honduran, with a Connecticut shade wrapper.

Camórra — (Honduras) Actually, this well made cigar's official name is Camórra Imported Limited Reserve, but nobody's going to remember all that. What you should remember is that this medium-mild cigar has an excellently blended Honduran filler, mated with a Honduran binder and then topped off with a delicate Ecuadorian wrapper. The end result is an exceptionally well rolled cigar with a wonderfully rich and smooth flavor, much of it due to the Ecuadorian wrapper. This cigar really seems to come into its own with the bigger ring gauges, such as the San Remo (7x48) and the Roma Robusto (5x50). A very pleasant HPH 2.5, making the Camórra ideal for afternoon or evening. Introduced in August of 1995, the Camórra name is taken from a region in Italy that was reputed to have mob connections, which no doubt explains the Italian red, white and green ribbon stretched across the bodies of all boxed cigars, so that they can't escape. There are eight sizes available, each one named after an Italian city. Oh yes, the 1942 date on all boxes and bands of Camórra cigars reflects — not the founding of the brand, which only occurred in 1995 — but the year in which one of the founders was born.

Canaria d'Oro — (Dominican Republic) Made of Mexican Sumatra wrapper with Dominican, Jamaican and Mexican tobaccos. A very light, sweet tasting cigar.

CAO — (Honduras) Introduced in 1995 by Cano A. Ozgener, an importer of meerschaum pipes who now also imports cigars. Filler is a Cuban seed Nicaraguan with a touch of Mexican leaf, the binder is Cuban seed Honduran and the wrapper is a Connecticut shade. Seven sizes are available with Connecticut shade wrapper: Petit Corona, Corona, Lonsdale, Corona Gorda, Robusto, Churchill, and Triangulare while a Connecticut broadleaf Maduro wrapper is available in the latter four sizes. The Connecticut wrapper is a pleasant HPH 2, while the Maduro comes in at HPH 2—2.5, pleasant and not overpowering. However, it tends to get a bit harsh near the end, so don't plan on smoking this one down to the band.

Caoba — (Dominican Republic) A faintly harsh tasting and spicy cigar that began in 1993 and was first imported into the U.S. in 1996. It has a Cuban seed Dominican filler, Dominican binder, and a claro Connecticut shade wrapper. Each box comes packed with a tobacco leaf, a novel twist for those who might like to try rolling their own.

Captain Black — (United States) I only put this in because every once in a while somebody asks me if there is a cigar that tastes and smells like pipe tobacco. Yes, there is! And this is it, a tipped cigar that is made in Jacksonville, Florida from a pleasantly aromatic and extremely popular pipe tobacco of the same name. Introduced in 1996.

Carat — (Holland) This elegant, high-grade, European-style cigar was introduced in the early 1990s. Manufactured by Schimmelpenninck, these medium tasting Dutch smokes (a 2 on the HackerScale) are machine made of Java, Brazil, Sumatra and Havana tobaccos. Yes, there is the forbidden "H" word, so you won't find these on American shores. However, when on the Continent, pick up a box of the Grand Coronas Imperiales; they come in an easy-to-carry cedar box that contains a cigar cutter, in case you left yours back home.

Carlos — (Dominican Republic) This is the name of the Juan Clemente cigar that is sold in Switzerland.

Carlos V — (Philippines) The European brand name for Calixto López.

Carrington — (Dominican Republic) A very mild HPH 1.5 cigar produced by Hendrik Kelner, the same master blender who creates Davidoff and Avo cigars. This well-made cigar is proof that you can't judge quality by its band.

Casa Blanca — (Dominican Republic) Originally created for use at the White House in Washington, D.C., this was the featured cigar at the Republican inaugural of Ronald Reagan. Unfortunately, with "politically correct" no smoking signs being plastered on the White House walls, Casa Blanca (which means "white house" in Span-

241

ish) has moved out into the mainstream, where it can now be enjoyed by Democrats and Republicans alike. It boasts Brazil and Dominican filler, Mexican binder, and a Connecticut shade wrapper. The size range of this cigar goes from a 4 x 30 all the way up to a mammoth Jeroboam that clocks in at 10 x 66. There is also a Half Jeroboam in case you can't stay up late.

Casa Blanca — (Mexico) A cigar that used to be made in the Canary Islands, but it is now manufactured in Mexico.

Casadores — (Cuba) An old Havana brand, no longer exported and now relegated strictly for local Cuban consumption.

Century Sam — (Canada) I discovered this inexpensive machine-made cigar during a speaking engagement at the first Great Halifax Smoke in 1995, when an anonymous Canadian admirer of this book fired two of them across my bow as I cruised the buffet table at the Chateaux Halifax hotel. Whatever it's soaked in, you can taste it even before the cigar touches your lips. Sweet, thick and unforgettable. Upon lighting up, the full, distinctive taste of homogenized wrapper comes through to the forefront, with essence of Sunday morning Times, and flavors of water, pulp, and dust. An HPH 1. Much maligned but very popular nonetheless, this ubiquitous little cigar was named in honor of British Columbia's centennial. It originally sold for a (Canadian) nickel apiece.

Chambrair — (Dominican Republic) A special cigar made by the A. Fuente company for restaurants and other establishments in Germany. Eight shapes are offered, including a Churchill, Lonsdale, Double Corona, and a Perfecto. In addition to Connecticut, Maduro wrappers are available in some of the shapes.

Charles the Great — (United States) This is an old brand that used to be made in Tampa, and it is still possible to find some of the colorful original labels for sale at antique shows. The cigars will probably not cost as much as the labels however, although they may be just as hard to find unless you live in Texas. The brand is now owned and manufactured by the Finck Cigar Company of San Antonio. These cigars, although newly made, still utilize the original, pre-World War II vintage bands that were made in Germany. The Charles the Great bands are historic works of art, and add a unique flavor to an already flavorful cigar. Obviously, you get them free with each cigar, unlike the antique label, which doesn't come with any cigars at all.

Christian of Denmark — See Nobel Cigars.

Churchill — (Switzerland/Dominican Republic) Not only is this a cigar size, it is also a brand, but one that doesn't often show up outside of Europe. Oddly enough, the first "Churchill" cigars were not anything like the large Double Corona sizes that used to be associated with the shape. Instead, these cigars were small and of the "dry" European style and were made in Switzerland by a tobacconist named Friedrich in the small town of Buelach, near Zurich. However, when the Prime Minister of England made his historic postwar speech in 1946 at the University of Zurich, Winston Churchill graciously consented to having these cigars (which were unlike anything he smoked) christened with his family name. In addition, the flattered Churchill agreed to have his portrait appear on the band. The small Churchill brand cigars were sold exclusively in Switzerland, and then gradually expanded their regions to Germany, France and Italy. More recently, in keeping with the growing trend towards humidified cigars in Europe, this brand has come out with their Churchill Latinos, which are made in the Dominican Republic by Fuente. An HPH 2, they deepen and smooth out as they are smoked. Since writing the first edition of this book, I have aged some for three years and found them to be a better smoke than when I bought them in Germany in 1992. Medium flavored, they are available in Corona Classica, Gran Corona, Panetela Larga and the largest, a 6¾ x 44 Double Corona — none of which are a true Churchill. Still, the glowering portrait of Sir Winston Churchill on a box of Latinos can be a friendly face for those Americans in Europe looking for a break from the ever-present dry cigars and cigarillos. In addition, Churchills are sometimes encountered in duty-free shops in airports. I picked up my first box out of curiosity at the well-stocked and super-friendly J. Schwarzenbach & Co. tobacco shop, located in the Zurich railroad station's underground shopping mall. They make for a very pleasant afternoon smoke while waiting for the train to Munich.

Cifuentes — (Cuba) A famous brand that is named after one of Cuba's premier cigar-making families before the revolution. Today, one of the members of that famous family, Ramon Cifuentes, oversees production of the Dominican-made Partagas and Macanudo cigars.

Cohiba — (Cuba) Yes, this is *the* cigar, the one that was originally reserved only for invited dignitaries to Cuba, and divvied out with great aplomb at select governmental functions. Never was it allowed outside of the Cuban borders, nor was it ever seen at anything other than sanctioned state affairs. Named after the Taino Indian word for "tobacco," Cohiba was supposedly created by Che Guevera (Cuba's first Minister of Industry after the revolution) at the express request of Fidel Castro to produce a cigar that would epitomize everything that the new Cuba was capable of achieving. However, Che Guevera died before this cigar officially came out, so that story — which was originally told to me in Cuba — is somewhat suspect. Another, slightly more plausible story is that shortly after the revolution, Castro was given an exquisite cigar by one of his bodyguards (he always had someone taste his food and "test puff" his cigars, as there was the constant fear of poisoning). Immediately impressed with the flavor and intrigued as to the origin of this particular cigar, which carried no brand name, he was told it was a special blend made and rolled by a man named Avelino Lara. Still another version names Eduardo Ribera as the originator of this blend. In any case, this talented *torcedor* (whichever of the two it was, for it was definitely one of them and they both admit to it) was contacted and put in charge of making these special cigars for Castro. And thus, the Cohiba was born. (Another version of this story has a man by the name of Edwardo Rivera being the creator of Cohiba and the personal roller for Castro.) No matter which of these stories is true, the fact remains that only the best tobaccos from the best regions of the Vuelta Abajo are used, and only the most skilled of Cuban artisans (which up until 1995 were only women) are permitted to cut, bunch and roll its judiciously cured and triple fermented leaves. Part of Cohiba's uniqueness is due to the fact that, while many of Havana's best brands are double fermented, only the Cohiba tobacco leaves go through a special third aging process of spending two to three weeks in oak barrels. As a result, the exquisite Cohiba emerged in 1968, one of the very first cigars to be made in the Castro regime. Its success was instantaneous. Word quickly spread among those fortunate enough to have savored its carefully honed and nurtured full rich taste. Cohiba's mystique was aided by the fact that only the very privileged were ever allowed to touch a match to this rarified treasure from the Vuelta Abajo. Finally, in 1982, Cuba's precious Cohiba was permitted to be shipped beyond its isolated shores. The occasion was the Cuban/Spanish Mundial Soccer games. Of course, the cigar was an immediate success, and Cubatabaco eventually realized the monetary potential of their newest native product. In 1984 the Cohiba appeared in Switzerland, no doubt (although nobody will confirm this) in the Davidoff shop in Geneva, which had a two decades old relationship with Havana. Initially, three sizes were offered to the public: Panetelas, Lanceros, and Corona Especiales. From there, the cigar went to Belgium, England, and finally to France. In 1989 the Robusto, Esplendido and Exquisitos were introduced. This completed The Classic Line or La Linea Classica. Then, in 1992, to commemorate the 500th anniversary of Columbus' discovery of the New World (and of Cuba), La Linea 1492 was introduced with a milder blend designed to attract newer smokers. This consisted of the Siglos (which means "century" in Spanish) I through V, representing each of the five centuries since Columbus' discovery. Today, the original 1968 Cohiba blend is still produced in the Lanceros, Panetelas, and Gran Coronas shapes. But a newer, slightly more refined (but still very heady) blend was created in 1988 for the Esplendidos, Corona Especiales, Exquisitos, and Robustos. Thus, there are three different blends for the same brand. Since 1982, Cohibas have been proudly produced in the El Laguito Factory, a former 1910-era mansion resplendent along a palm-tree lined suburb of Havana. Prior to Cohiba, El Laguito had been used as a training school to teach women how to roll cigars. The former tenant of this mini-palace was the Marquesa de Pinar del Rio; for the significance of this name, the Pinar del Rio is one of the

245

top two tobacco growing sections of the Vuelta Abajo. However, some sizes, such as the Robusto and Esplendido, are now also rolled — under strict supervision — in the Partagás and H. Upmann factories (check the stampings on the bottom of your boxes). And not all Cohibas are made in Cuba; an all-Havana cigarillo is made in France under license to Cubatabaco. But no matter in which factory they are made, for cigar connoisseurs the world over, Cohiba's well recognized logo — a black silhouette of a Taino Indian surrounded by an orange and black band with white dots — has come to symbolize the very best that Cuba has to offer. As verification of the Cohiba's rarity, of a total Havana cigar production of 30 million cigars in 1989, only 1.5 million were Cohibas. In 1993, with total cigar production at around 40 million, Cohiba production was just a little over 2 million. It is by far the most expensive of all the Havanas offered for public sale, but one that is truly worth the price. It is also the most counterfeited cigar in the world, so *cuidado* (be careful)!

Cohiba — (Dominican Republic) In 1993 this cigar was introduced to U.S. cigar smokers via the Alfred Dunhill stores on a limited basis. This marked the first time that the Cohiba brand was made available in the United States (even the Cuban brand was not publicly sold until 1982, well after the embargo). The new version is completely handmade, with a Connecticut shade wrapper, Mexican binder, and Dominican, Jamaican and Mexican tobaccos in the filler blend. It is decidedly heavier in taste than the Macanudo (which is made by the same company), possessing a medium yet full-bodied flavor. The initial run of these cigars was not banded, and the box simply had the brand name stenciled on the cover. Judging from the initial reaction to the appearance of the new Dominican Cohiba, I expect this cigar to be around, in one form or another, for a long time.

Condial — (Canary Islands) A humidified cigar that has been around since 1885. It formerly was sold only in Europe, most notably Germany. But in 1995 this 19th century brand was brought into the U.S., albeit in small numbers. It is made in 20 individual shapes, ranging from a 20 ring cigarillo all the way up to a 50 ring Churchill. It features a Brazilian and Dominican filler,

Mexican binder, and a Connecticut shade wrapper. Medium flavored (HPH 2), it is a good daytime cigar.

Coroa — (Portugal) Handmade in the Azores, this corona-sized cigar from the Fabrica de Tobacco Estrela has a tasty filler blend of Havana, Dominican, and Brazilian tobaccos, nestled inside of a Dominican binder and wrapped with Connecticut leaf.

Corps Diplomatique — (Belgium) An excellent upscale all-tobacco European cigar. It is of the dry type variety, but many shapes have a thicker ring gauge than most. The Panetela-style International is elegantly wrapped in tissue and blended with Sumatra wrapper and Java and Brazil filler. The smaller After Dinner, Panetela, and Deauville sizes are available in the U.S.

Credo — (Dominican Republic) If the name seems familiar, it is because this cigar brand is owned by the same French family that also owns the reliable Credo humidifier. Introduced in 1993, the Credo cigar sports a distinctively flavored blending of Dominican and Cuban seed filler, an aged Dominican binder and a smooth Connecticut shade wrapper. I find it a bit on the stronger side of mild (an HPH 2.5) with a pleasantly rich and slightly pungent smoke. Although mild, it asserts its individuality in flavor. In fact, it teeters on the brink of being a strong cigar but doesn't quite topple over into that category. Some may find it a bit rough around the edges, but I find it consistently enjoyable. It is perfect for an after dinner repast — especially in the larger ring gauges — with a snifter of one of the more muscular Highland malt whiskeys. It you are into nouveau-moderne stylings, you will also enjoy its very distinctively-shaped blue-grey box.

Creme de Jamaica — (Jamaica) Produced in the General Cigar factory, this mild tasting cigar features filler from the Dominican Republic and Brazil, a Mexican binder, and a Connecticut wrapper.

Creston — (Honduran) A super premium cigar brought out in 1996 with Alex Trebek, host of TV's popular "Jeopardy" as one of the founders. Made of Honduran filler and binder with an Ecuadorian shade-grown wrapper, these cigars have a "Habana sweet cap," a small drop of pure cane sugar placed on the tip of each cap after rolling. The purpose of this added sweetener, the Creston cigar makers say, is to allow the palate to acclimate from dessert to the full rich taste of the cigar. But if you think about it, your palate already has a sweet sensation from the dessert, so why stretch it out? Better to plunge directly into the pool and get those taste buds instantly acclimated. As you might have guessed, I'm not in favor of augmenting a good cigar (which the Creston happens to be) with any non-tobacco flavor. Nevertheless, with all this attention to palate, it is not surprising to learn that these cigars are distributed by Creston Vineyards, located in Creston, California. In addition to the Creston Prestige Cuvèe there are two "special order" cigars, a Pyramid and a 9 x 50 Farouk Gigante. The first run of cigars that I test smoked were slightly overpacked; i.e., rolled a little too tight. And you have to get past that "Havana sweet cap" to really appreciate what a good blend this really is. A nice, healthy HPH 2. Definitely worth checking out. Like their wines, custom labels are available if you order sufficient quantities.

Cruz Real — (Mexico) This is one of the newest cigars from Mexico, and is the company's entry directly into the premium cigar market. Cruz Real was introduced first in Belgium in 1990, and then France, Germany, and Spain. It made its initial appearance in the United States in 1993-94. The Cruz Real cigar is made with two types of Mexican-grown wrappers: Sumatra and Maduro. All wrapper, binder and filler tobaccos are grown in the San Andrés Valley. And in keeping with government requirements, even the Honduran cedar boxes are made in Mexico. The cigar comes packaged singly, in a 10-cigar presentation box, and in boxes of 25. A Cruz Real Special Edition was introduced in 1995 with a Mexican-grown Connecticut shade wrapper. The cigars are full tasting with just a hint of roughness, which brings it into the HPH 2—2.5 range. In terms of flavor, they are by far one of the most elegant of all Mexican cigars.

Cuaba — (Cuba) The first new cigar to be introduced under the Habanos banner. Launched in November 1996, it is made in four distinctive *figurado* shapes.

Cuba Aliados — (Honduras) One of the truly great cigars, with Brazilian and Dominican long leaf filler, Cuban seed Honduran binder, and a beautiful Ecuadorian wrapper that is available in Claro, Double Claro and Colorado. This handcrafted cigar was started in New Jersey, where it was being made in an incredible array of *figurado* sizes by a talented Cuban exiled cigar maker named Rolando Reyes, who has since gained an identity and a following of his own. Eventually the fame of his cigars spread and he moved to Honduras to be closer to his sources for tobacco. Rolando and his son are now making their own cigars and the Cuba Aliados brand is being manufactured by another factory, but with the same attention to detail and blend. In the larger sizes, this rich tasting cigar starts out an HPH 2 but ends up with an HPH 2.5. And with a big finish you need a big cigar, such as the 18 x 66 "General," which lays claim to being the largest commercially produced cigar in the world. But if you feel you can't spend the entire weekend smoking just one cigar, try the Figurin. It is "only" 10 inches in length.

Cubita — (Dominican Republic) Introduced in 1995, with a Dominican filler and binder and a Connecticut shade wrapper. A full, rich cigar, clocking in at HPH 2.5. Actually one of the best in its price range.

Cuesta-Rey — (United States/Dominican Republic) One of the great 19th century cigars that is still very much with us today. The brand was founded in 1884 by Angel LaMadrid Cuesta, a Spanish cigar maker who had apprenticed in Cuba. He eventually took in a partner, Peregrino Rey and thus, the famed Cuesta-Rey brand was born. In 1893, following the trends of the times, the Cuesta-Rey cigar-making operations moved to Ybor City, the famed center of cigar rolling in Tampa. In time, Angel Cuesta's son Carl entered the firm and eventually assumed responsibility for its operations. In 1958 Carl Cuesta sold the Cuesta-Rey cigar firm to M&N Cigar Manufacturers in Tampa. Today, the well-recognized Cuesta-Rey brand is still being produced, with the short filler cigars being made in Tampa on machines, while the long filler cigars have been made in the Dominican Republic since 1986. The firm has also brought out their Centennial Collection, completely handcrafted cigars of Dominican tobaccos and Connecticut wrapper which are aged for 35 days before being packed in a dress box. These commemorative smokables are specially banded, offered in Natural or Maduro wrappers, and are available in 6 sizes. The Cuesta-Rey Cabinet Selection, with its Dominican filler and Connecticut binder and wrapper, is aged 65 days and comes in a cabinet box; hence the name. The first full cedar cabinet box of cigars that I ever bought were a complement of Cuesta-Rey #95s back in the mid-sixties. Those cigars are long gone, but I still have that box.

Dannemann — (Germany) Established in 1873 by Geraldo Dannemann in Brazil. Their wide assortment of cigars are made in Germany, including their Espada and Lights which were formerly manufactured in Switzerland. Dannemann cigars are made with Brazil and Sumatra tobaccos and are found worldwide. Available in a single cigar aluminum foil humidity pack, in handy tins for cigarillos, and as a 12-cigar gift pack assortment.

Davidoff — (Dominican Republic) This is the *ne plus ultra* of cigars, featuring a Rolls Royce quality, with what many feel to be a Rolls Royce pricetag. Nonetheless, Davidoff cigars are the embodiment of getting what you pay for. Their quality control is among the highest in the industry and the factory supervisor who oversees their handrolling workmanship once complained to me that Davidoff is the only company that seems to reject more cigars than it accepts. All of this is reflective of the exacting personality of the late Zino Davidoff, who helped set new standards for the cigar industry. Davidoff was born in 1906 in Kiev, Ukraine, Russia. In 1911 his family moved to Geneva, Switzerland; this was very fortunate for cigar aficionados, for somehow, a Russian Davidoff cigar would probably not be too well received today. Zino's father specialized in cigarette and pipe tobacco blending and young Davidoff began to learn the trade. But this wasn't enough for him, so at 19 he decided to see the world. As fate would have it, he ended up in Cuba and from 1924 to 1929, became a devoted student of tobacco. Buoyed with this knowledge, Zino returned to Geneva and convinced his father to install a cigar section in his tobacco shop. Then, using the contacts he had made in Cuba, Zino began importing cigars. The Geneva store proved to be the perfect location for Zino's new enterprise. High ranking dignitaries were among his clientele. Precious contacts were made and soon Davidoff was the "in" place to buy cigars. He began shipping cigars all over the world. During WWII, Davidoff was one of the few places in Europe where Havanas could still be obtained. After the war, Zino Davidoff scored a coup that was destined to bring him a sense of immortality among the cigar world; he was given permission to create his own Cuban line of cigars. He hit upon the idea of naming each cigar after a famous French winemaking *château*, as these names would be instantly familiar to connoisseurs. Thus, in 1946 he introduced Château Latour, and the rest soon followed. Of course, he had neglected to obtain permission from the owners to use their names on his cigars. But in those pre-litigious days, the diplomatic Zino simply sent a gift of cigars to each individual. When they saw their *château* immortalized on a box of Havanas, all was forgiven. Through the years the Davidoff line continued to grow, necessitating three different moves of the original shop in Geneva. Finally, in 1970, Davidoff cigars were launched worldwide. Today there are over 60 "depositaires" selling Davidoff products throughout the globe. The first was in Switzerland, then came Germany and Belgium in 1974, Canada in 1977, Asia and finally the United States in 1987. Davidoff cigars are currently sold in 35 countries worldwide. Following a much-heralded break in relations with Cubatabaco in 1989 (see Chapter 1), Davidoff unveiled their Dominican line in 1990. Interestingly, these cigars were launched in the United States first, because Europe still had a three-year supply of Davidoff Havanas that had to be used up before the new line could be introduced. The Dominican line includes three series: Aniversario — extremely mild, even the large 8⅜ x 48 No. 1 size; Grand Cru — my personal favorite, these are full-flavored cigars; Thousand — medium flavored, and designed to fall between the Aniversarios and the Grand Cru. Their Special R (a Robusto), Double R (double corona), and Special T (a Pyramid) are all perfect after dinner cigars that are befitting the most elegant occasion, or can add elegance where there is none. Although meticulously handmade in the DR, all Davidoff cigars are shipped either to Holland (for the European market) or to Connecticut (for the U.S.), where they are reinspected and then aged for one to one and a half years before being sent to stores that are as care-

251

fully selected as their cigars; Davidoff is the only company that requires its dealers to sign a written agreement on cigar display and maintenance. Although the flamboyant Zino Davidoff passed away in 1993 at the still-active age of 87, the company that carries his name lives on. In keeping with its founder's elegant lifestyle theme, Davidoff has now expanded into fashion accessories, colognes and other men's toiletries.

De Nobili — (United States) You might wonder what an Italian dry cigar is doing being manufactured in Scranton, Pennsylvania, but the brand was purchased in 1947 by the Avanti Cigar Company, the same folks who make the Europa cigar. This one is mainly found in the mid-Atlantic states.

Diamond Crown — (Dominican Republic) This is the first super-duper premium cigar made by Cuesta-Rey, which is really made in the Fuente factory. No cigar other than the Opus X has created such excitement. The Diamond Crown was introduced at the Grand Havana Room in Beverly Hills on April 21, 1995 to honor the Newman family's 100th anniversary in the cigar business. Only 150,000 cigars were available initially, and anxious purchasers were shocked to find that they were limited to two cigars per person and that there was a limit of ten boxes per store, unheard of stipulations in the cigar business. But it worked. In fact, it was not unusual to find twelve shrewdies hitting a tobacconist at once so they could commandeer a full box. And it was not unusual to see Diamond Crown boxes, in all their colorful Holland-designed glory, picked clean and sitting empty and forlorn on many a dealer's shelves. Such is the continuing demand for this carefully honed cigar. The wrapper is a double fermented (that means after aging in bulks they are inspected, and fermented again) five-year-old Connecticut shade with a very well balanced Dominican binder and filler blend composed of the top primings — leaf that is picked nearer the uppermost part of the plant. After completion, the cigars are aged for a full year. The cigars are then boxed with a numbered certificate of inspection. There are five sizes, all in 54 ring and ranging in length from 4½ to 8½ inches. This is called the Robusto Series and it is likely that other ring-gauge inspired series will be forthcoming.

The careful selection of leaf and double aging brings out a light, creamy smooth flavor in this cigar. In fact, it is surprisingly mild, an HPH 1.5—2. This is one rarified cigar that can really give you your money's worth, as it can be smoked practically right on down to the band.

Diana Silvius Diamond Vintage Selection — (Dominican Republic) Named after its creator, Chicago (USA) tobacconist Diana Silvius Gits, this medium-full tasting cigar has a slight hint of sweetness, which brings it well into the 2 HPH range, except in the larger Churchill and Robusto sizes, where it hovers around a 2.5 reading. Having first appeared on the market in 1993, the Diana features a Connecticut shade wrapper and Dominican-grown filler and binder. The unique boxes that house these cigars all sport a "diamond" set within the lids, thus making it a jewel of a smoke. A thoroughly enjoyable cigar but it is rarely encountered outside of the U.S.

Diplomáticos — (Cuba) One of the few Havana cigars in which every shape is handrolled.

Don Alfredo — (Honduras) A old Cuban brand that was made exclusively for Dunhill, and is now being revived by that historic firm, but this time with Honduran tobaccos.

Don Diego — (Dominican Republic) Created by noted Cuban cigar maker Pepe Garcia, one of the first Cuban expatriates to resume his cigar-making skills outside of Cuba. This handmade cigar was created in 1964, to fill the niche left by the embargoed departure of all those great Cuban "Don" cigars, most notably the Don Marcos. Some sizes of the Don Diego, such as their Coronas and Lonsdales, are offered in both AMS and EMS wrappers. With Santo Domingo filler and binder and a Connecticut wrapper, it is a mild to full-bodied cigar (depending on shape) and ages very well. The European version is slightly heavier in taste, an HPH 2.5. Of special interest is their limited production Don Diego Connoisseur vintage cigar. Also worth noting is their first-ever ladies' cigar, called the Cleopatra. It will have a tapered foot for easy lighting and has the same Don Diego blend as the rest of the U.S. line, so guys can smoke it too. It had to happen — a unisex cigar!

Don Elito — (Dominican Republic) Introduced in 1996 and christened after the nickname of Joaquin Balaguer, president of the DR at that time, just prior to the elections. In case you're wondering at the wisdom of naming a cigar after an outgoing president of a third world country, I can assure you that certain ex-presidents will never lose their influence. But politics aside, this unusual cigar features a unique candy cane wrapper design created by double wrapping with dark Dominican and light Connecticut shade leaves. The interior is composed of a Dominican binder and filler.

Don Gonzalez — (United States) Originally made in both Florida and the Dominican Republic, this cigar is now only being manufactured in Miami.

Don Juan — (Nicaragua) Made with Nicaraguan and Mexican filler, and a Nicaraguan binder and wrapper.

Don Julian — (Canary Islands) A mild HPH 1.5—2.0 that is quite popular in Spain, although difficult to find in most other countries.

Don Lino — (Honduras) Handmade, with a Havana seed filler, Sumatra binder, and choice of Connecticut, Sumatra, or Maduro wrapper. A variation of the Don Lino, the Don Lino Oro cigar features a Seco filler, Connecticut binder and Cameroon wrapper. Top of the line is the Don Lino Havana Reserve, a mild tasting silky cigar with all Connecticut filler, wrapper and binder. A light to medium taste (1.5 to 2 on the HackerScale).

Don Marcos — (Dominican Republic) Made in seven sizes.

Don Melo — (Honduran) The first thing I wanted to know about this cigar is who is Don Melo, the elderly gentleman pictured on the namesake band. Turns out he is Don Melo Bueso, the father of the man who currently runs the La Flor de Copan factory where this cigar is made. (See? There is no *limit* to what you can learn by reading this book! And just like the first edition, pretty soon, other people will begin copying this information and putting it in their articles and books.) It is a brand that has been around since 1896, so it is not surprising that this Honduran puro came out with a centennial edition vintage cigar that was only offered in 1996-97. This limited edition cigar was made with aged tobaccos, featured a specially designed box and band, and came in four large ringed sizes.

Don Pepe — (Brazil) Made by Suerdieck, this short filler handmade cigar comes in four sizes, a Robusto, Slim Panetela, Double Corona, and a Half Corona. Its filler blend of Brazilian and Dominican tobaccos, plus a Brazilian-grown Bahia-Mata Fina binder and Brazilian-grown Sumatra wrapper all combine to produce a very mild taste. HPH 1.5

Don Ramos — (Honduras) Supposedly the most popular Honduran cigar in Great Britain.

Don Rex — (Honduras) Started in 1987. Handmade.

Don Tomás — (Honduras) Introduced in 1974, this cigar takes its name from the president of the company at that time. The blends and overall makeup of the cigar has changed through the years, but the Don Tomás is currently a medium strength cigar with Honduran filler and binder and Sumatra wrappers in a choice of Claro/Claro, Natural/Colorado, and Maduro. The Don Tomás Special Edition is a much higher grade cigar with a Connecticut shade wrapper and hence, a milder and more refined taste. Both cigars fall into the HPH 2 category of strength. There is also a new International Series that was brought out in 1996.

Double Happiness — (Philippines) Worth getting just for the artwork on the colorful band and box, which feature a contented sun and moon facing each other and smoking cigars. The cigar's name reflects the Yin/Yang symbol for opposites and is usually associated with the blessings given at Asian weddings. Created by Chuck and Charles Alcorn, Jr., a father and son team of cigar lovers, Double Happiness is manufactured by Gabriel Ripoll, Jr. and Armando Espera, two long-time Filipino cigar makers. Available in a Robusto, Churchill, Pyramid and a Perfecto, each of the four sizes are housed in an attractive, heavily lacquered box that only the Filipinos can make. These cigars are handmade with Philippine filler and binder grown in the Cagayan Valley and topped off with a Connecticut shade wrapper. The Bliss, a pig-tailed Perfecto, is one of the most interesting in this mild tasting HPH 1.5 brand, but I have found that some were too tightly wrapped. You might have better luck with the larger 6½ x 50 Euporia, which is a box-pressed Double Corona. Other great names in this brand are Nirvana (a Pyramid) and Rapture (a Robusto). Besides being good conversation starters (especially if you bring out a whole artistically designed box instead of just one cigar), Double Happiness is actually a good smoke.

Ducados — (Spain) A small, Sumatra wrapped cigarillo manufactured by Tabacalera, the state-owned tobacco agency.

Dunhill — (Canary Islands) These cigars, with the dark brown (formerly black) oval on the band, were originally developed in 1986 for the U.S. market, which remains the only country in which they are sold. Tobaccos used are Brazil and Dominican in the filler, with a Dominican binder and a Connecticut shade wrapper. The Canary Islands cigars are well constructed of long filler and are handrolled, but are overshadowed by the wider acceptance among smokers of the Dunhill Aged Cigars.

Dunhill Aged Cigars — (Dominican Republic) These cigars have the blue oval on the band. They were first introduced in 1989, following Dunhill's amiable departure from their Cuban connections (see Chapter 1 for more on this). More appropriately identified on the box as the Dunhill Aged Cigar, the first offering was made with vintage 1986 tobaccos. Because there were still some Dunhill Havana cigars left in Europe, the new Dunhill Aged Cigars were launched in the U.S. and have since become overwhelmingly successful. Part of their lure is the fact that each year's vintage is printed on the box. The 1987 vintage was made available on a worldwide basis in the fall of 1991. Starting in 1996, the vintage years on the boxes were changed much more frequently, which obviously means there are fewer cigars being produced of any given crop. So if you find a year that you like, buy it now! Today, this superbly constructed cigar is sold throughout Europe, the Middle East, the Far East, and duty-free shops, although some of the bigger ring gauges are not available in Germany or Switzerland. And two of the shapes (a Demi-tasse and a Petite Corona) are not sold in the U.S. There are three different tobaccos used in the filler blend: Dominican grown Piloto Cubano, Olor, and Brazil. The binder is of Dominican leaf, while the wrapper is the very best of the Connecticut shade. Meticulously handrolled by one of the largest factories in the DR, every cigar is aged in cedar for a minimum of three months, and sometimes even longer. In 1993, to celebrate the centenary of Alfred Dunhill Ltd., a special Dunhill Aged "Centena" cigar (a 6 x 50 Torpedo) was brought out. No, it wasn't aged for 100 years, but it does feature a special 1893-1993 date on the band and each box is individually numbered with a Master Blender's serial number. The shape is a very smokeable 6 x 50 Belicoso with a curly head. No matter which of the Dominican Dunhills you select, with its extra aging, superb construction, and strict adherence to using only the best vintage years for its tobacco, these are one of the best medium-flavored cigars on today's market.

Dunhill Small Cigars — (Holland) Introduced in 1986 to European and Far East markets, these "dry" type cigars were not sold in the U.S. until 1991. Made by the famous Schimmelpenninck factory located in Wageningen, in the south of Holland, all Dunhill Small Cigars are fashioned of 100% tobacco and feature a mild Sumatra sandleaf wrapper with Java binder and natural Brazil Bahia and Java tobacco leaf filler. There are three sizes available: Miniatures, Señoritas, and Slim Panetelas; an after-dinner Corona size was brought out for the Far Eastern market in late 1996. While one might run the risk of an altercation by walking into a bar and asking for a "pack of Señoritas," I find this size the most practical for a satisfying short smoke.

Dutch Masters — (Puerto Rico) The cigar made famous in the '50s by Ernie Kovacs. Produced on machines, of short filler and homogenized binder.

8-9-8 Collection — (Jamaica) If you spell out the number "eight," it starts out with an "E," which is why it is listed here alphabetically. Made in the General Cigar factory with a Jamaican and Dominican filler, Mexican binder, and a Connecticut shade wrapper.

Ejecutivos — (Mexico) A powerhouse of a little cigar, with a satisfying although somewhat unrefined finish. Made in the San Andrés Valley and sold in Australia and USA. One of these at a time is enough. Stops just short of being overwhelming.

El Glorioso Dominicano — (Dominican Republic) If there is such as thing as medium full, this cigar is it. One of the most consistent smokes from after lunch until after dinner. Started in 1986, this family-owned brand is completely handmade with a filler blend that is a mixture of Honduran and Dominican leaf, and sports a Dominican binder, all of which, when combined with the Connecticut shade wrapper, creates a pleasant 2.5 on the Highly Prejudiced HackerScale. The fullest taste comes from the 54 ring Pyramid. The El Glorioso name was inspired by Havana's famed El Cubano Glorioso brand. The El Glorioso cigar started out in New York, but ironically, just as the first edition of this book was published, this excellent cigar became semi-dormant. From 1993 until 1995 it was not to be found, just as the cigar boom was booming. What a mistake, as it was one of the finer, if lesser-known, smokables. Then in 1996 it once again resurfaced, made in a new factory (the same one where the excellent Romeo y Julietas are made) and with a similar medium-full blend. The cigars are uncellophaned and six shapes are offered: Lonsdale, Robusto, Pyramid, Churchill, Corona, and Panetela. A Maduro in three sizes was introduced in 1996. I can attest from experience, this cigar ages extremely well, as some of the original cigars I put down in 1993 are now richer and smoother in flavor and have developed a wonderful oily sheen on the wrappers. These new cigars should be worth trying as well, as long as they don't disappear from the scene like their predecessors.

El Producto — (Puerto Rico) This mass-market favorite, which was started in the United States in 1916, is now being machine made in Puerto Rico. The El Producto Queens were a favorite of the late George Burns.

El Rey del Mundo — (Cuba) The name literally means, "The King of the World." Started in 1882 by Antonio Allones, at one time this was the highest priced Cuban cigar you could buy, and the picturesque Victorian factory turned out from seven to eight thousand cigars a day. It was originally sold in Europe by Tabacalera, the Spanish tobacco consortium. The same factory also made the Rafael Gonzales cigar and produced one of the first (although not the original) Lonsdale shapes. One of most popular cigars in England, it gradually lessened its production but used the very best tobaccos available. This historic Havana brand is surprisingly mild, with an HPH of 1.2—2, and would be a good introductory cigar for anyone who wishes to enter the Cuban realm gently.

El Rey del Mundo — (Honduras) Introduced to U.S. smokers in late 1993, this 100% handmade cigar is a "puro," being completely made from Honduran-grown tobaccos. It is a heavy, musky, and deep flavored cigar, and is available in a wide variety of 47 standard (and some not-so-standard) shapes and sizes, including cello'd and uncello'd cigars and a great number of glass and aluminum tubed variations.

El Rico Habano — (United States) A Cuban brand that started out relatively late — 1948 to be exact — and ceased production during the revolution. It is now being made by hand in Miami. It is a pleasant, medium to medium strong tasting cigar, with a red and white "RH" band that I find personally appealing. Now, if they had only called it Rico Cigaro Habano the band would have had all three of my initials and I could have claimed it as a personalized cigar.

El Sublimado — (Dominican Republic) Although rather pricey, this cigar did make some notable headway from its birth in 1993 until it ceased to legally exist as a brand in 1996, when it changed its named to La Diva. But the origins of this cigar are as follows: In Spanish, El Sublimado means "the sublime." The name originated when a cigar roller, upon smoking one of the first test cigars in the early 1990s, exclaimed, "Este puro tiene un savor sublimado." Translated, it simply means, "This cigar has a sublime flavor." Everyone in the room immediately agreed that the word "sublimado" was an ideal description of the new blend, and thus, in 1993, a cigar was born. El Sublimado owes its claim to fame to a unique and highly guarded manufacturing technique that actually marries the flavor of 50-year-old "Noces d'Or" Grande Champagne cognac with carefully chosen Dominican filler and binder leaves during the curing process. After aging, the fermented tobaccos are paired with an excellent Connecticut shade wrapper. The handmade cigars are then aged for six months to a year, depending on shape. It is interesting to note that all single cigars (that is, those cigars that were not boxed) were only available in tubes, including a handy five-pack. This, of course, was to keep the pungent cognac fragrance away from the non-El Sublimado cigars. The cigars were available in the most popular U.S. shapes, including Corona, Robusto, Churchill and Pyramid. El Sublimado cigars did indeed have a very light, but distinctive cognac undercurrent of taste and saved precious time for the smoker who was partial to dipping his cigar in cognac, as the El Sublimado was already anointed from the very first puff. They were a bit heady and rated a tasty 2.5 HPH. You can find out how the new La Diva differs from the El Sublimado by flipping the pages over to the "La's" in this chapter.

Encanto — (Honduras) A full-bodied, long leaf cigar, popular in New England, and introduced during the 1970s. It is an excellent value for the money.

Europa — (United States) A short filler, machine made all-tobacco cigar that came out in mid-1994 to try and crack the premium cigar market. Don't let the lack of a long-leaf pedigree stop you from trying this very affordable Scranton, Pennsylvania product. It is rather tasty, in a rough and tumble way. It utilizes dark, fired cured tobaccos from Kentucky and Tennessee and instead of having a binder, it is double wrapped, the same technique used for some of the dry cigars in Europe. Hence its name. Europa is made by the Surachi family, owners of the Tannhauser Cigar Company, a division of the Avanti Cigar Company, which has a virtual monopoly on almost all of the Toscani styled dry-cured cigars made in America. Europa comes in only one size, a 5½ x 34 long cheroot. Of course, these measurements are only approximate, as dry cured cigars always have a degree of variance in their structure. It's an effortless cigar to smoke, as the only wrapper shade to chose from is Maduro, the cigars come already clipped, and you don't have to keep them humidified. The curing process brings out a natural sugar sweetness in the wrapper and the taste is akin to a charred steak. Right around an HPH 2.5. You probably won't want to fire one of these babies up while decked out in your tux, but during a flannel shirt type of autumn afternoon or sitting around the campfire or while playing the lead role in a Spaghetti western, they're just the right kind of smoke.

Excalibur — (Honduras) The name given to the Honduran-made Hoyo de Monterrey cigars that are sold in Europe, Great Britain, and Canada. (For a complete description of this excellent cigar, see its listing in this chapter under Hoyo de Monterrey — Honduras.)

Falstaff — (Austria) A rich tasting non-humidified cigar with Brazil wrapper. Made in Vienna by Austria Tabak, it is only available in Europe.

F.D. Grave & Son — (Honduras) For the first time since 1954, this famous American cigar making company is once again selling a long leaf handmade cigar. But due to the high cost of labor in the U.S., their new cigar is being made in Honduras, where it is fashioned of Honduran, Mexican and Dominican filer, a Cuban seed Honduran binder, and Connecticut broadleaf wrapper. It is a pleasantly meaty cigar that hovers around the HPH 2.5 mark. Well worth investigating.

F.D. Grave & Son — (United States) Founded by Frederick D. Grave in 1884, this historic company is one of the last of the old time U.S. cigar manufacturers. However, the company is still very much in business and still produces classic cigars and shapes, including their original cigar, Judge's Cave (1884), as well as their Muniemaker series (1916), and their glass-tubed, cedar wrapped Bouquet Special (1916), which still proudly boasts it is "the millionaire's cigar at an average man's price." Still owned and operated by the founding family, brothers Richard and Frederick Grave III and Fred's daughter Dorothy Grave Hoyt have maintained an all tobacco quality with both handrolled and machine-made cigars among the ten shapes they produce. The only concession to modern times has been the change from long filler to short filler in 1964. In 1996 the company brought out their first hand-rolled cigar since the 1950s, but due to the high cost of labor in the U.S., this new Graves cigar is being made in Honduras (see above). Aside from their offshore cigar, the high quality Grave cigars are still made with sun-grown Connecticut broadleaf wrappers, selected broadleaf binders and domestically grown filler. Located in New Haven, Connecticut, the factory has occupied the same brick building since 1901. Even their cigar boxes are classics, and the colorful Judge's Cave label is a nostalgic reminder of the days of the five-cent cigar. The cost of a box of F.D. Graves is still comfortably affordable and makes for a refreshing change-of-pace smoke. All of their machine made cigars fall easily within the HPH 2 range, but their new Honduran is a robust and feisty 2.5.

Fighting Cock — (Philippines) You probably won't see many Friends of Animals smoking this cigar, but cock fighting is almost a national sport in the Philippines. And so it is that each of the four shapes is named after a champion rooster who literally had to kill to escape from becoming Sunday dinner. There's Texas Red (Lonsdale); Smokin' Lulu (Perfecto), Rooster Arturo (Robusto), and C.O.D. (Churchill). Ingredients are Philippine filler and binder and Java wrapper, which gives this otherwise mild cigar a bit of a bite...but nothing like the bite from a real fighting cock.

Fleur de Savane — (France) One of the most popular cigars in France. Made in one of the two government factories owned by SEITA, the French tobacco consortium, Fleur de Savane is a blend of Central African tobaccos with a Cameroon wrapper. A very wide range of cigars is offered, including their petit mini-cigars, cigarillos, and "full sized" cigars, of which the largest is a half Corona with an unfinished foot. This brand is one of the few SEITA-made cigars that is exported, in this case, specifically to Spain.

Felipe Gregorio — (Honduras) A "puro" cigar. Named after its creator, Phillip Gregory Wynne.

Flor de Cano — (Cuba) Started in Havana by Tomás and José Cano. It is not widely found today. But I found one, so I can report that it is an HPH 2.

Flor de Filipinas — (Philippines) A very mild tasting and inexpensive "puro." HPH 1.5.

Flor de Florez — (United States) A mild Florida-made cigar with Nicaraguan and Dominican filler and Equadorian wrapper.

262

Flor de Honduras — (Honduras) A cigar with Sumatra wrapper but two different filler blends. A special Havana blend is used for European exports. Non-Havana tobaccos are used for the rich-tasting U.S. imported cigar.

Flor de Jalapa — (Nicaragua) The name translates to "flower of Jalapa," which is one of the two great tobacco-growing valleys in Nicaragua.

Flor de Machado — (Portugal) Made in the Azores Islands.

Flor de Manila — (Philippines) One of the newest of the handmade cigars to come out of the northernmost Cagayan Valley, with its rich volcanic slopes, this brand was introduced in 1994. Much of the filler is grown from Cuban seed. Available in five different small ringed sizes, the Sumatra wrappers and a unique European-style pyramid are my favorites of the offering, even though they are a mild HPH 1.5.

Flor de Orlando — (United States) One of the first machine-made short filler non-Havana cigars to appear after the embargo. Tobaccos used were Columbian, Dominican and Pennsylvanian tobaccos. In the mid 1970s it became a popular handmade Nicaraguan cigar sold in the U.S. and Europe by Fuente. But workers' strikes, student protests, civil unrest and the overall political situation in Nicaragua resulted in the factory being burned, thus temporarily ending the current story of this cigar. It may soon show up, however, as a Dominican.

Flor del Caribe — (Honduras) An early day Cuban brand that surfaced in Honduras shortly after the embargo. Still completely made by hand.

Flor del Isla — (Philippines) Made by hand, with long leaf filler.

Fonseca — (Cuba) Established in 1891 and named after the brand's creator, F.E. Fonseca. Not one of the most popular Havana names, the Fonseca nonetheless enjoys a following of cigar smokers who prefer a very mild (in Havana terms) taste. There isn't a lot to chose from in the Fonseca line, as Cubatabaco only makes two sizes, a Lonsdale-shaped No. 1, measuring 6¼ x 42, and a smaller Corona sized Cosacos. Not easily found, unless you happen to be in Spain, where most of the production is exported (although I have also encountered the No. 1 in Canada). Each individual cigar is hand wrapped in a thin sheet of tissue paper which is secured by the band, as a tribute to the old ways of doing things.

Fonseca — (Dominican Republic) Like many of the old Cuban brands, this one is also being made in the DR, with a Dominican filler, Mexican binder and Connecticut shade wrapper. There is also a Connecticut broadleaf maduro. The aged versions of this cigar are called Vintage Vitolas and are available in three sizes. An HPH 2—2.5, it is one of the best of the "new breed" of cigar brands, but then, it is made by the same expert blenders and rollers who make the great Romeo y Julieta, so what else could you expect?

Fuego Eterno — (Dominican Republic) A strong HPH 2.5 cigar whose name, appropriately enough, means "eternal fire." Made with a Dominican filler and binder and a Connecticut shade wrapper.

Galiano — (Dominican Republic) A very pleasant and mild cigar (HPH 1.5—2) with Dominican filler and binder and Connecticut shade wrapper. It has been made since 1992 and is quite popular in the Caribbean area. This cigar was first imported into the U.S. in 1996 and is made in eight sizes.

Gallaher — (Holland) One of the world's major manufacturers of European-style non-humidified cigars, utilizing primarily Java, Sumatra, and Cameroon tobaccos.

Garcia y Vega — (United States) Named after the two Cuban families who started the brand in New York during the late 19th century. At first it was only known locally, but then, after moving the operation to Tampa, the cigar took off nationally. Today it is made in Alabama by machine, and offers a choice of four different wrappers: Connecticut, Mexican in Candela and Natural, and a Mexican Maduro wrapper that was introduced in 1993. The Garcia y Vega incorporates some of the best Mexican grown Sumatra in their cigars. It is a difficult cigar to categorize, as it is one of the few that falls in the twilight zone between a mass market and a premium cigar.

Garo — (Dominican Republic) Conceived by a chiropractor named Garo Bouldoukian, this non-bone crusher is a relaxed and tasty HPH 2, with DR filler, binder and Connecticut shade wrapper.

Gispert — (Cuba) An old name, noted for its mildness. Today, it is one of the new Havanas in which every shape is completely machine made.

Gispert — (Nicaragua) A Cuban brand once made in Jamaica and now being made in Nicaragua for select tobacconists in the U.S..

Griffin's — (Dominican Republic) Named after a famous nightclub in Geneva. The nightclub's owner began achieving a fair amount of fame, not only for his popular establishment, but also for the special cigars that he had made for his patrons. It was only natural that soon the Griffin cigar would transcend the shoreline of Lac Léman. Originally a medium-light taste, the Griffin's blend was updated in 1995 and improved to appeal to a slightly spicier palate. As a result, the Robusto has become one of my favorite "sundown cigars." There are two to three different tobaccos in the Dominican filler, depending on the size and taste of each individual cigar, and a Dominican binder and Connecticut wrapper are used for the complete line. To complement this new blend, two new sizes have been added, a 5 x 43 No. 500 and the aforementioned 5 x 50 Robusto. More are sure to come.

H. Upmann — (Cuba) In case you've always wondered what the H. stood for, this cigar was started in 1844 by Herman Upmann, a European banker who loved Havana cigars so much, he quit his job at the bank, moved to Cuba, and started his own brand. In its heyday, the H. Upmann Cigar Factory produced more than 200 different sizes. During the pre-Castro years of this century, the H. Upmann brand was owned by the respected Menendez and Garcia families. The original factory is still in operation, although now additional brands besides H. Upmann are produced there. As one of the oldest continuously produced cigars in Cuba, the H. Upmann has a deep, earthy flavor that seems to come directly from the richest topsoil of the Vuelta Abajo itself. It is one of the all-time great Havanas, with a pleasant medium strength HPH reading of 2.

H. Upmann — (Dominican Republic) A consistent classic among cigar smokers, even though up until 1985, some cigars were machine bunched (they became totally handmade by 1987). And starting in 1990, the wrapper was gradually switched from Cameroon to Indonesian leaf. Burt Reynolds is no stranger to the Upmann 2000, nor are countless other cigarmen who have made this the most popular shape in the line. All H. Upmanns have a very pleasant but definite undertaste of sweetness. For years I had a theory that this was because the cigar was made on the same site where a sugar cane plantation once stood. However, upon personal investigation in La Romana, where the Dominican H. Upmanns are handmade, I found there was no correlation; the tobaccos used in this cigar — a blend of Olor and Cuban seed Piloto Cubano with a Santo Domingo — are grown elsewhere on the island. So much for theories. It's a great cigar anyway, a 2 to 2.5 on the HPH. Worth investigating, if you like small ring-sized cigars, is the new Chairman's Reserve, a 7 x 38 curlyhead that duplicates the special cigars that entrepreneurial businessman (and chairman of Consolidated Cigar Corporation, the company that makes H. Upmann) Ron Perelman smokes. Also available in this new range will be a Torpedo, Robusto, Churchill, and Double Corona. These limited edition cigars, which first came out in the summer of 1996, are only sold through Dunhill. They feature a Dominican filler, Indonesian binder, and a Connecticut wrapper. As a final matter of interest, Upmann has one of the largest selections of humidified tubed cigars, with 5 different varieties and 6 variations.

Habana Gold — (Honduras) A medium-range (HPH 2) cigar with a dual personality in the form of black and white bands. The black band came out first and signifies an Indonesian-grown Sumatra wrapper; the white band is a Cuban seed Nicaraguan wrapper. Black or white, both bands surround a Cuban seed Honduran and Nicaraguan filler and Nicaraguan binder. Introduced in 1993, the name of this cigar was inspired by the Cuban seed that is "mined" from the ground and is as precious as you-know-what.

Habanica — (Nicaragua) A true "puro," with all Nicaraguan components grown from Havana seed in the wonderful rich soil of the Jalapa Valley and made in Condega. The name comes from a compilation of two words: Habana and Nicaragua. It starts out a little coarse at HPH 2.5 but about ten minutes into the smoke it settles down to an HPH 2 with a hefty smoothness and a pointedly sweet undertaste. A great cocktail cigar, if you happen to be drinking bourbon.

Hamilton — (Dominican Republic) Thespian George Hamilton, star and producer of such hits as *Love At First Bite* and *Zorro, The Gay Blade*, has had a lifelong love affair with...cigars! So it was only natural that this talented actor and perpetuator of The Eternal Tan would eventually come out with his own brand. Basically a slightly augmented Upmann blend, the Hamilton is available in no less than 16 different shapes. The George III (a Pyramid) is hearty and robust, an HPH 2.5; the Robusto is a medium HPH 2; the specially aged Churchill Reserve is extremely mild and pleasant. First introduced at Hamilton's Wine Bar in Beverly Hills in 1996, these cigars have gradually spread throughout California and soon may go national. And don't be surprised to see a Honduran and perhaps even a Nicaraguan Hamilton in the very near future. Like its namesake, the Hamilton cigar, in all its roles, is a very refined and social smoke.

Hamlet — (Great Britain) A popular and mild tasting British small cigar. Easily found in pubs. Does not smoke well when accidentally dropped in beer. I discovered this through personal investigation and observation.

Havana Classico — (United States) Made in Miami.

Havana Reserve — (Honduras) A cigar that is purportedly aged for five years.

Havanitos — (Austria) An extremely popular European cigarillo, with a Java wrapper, and a filler blend of Indonesia, Brazil and Havana leaf. Widely distributed throughout Austria, France, in fact, most of Europe. Easily recognized in its gold colored tin, it is medium mild in flavor.

Hav-A-Tampa — (United States) This extremely popular little cigar had its beginnings around WWII, when the company started out with Tampa Nuggets and Tampa Straights. They became enormously popular. Then, in the late 1940s, a Tampa fellow by the name of Gene Pride developed that famous wooden tip. The handy shape and unique self-contained wooden mouthpiece made the Hav-a-Tampa an instant hit with smokers. Today, Hav-a-Tampa is manufactured in a fully automated factory.

Henri Winterman — (Holland) This brand helped popularize the affordable small, European-style cigar in most of the world. Their Cafe Creme is one of the most popular sizes.

Henry Clay — (Dominican Republic) Named after the 18th century U.S. senator and statesman who dominated the Whig Party in the 1820s through the 1830s, whose platform was to transform the U.S. from an agricultural bartering nation into a country that relied more on economic principles. Who says you can't learn history from cigars? Like its namesake, this brand is an unsung hero among those who know affordable cigars and like a full, semi-heavy taste. Originally a Cuban brand, the label and band have remained unchanged over the years, except for the obvious omission of "Havana" in both word and contents. Today's cigar is a tasty combination of long leaf Dominican filler complimented by a Dominican binder. A slightly stronger blend is used for Europe. The Connecticut broadleaf wrapper is not the prettiest in the world, but it is made of choice tobacco, nonetheless. It is purposely made "out of round," in a style that was popular many years ago. This cigar comes in three sizes, of which the Brevas a la Conserva is my favorite. The HPH 2.5 Henry Clay cigar is well worth investigating for a change-of-pace affordable smoke.

Hirschsprung — (Denmark) A delicious Dutch-type tubed cigar that is both full sized and full-bodied. It incorporates Brazil and Havana tobaccos in its blend, and is made by Nobel.

House of Lords — (Canada) A Havana-blend, short-filler machine-made cigar that is produced for the Canadian market.

Hoja de Oro — (Mexico) Contains both Mexican and Cuban seed San Andrés tobaccos in the filler, a Moron binder and a wonderful Mexican-grown Sumatra wrapper.

Hoyo de Casa — (Mexico) Made in both natural and Maduro wrappers in the San Andrés region of Mexico.

Hoyo de Monterrey — (Cuba) One of the most famous of Cuban brands, Hoyo de Monterrey was originated by José Gener (whose name is still on the box) in either 1865 or 1867 — the records vary. Nonetheless, this was one of the first of the "brand name" cigars to be made in Cuba. Prior to that time, most cigars were sold by shape and size, without trademarked names. The name Hoyo (which means valley or low spot) de Monterrey was inspired by the San Juan y Martinez Monterrey valley plantation, which was located in the Vuelta Abajo's Pinar del Rio region of Cuba, where the cigar's tobacco was grown. The flavor of today's Hoyo is quite a bit different than that of the original brand, being lighter and much more subtle in taste. (As an aside, it is a bit ironic that the Honduran version of this brand seems to carry a bit more "meat" in its flavor, while the Cuban brand is now a medium strength cigar.) The Hoyo de Monterrey brand also carries a sub-brand (much like the Honduran's Excalibur), which is simply called "Le Hoyo," which is listed elsewhere in this chapter. It is a much headier cigar than the regular line, which hovers around the HPH 2—2.5 ranges, depending on size.

Hoyo de Monterrey — (Honduras) The Cuban version of this cigar dropped from sight almost immediately after the Cuban embargo, as all available supplies were quickly snatched up. But by 1963, this hearty cigar resurfaced as a handmade Honduran product that continued to be made with Havana leaf, which had been judiciously stored in the U.S. since before the embargo. The Honduran Hoyo de Monterrey "made with real Havana leaf" boxes and cigars could still be found in tobacconists' humidors as late as 1971, and I have vivid memories of greedily buying these cigars and squirreling them away for months at a time. It was the closest thing to brand loyalty that I ever knew. Today this richly, satisfying cigar is blended with Nicaragua, Honduras, and Santo Domingo Cuban seed filler, flavored with a Connecticut binder, and topped off with a superb Ecuadorian-grown Sumatra wrapper. In addition, the special Excalibur sub-brand of the Hoyo de Monterrey is one of the finest after dinner cigars on the market, especially

269

the Number 1, which I buy by the box. And for a quick change of pace smoke, try their miniatures, which come packed 20 to a pocket-sized tin.

Hugo Cassar — (Dominican Republic) A series of cigars named after the importer. Comes in two versions: the Diamond Line, with Dominican filler and binder and Connecticut shade wrapper, and the Private Line, a Dominican puro, whose most intriguing offering is the double wrapped barber shop pole cigar called the Mystic, a rather mild concoction which unfortunately, does not taste as good as it looks.

Hugo Cassar — (Honduras) Includes a Diamond and Private Collection made with Ecadorian wrappers.

Indian Cigars — (Honduras) If you are into vintage motorcycles, you will recognize the name of this excellent cigar. Originally inspired by the 1921 Indian Motorcycle Company (one of the partners in this venture, Phillip Zanghi III, president of the Indian TabacCo., is a recognized authority on Indian bikes), this cigar is a spin-off of that famous name. Although the motorcycle company no longer exists, the cigar does. It is available in a variety of Native American configurations: Warrior (Lonsdale), Arrow (Panetela), Chief (Double Corona), Boxer — how'd that get in there? (Robusto), and the appropriately named Teepee (Pyramid). Blends vary by size, with Honduran being augmented by a Nicaraguan base. A Connecticut wrapper is found on the Chief and the Warrior. The Teepee, Boxer, and Arrow sport an Ecuadorian Sumatra leaf. Long leaf and handmade, these are fun cigars to smoke, well constructed and economical, with strengths in the HPH 2—2.5 range.

Irasema — (Brazil) A non-humidified cigar from the 1970s and brought back in 1995. It is allegedly named after an Indian maiden with a legend much too contrived and complicated to print here or in any other book. A rather mild cigar, an HPH 1.5, but it goes well with certain American beers (see Chapter 7).

J. Cortes — (Belgium) Made in Belgium in a modern, sprawling blue and white factory that matches the colors of their banded and tubed high-end cigars, the J. Cortes brand is made by the Vandermarliere family and is a relatively new entry to the world market, even though

270

the company itself has been making cigars since the 1920s. Made of 100% tobacco, these mild tasting cigars (a pleasant HPH 2) range in size from the Mino cigarillo all the way up to the 140mm x 15.1mm Longfiller. Their tubed High Class is one of my favorites. Up until recently, the Vandermarliere family, one of the few family-operated cigar making businesses left in Belgium, was only known for their less expensive machine made Neos, Nic, Taf, and Don Carlos cigars. Tobaccos used in their various machine made cigars (depending on the brand)) include leaf from Cuba, Java, Sumatra, Paraguay, Brazil, and Cameroon. Approximately 220 billion cigars are produced annually, of which 75% are exported, primarily to Germany and France, as well as approximately eighteen other markets, including America.

John Aylesbury — (Germany) One of the most renowned and widespread brands in Germany. Not really one factory, but a consortium of 42 tobacconists throughout Germany as well as numerous factories and importers who have assembled a vast array of cigars from Holland, Germany, Honduras, the Dominican — just about anywhere cigars are made, as long as there is quality. Most are made by the various factories under the John Aylesbury name. A few are now being imported to the United States.

José Benito — (Dominican Republic) Basically a Central American Connecticut seed binder with an Indonesian wrapper and a blend of Olor and Cuban seed Dominican fillers. It is right between the Dominican Romeo y Julieta and the Pléiades in taste. A good medium-strength cigar that has it origins with the Cuban tobacco growers of long ago. The Benito family moved from Spain to Cuba in the mid 1800s and soon became one of the largest exporters of Havana tobacco. Eventually they made their way to the Dominican Republic in 1941 and became one of the first cigar makers there. Today the company is run by the namesake's direct descendants.

José Llopis — (Panama) A long filler cigar made with a unique blend of tobaccos from Honduras, Panama, Dominican Republic and Ecuador. Priced right, this is an excellent cigar for the money. The Llopis Gold is their top of the line, and its gold band and slightly more refined taste sets it apart. You are more likely to find this cigar in the midwestern United States, although it does show up in other parts of the country. Worth searching out if you've never smoked a Panamanian cigar.

José Martí Cubre Libre — (Dominican Republic) A Dominican filler, Mexican binder and Connecticut wrapper. A very light, transparent tasting HPH 1.5. The band looks like a Punch, but this is definitely not a Punch-tasting cigar.

José Melendi — (United States) José Melendi was a master cigar blender from Cuba who established a factory that handmade clear Havana cigars in New York. Eventually, he decided to create a cigar using his own name. In time, Melendi became a consultant to other cigar manufacturers. Today, this cigar is machine made of imported long filler, with a broadleaf binder and Cameroon wrapper. However, it has been discontinued as of 1997.

Joya de Canarias — (Canary Islands) Introduced in August 1990. Shade grown wrapper, long leaf filler.

Joya de Nicaragua — (Nicaragua) This interesting cigar was the direct result of Cuban expatriates emigrating to Nicaragua right after the U.S. embargo. Here, they discovered soil very close to their own back in Cuba. They made their discovery known and consequently, Joya de Nicaragua was created in 1965 by General Samoza and his partners. Ever since then, this cigar has experienced tremendous rises and falls in its imagery. Its name means "Jewel of Nicaragua," and for a great many years, it was one of the most consistently great tasting cigars on the market, although it has never been as well known as it deserves to be. Part of this problem is with the country of origin. The Nicaraguan revolution of 1979, and its resultant confiscation of the Joya factory did not help much. Nor did a subsequent firebombing of its factory, or the U.S. embargo of 1985-90, during which time the last available supplies of Joya de Nicaraguan cigars were rapidly snatched up. After all, it was a delicious cigar, utilizing tobaccos from Nicaragua's most fertile valleys, Esteli for the Connecticut seed wrappers and Jalapa for the Havana seed binder and filler. Unfortunately, after the embargo was lifted in 1990, quality and

consistency began to suffer. But then, it must be difficult rolling a cigar with any consistency when bullets are
ricocheting off your worktable. Today, there is a delicate balance in Nicaragua between the Sandinistas and
the Contras and a new government promises reforms.
The factories have been turned back to the workers and
changes are supposedly under way. But tobacco growers still do not get paid until the end of each year and
money problems always mean production problems.
Whether the Joya de Nicaragua will ever regain its excellent quality on a full-time basis is still unknown.
However, as a matter of interest, just before the first
U.S. edition of this book was published in 1993, I was
able to smoke two Joya de Nicaragua cigars, as well as
a "Habano Maduro," that were all made in 1991. They
were superb, as was a very dark and rich tasting Costa
Rican Maduro that I smoked shortly after the fourth
U.S. printing of *The Ultimate Cigar Book*. And in the
summer of 1996 I smoked a current batch of Joya's that
were as good as any cigar ever produced by that country. In fact, I immediately went out and bought some
boxes to age. These cigars feature a new blend that is
not as strong as in the past but are very flavorful and
refined. There is also a new Maduro Delux, made with
a Costa Rican wrapper in three large ring sizes that are
worthy of exploring. So the tobacco and the skill are
still there. Now all the country has to do is get rid of its
political problems so that we can start enjoying its cigars on a regular basis.

Juan Clemente — (Dominican Republic) One of the all
time great premium cigars of the new generation, and
one that can be aged extremely well. It is also a bit of a
black sheep among the Dominicans, as you shall see. The
Juan Clemente brand was launched on April 1, 1982 in
Switzerland and France, but it wasn't introduced to the
U.S. until the autumn of 1985. Today, these cigars are
also sold in other parts of Europe, as well as Australia
and Japan. Like the ads say, there really is a Juan
Clemente, except that his name is Jean Clement and
he is French. But he had become so enamored with the
Dominican romance and expertise of cigar making, that
he Latinized his brand's name. Prior to creating his
much respected cigar, Jean — or Juan — spent many

273

years in Latin America and in 1975 he realized the cigar-
making potential of the DR. An entrepreneur by nature,
he established a small factory in Santiago, but unlike
most cigar makers, he purposely located it outside of
the Free Zone. Because he is not within this export-ori-
ented, lower-taxed zone, Juan Clemente is one of the few
Dominican-made cigars that can be sold to tourists visiting the DR. That, plus the fact that the factory employs fewer than fifteen rollers (up from ten back in the
early 90s), makes it hardly surprising that these cigars
are occasionally in short supply. But by the same token,
the relatively small output of the Juan Clemente workers means that the factory can often afford to buy small
quantities of the very best Santiago Domingo leaf, tobaccos that would normally be passed up by the larger
companies because there are not enough bales to meet
their production schedules. Juan Clemente makes about
450,000 cigars a year, which is not a large amount by
cigar standards. Aside from not being in the Free Zone,
another quirk of this brand is that they are packed 24
cigars to the box, because Jean feels that the standard
25 cigars in a box "looks wrong." Also unique to Juan
Clemente is the fact that there is no band, in the traditional sense, which is usually located about one-sixth
of the way down from the head of the cigar. Instead, it
is the foot of every Juan Clemente cigar that is banded,
so that the tuck end is protected from the moment it
leaves the worker's bench until it is finally graced by a
flame in the consumer's hands. A final observation:
there are no less than four different tobaccos used in the
Juan Clemente filler blend, a notable number of varieties
of leaf in a single cigar. The filler contains the hearty
Ligero and a smaller percentage of Seco tobaccos, with
a Dominican binder and a Connecticut shade wrapper.
The completed cigars are then aged for a full six months,
all of which combines to produce a 2.5 on the Highly Prejudiced HackerScale, and if you age them for three to
five years as I have done, you can boost the taste up to
a full-bodied 3. On July 1, 1992, Juan Clemente introduced his first vintage cigars, called the Club Selection
(see my comments in Chapter 4). Only two rollers out
of the fifteen are allowed to make these extra-premium
smokes, which consist of five shapes, including a new
6 x 54/30 Torpedo. The Club Selection has gold foil cov-

ering the end of the tuck. Frankly, the initial cigars were a bit rougher in the filler recipe than I would like, but they have since been smoothed down. For my money, I much prefer the standard Classic line, especially the larger ring sizes such as the Rothschild, the Churchill, and (when you can find them) the Gigante. Newly added to the standard Classic line is the Mini, which might very well be the smallest handrolled cigar in the world. Whether Classic or Club Selection, these are very individualistic cigars, made by a very individualistic individual. You might also want to search out the Por Matamor, a very special cigar made in an entirely different factory and in very limited numbers; it is a rich, creamy HPH 2.

Juan López - (Cuba) A light, almost aromatic cigar — unusual for a Havana — that is clearly aimed at bringing the non-Havana smoker into the fold. This is a very old brand, whose full name is "Flor de Juan López," now being made with a decidedly new blend of tobaccos.

Julia Marlowe — (Dominican Republic) Introduced in 1991, this cigar features one of the most elegant of the "new breed" bands and packaging. That is because the previous owner of the brand spent virtually all of his money in creating a glorious four-color persona with gold embossing. It was truly a tribute to the 19th century cigar label art. Except that this was the 20th century. So when all the artwork bills came in, there wasn't enough money left to produce the cigar. A few years later, the name, bands and labels were bought by an enterprising fellow who knew good cigars. The result was a cigar created especially to fulfill the image of the brand (usually it works the other way around). This mild tasting cigar (an HPH 1.5—2), which is sold throughout the U.S. and in Europe, utilizes Ecuadorian shade grown Connecticut seed wrapper seasoned with four different types of Dominican filler and a Dominican binder. A very economically priced cigar, offered in a variety of shapes, for which you'll probably be getting more than your money's worth in the band alone.

Kentucky Cheroots — (United States) The name says it all; that's what these stogies are. Made of 100% Kentucky and Tennessee tobacco, so maybe they should be called Kentucky/Tennessee Cheroots. A dark fired-cured dry "seegar" that's jest right for firing up after a hard day plowin' the back forty.

King Edward — (United States) One of the most popular Christmas gifts you can give in England is a box of King Edward cigars. The brand, of course, pays tribute to Queen Victoria's son, who first uttered those famous words shortly after his succession to the throne, "Gentlemen, you may smoke." At one time, this was the best selling mass-market cigar in the world. Still being made, although now by machine, in Georgia. An identical short-filler cigar is also made in Canada for exclusive distribution in that country.

Knockando — (Dominican Republic) I debated whether or not to put this cigar in this chapter, as it tends to come and go with the seasons. It is named after the peaty malt whiskey distilled in the famed Speyside region of Scotland. Like the malt whiskey, the cigars (when they are being made and distributed) carry a rich, earthy flavor. With a Connecticut wrapper and Dominican binder and filler (at least, the last time I looked) they are an interesting addition to our cigar compendium. I list them here because I would not be surprised if they resurfaced again, although their composition may have changed.

La Aurora — (Dominican Republic) One of the very few cigars that was being made in the DR before the Cuban embargo. It was named after General Trujillo's daughter, Aurora. The quality of the recent cigars is decidedly better than the original blend, although the last ones I smoked were medium strong, with a heavily textured, non-oily wrapper. These HPH 2.5 cigars have a Dominican filler and binder topped of with a Cameroon wrapper. By the way, if anyone should ask, La Aurora means, "the dawn." It was also the name of the first Cuban newspaper written expressly for working class cigar makers in 1866. How's that for cigar trivia?

La Corona — (Cuba) Started in Cuba in 1844.

La Diligencia — (Honduras) Hand rolled in five shapes. A very mild tasting cigar (HPH 1.5) with Nicaraguan, Dominican and Honduran filler, Dominican binder, and Ecuadorian wrapper; a Maduro version uses Mexican leaf.

La Diva — (Dominican Republic) Formerly known as El Sublimado (see additional notes under that heading). Gone is the metal tube, replaced now by a glass tube for single cigars and wooden gift boxes in three and twenty-cigar sizes. Even the cognac has been changed; the filler is now aged in thirty year old "Selection des Angeles" (Selection of the Angels) Pierre Ferand Cognac. Not inexpensive, it has a heavy-handed HPH 2.5 strength and does make for an interesting alternative for those who would rather smoke their cognac than drink it.

La Escepción — (Cuba) This once famous old brand was started by José Gener, the same enterprising individual whose name we also find on the Hoyo de Monterrey and whose JG initials can be found on some of the Cuban and Honduran Punch bands. Only a Panetela and a Gran Corona remain in the line. Both use the same blends of tobaccos, which is extremely strong.

La Finca — (Nicaragua) A "puro" handmade cigar with all-Nicaraguan filler, binder and wrapper. Introduced in the winter of 1993. This was one of the very first cigars to be made after the elections, when Violete Chamorro became president of Nicaragua.

La Flor de Cano — (Cuba) A relatively new brand on the market. With its sweet, mild taste, it is a cigar designed to please the new smoker just entering the Havana ranks.

La Flor Dominicana — (Dominican Republic) Formerly known as Los Libertadores (see listing under that name).

La Fontana — (Honduras) A vintage cigar made in the same factory as Baccarat. Introduced in 1992, it has a Connecticut shade wrapper that has been aged for three years, with a Mexican binder and Honduran filler. It is named after Sal Fontana, the importer. Rich and slightly sweetened. The cigar, not Sal.

La Gloria Cubana — (Cuba) One of the most famous of the old time Cuban brands, seeing its yellow band with the Cubana señorita is always like meeting an old friend. The cigar was not produced for many years, during which time a Tampa cigar, featuring the identical band, was started up and has since made tremendous inroads among American smokers. However, the Havana brand has been resurrected, and the new La Gloria Cubana is now a much more mellow, entry-level Havana than its predecessor ever was. In fact, it is one of the few Havanas you can smoke in the morning without the need of a heavy breakfast beforehand.

La Gloria Cubana — (United States) Not to be confused with the famous Havana brand of this same name, even though the bands are practically identical (enough to fool a collector at a recent antique show). The cigar is handmade in the "Little Havana" section of Miami, Florida by the same company that originally brought the brand to the United States after Castro took power. However, in order to meet demand some production is now being transferred to the Dominican Republic, in a factory with 42 rollers. Affordably priced, this medium-flavored cigar boasts a Nicaraguan, Dominican, and Ecuadorian filler blend, Nicaraguan binder, and an Ecuador-grown Sumatra wrapper. These cigars rate a 2 to 2.5 on the Highly Prejudiced HackerScale, with a special affinity towards the pyramid shape, especially in Maduro.

La Herencia — (United States) Once in a while a new cigar finally comes out that is worth the word "new" and adds something to the cigar smoking hobby. This is one of those cigars. La Herencia means "The Heritage," in Spanish and it is the creation of a Miami roller named Roberto Ramirez, who, for thirty years before the revolution, was one of Cuba's *torcedors* in the Santa Clara factory. This is a full-bodied cigar and comes with a Dominican, Nicaraguan and Ecuadorian filler blend, a Cameroon binder (a rarity in itself), and either a Connecticut shade or an Ecuadorian EMS wrapper. But, some of the Ecuadorian wrapper is also available in a chocolaty red "rosado" wrapper, which traditionally is some of the oiliest and most flavorful tobacco one can hope for. I've only seen consistently superb examples of this wrapper on a very few cigars (the Honduran Punch being one of them), but this new cigar exhibits the rosado color and flavor in all its glory. Not a beginner's cigar, but one that demands a hearty meal beforehand to lay a base for the rich flavor it offers.

La Hoja Selecta — (United States) Originally a Havana brand that was only sold in Cuba. Today it is made in Tampa with Dominican, Brazilian, and Mexican filler, Dominican binder, and a Connecticut shade wrapper. The cigar enjoys a small following in various tobacco shops across the country.

La Invicta — (Honduras) A handmade cigar that was initially made in Jamaica but is now being produced in Honduras. From what I can tell, it concentrates on the larger ring sizes.

La Maximiliana — (Honduras) First brought out in 1996, with a Nicaraguan filler, Honduran binder, and Connecticut seed Honduran wrapper. Available in three 44 ring sizes.

Lamb's Club — (United States) Started out as a private label cigar for The Lamb's Club, a theatrical association in New York during World War II. Still being made by the Finck Cigar Company of San Antonio, Texas.

La Paz — (Holland) Famous for their "Wilde" Cigarillos and small cigar brands; in tobacco trade parlance, wild means a ragged foot of tobacco, as opposed to one that is smoothly trimmed. The tobaccos are from Cuba, Brazil and Indonesia.

La Plata — (U.S.) Although their leaf comes from the Dominican Republic, Honduras, Ecuador and Mexico, all cigars are hand made right in the heart of downtown Los Angeles. Victor Migenes,Sr. started this "neighborhood" cigar making shop in 1947. His son, Victor, continues the tradition and has now taken the brand national, although a large portion of sales are still done via a telephone for orders shipped all over the world. Due to its proximity to Hollywood and the fact that the four rollers in the store's tiny "back room *galeria*" can roll virtually any size of standard or *figurado* cigar imaginable, La Plata is often called upon to create customized smokables for flicks such as *Naked Gun 2½*, *Die Hard 2*, *The Flintstones*, and *The Quick And The Dead*. In fact, it was Victor, Sr. who first rolled a "Hacker Special" for me as a young advertising executive, newly arrived in L.A. many years ago. Back then, I could only afford one cigar a week, so every Friday, Señor Migenes would gather up all the leftover tobacco and roll me what must have been the world's first Churchill Gigante. For a special treat from La Plata's current line, try their 5½ x 54 Hercules, with its Dominican filler and Connecticut shade wrapper. Because all La Plata cigars are freshly rolled, it is best to let them age for a few weeks before smoking them.

La Primadora — (Honduras) What was once a Cuban brand is now a Honduran "puro." A dusty, coarse wrapper that provides a dusty, coarse flavor. HPH 2.5, this is a good, rough tasting campfire cigar.

La Prueba — (Mexico) A popular cigar in Mexico, which takes its name from the factory in which it is made.

La Real — (Honduras) Introduced in 1996, it has a Nicaraguan filler, Honduran binder and a Nicaraguan wrapper. It comes in three sizes, all with 50 ring gauge.

Las Cabrillas — (Honduras) A well-made boxed cigar introduced in 1993. A nice sturdy smoke with an HPH of 2—2.5 Really rich and creamy, like a hot fudge sundae right from the first puff. Definitely a sundown cigar, great with steak or bourbon or...a hot fudge sundae.

Le Hoyo — (Cuba) An offshoot of the Hoyo de Monterrey brand, started in the 1970s to answer the call for a stronger cigar from the all-important (to Cubatabaco) Swiss market. It has now gained a loyal following in other countries as well. An HPH 2.5.

León Jimenes — (Dominican Republic/Honduras) Made with a Dominican filler and binder and a Connecticut wrapper. An HPH 2.

Licenciados — (Dominican Republic) One might wonder at the wisdom of having a cigar with a name that few people can pronounce, but in pre-Castro Cuba, Licenciados was a very popular brand. In Spanish Licenciados means "attorney," and it is a fair guess as to which group of professionals this cigar was originally targeted. Selling for a very affordable fifteen cents apiece in those early years, this cigar was only available in Cuba and was never exported. But times — and costs — change. Since 1991, Licenciados has been made in the Dominican Republic. It is currently offered in twelve different shapes, five of which feature a Connecticut broadleaf maduro wrapper. The rest of the line features a Connecticut shade wrapper, with Dominican filler and binder. This produces a rather refined, delicious and spicy flavor in the HPH 2 range, which, to my tastes, makes it perfect for late morning and early afternoon. In fact, I often make it my designated "daytime cigar" and usually keep some in my car humidor. You'll find these cigars in the U.S, Canada, and France. They also make a "Segundo," which means "seconds," and which may sometimes be easier to find than the "firsts," which are always in great demand.

Lord Beaconsfield — (United States) Was originally made in Havana for the British market. Later, the factory moved to Tampa. Today, it is a competitively priced machine-made cigar, utilizing short filler and a homogenized binder. Its Honduran filler blend gives it a full flavor.

Los Libertadores — (Dominican Republic) A real freedom fighter's cigar introduced in 1995. Contains a Dominican filler and binder and a Connecticut shade wrapper, blended to encompass the full range of tastes, from medium to heavy: Los Macheteros and Los Exilados are full flavored (HPH 2.5); Los Insurrectos is medium to full (HPH 2—2.5); and Los Mambises are mild to medium (HPH 1.5—2). Name changed to La Flor Dominicana in 1996.

Macabi — (United States) Made in Miami by Juan Sosa and available in seven sizes.

Macanudo — (Jamaica/Dominican Republic) One of the most popular cigars in America, the Macanudo started out as a Jamaican cigar in 1868, where it was made by a Cuban-owned factory. In fact, this famous cigar was originally the name of the largest selling size being made by the Havana Punch for British export. The Punch Macanudo gained an identity of its own during World War II, when Cuba was no longer permitted to sell their cigars to England due to a U.S. dollar embargo by Great Britain. Consequently, the five major Havana factories in Jamaica (a British colony) decided to legally make cigars for the U.K. Because the Punch Macanudo was the most popular size in Great Britain, the Cuban/Jamaican factory decided to spin off the name and create a separate Macanudo brand for their Jamaican-made cigar. By the end of the war, Jamaica was selling fifteen million cigars to England. In 1960, pressure from Castro forced the Cuban owners of Macanudo to divest themselves of their famous cigar-making operations, which were subsequently sold to a

281

Jamaican concern. In 1964 the Macanudo brand was again sold, this time to a company in Tampa, which was eventually acquired by one of the industry leaders, General Cigar Company. Under General's guidance, the Macanudo soared to new prominence. From the very beginning of its reintroduction to American smokers in the 1970s, Macanudo quickly became the best-selling cigar in the U.S. It was the first Jamaican cigar introduced to American smokers on a wide scale, and it started the trend away from Canary Islands cigars. Although it has historically been a Jamaican cigar since being spun off as a separate brand, since 1983 a number of Macanudos have been made in the Dominican Republic, in General Cigar's Santiago factory. It is virtually impossible to tell the Jamaican and Dominican cigars apart, as the exact tobaccos, recipes and aging processes are used in both countries. Which is why the Macanudo has such a great reputation for consistency. In fact, the only way to tell in which country the cigar is made is to turn the box over and look at the stamp on the bottom. The reason for this dual-nationality of the Macanudo involves the sometimes shaky political climate of Jamaica (after all, we would not want to be without our Macanudos should trade with Jamaica suddenly become interrupted), and the fact that the DR, like Jamaica, is now a part of the Lomé Agreement, which means a more favorable tax situation. There are still more Macanudos being handmade in Jamaica than in the DR, although that situation could eventually change. Because Jamaica is a crown colony, with valuable tax credits built up, most of the Macanudos made there are shipped to England as well as to Europe. Almost all of the Dominican-made Macanudos, however, are exported to the United States. Whether made in Jamaica or the DR, all Macanudos use Jamaican, Dominican and Mexican filler, Mexican binder, and Connecticut shade wrapper. Macanudo tobaccos go through an aging process of two years, from harvest to finished cigar. After that, the cigars are aged for another four to eight weeks. Part of the reason for Macanudo's success is the variety of Connecticut wrappers that this brand offers to the smoker: Jade (Candela) is a greenish-brown wrapper with a very mild taste; Cafe (Natural) is the classic Connecticut, golden brown in color and grown

282

from the Hazelwood variety of Cuban seed; and finally, Maduro, a dark rich brown sweetness derived from Mexican leaf. Ranging from 1.5 to 2.5 on the Highly Prejudiced HackerScale (depending on size and wrapper), the Macanudo is a perfect everyday smoking companion. In addition to their regular line, there is also a Red Label variation, with a White Spot in the center of the band, which is sold exclusively in the Dunhill shops. But for an epicurean's delight, the most flavorful Macanudo of all is their Vintage Cabinet Selection, especially the Number 1 and 8 sizes (a Churchill and Robusto, respectively), which should be reserved for special occasions. Mild and creamy in flavor, they are among the most perfectly constructed of all cigars.

Marsh Wheeling — (United States) These cigars have changed little since they were first made by Mifflin M. Marsh in 1840 for riverboat passengers and overland pioneers heading west. M. Marsh & Sons sold their stogies four for a penny. They were a bargain even back then, and they quickly became popular. The long, thin cigars, which many likened to the spokes of a Conestoga wagon, haven't changed much today. Originally packed in shoe boxes and later in wooden containers, the factory eventually began making its own distinctive blue and gold box, which also hasn't changed much over the years. In fact, the big Marsh Stogies sign on the side of their five-story brick factory building has been a prominent fixture in Wheeling, West Virginia since the beginning of this century. About the only thing that has changed is the fact that these famous short filler stogies used to be handmade; now they are machine made. The company makes 13 different cigars. Depending on the type, Marsh Wheelings are made with Connecticut or Cameroon wrappers, homogenized leaf for binder, and filler grown in the Miami River Valley of Ohio and in Lancaster, PA. They are extremely mild in taste. More than half of their sales are in West Virginia, Ohio and Pennsylvania. Basically a mass-market cigar, there's still nothing wrong with lighting one up in hunting camp or even as an authentic accessory for western re-enactments. Considering that they haven't changed much in over 150 years, it isn't surprising to learn that Marsh Wheeling Stogies appeared in the movie, *How The West*

Was Won. It was a fitting tribute for a piece of American history that you can still smoke today.

Martinez y Cia — (United States) This is a cigar for those who want to smoke affordable Havanas in the U.S. In 1967, the factory purchased enough Havana tobacco from the Cuban crop of 1959 to make a special Havana Blend cigar. Today, Martinez y Cia Havana Blend is a short-filler, machine-made cigar with a Connecticut wrapper and imported Cuban seed and real Havana tobaccos; the filler is still made with 20% Havana! The HPH 2 cigar is a little rough around the edges and it becomes intense as it sees the end nearing. But through it all you can still taste a hint of the old pre-Castro leaf that lies hidden beneath the surface. Why don't more people know about this?

Match Play — (Dominican Republic) Connecticut light shade wrapper, Olor Dominicano binder, and a Cuban seed and native Dominican filler. Most golfers are cigar smokers, so it should not be surprising that an aficionado of both, a tobacco professional (who also happens to be a scratch golfer) named Thomas Whitaker would eventually combine these two great pastimes to create this wonderfully mild and flavorful smoke that is perfect on the greens or off. Match Play is named after the original game of golf, in which each hole is a game in itself, and the total number of "wins per hole" determines the overall champion. Each of the six shapes are named after a famous golf course: Cypress (4¾ x 50); St. Andrews (6¼ x 43); Turnbery (6 x 50); Prestwick (6⅞ x 46); Olympic (7½ x 50; and Troon (7 x 36/54). If a line of small cigars were ever introduced, they would probably be named after miniature golf courses. This wonderful cigar with the great 1930-ish country duffer on the band starts out sweet, turns spicy and then remains steady with a flawless follow-through, just like the game it was named after. Par for this cigar is an HPH 2.

Medal of Honor — (Honduran) Made in three shapes, with Nicaraguan, Honduran and Dominican filler, Costa Rican binder and Ecuadorian wrapper. The Maduro version uses an Ecuadorian binder and a Costa Rican wrapper. A nice, quiet cigar that came out right at the beginning of the cigar renaissance and seems to be riding along quite well with it.

Meia-Coroa — (Portugal) Handmade in the Azores Islands, this smallish cigar is packed with a Havana, Dominican, and Brazilian filler, Java binder, and a Connecticut wrapper.

MiCubano — (Nicaragua) A powerhouse of a cigar, first unleashed in 1995. It thunders across your palate and doesn't let go. It is all Cuban seed Nicaraguan and comes in a stand-up cedar box that makes each MiCubano look like a miniature missile on a launching pad. Wash this HPH 3 cigar down with a beaker of 16-year-old Lagavulin malt whiskey or 100 proof Knob Creek small batch bourbon. Woof!

Mocambo — (Mexico) A little rough around the edges for American tastes, I find the Maduro version a perfect cigar for a hot summer night and a cold Pacífico *cerveza*.

Montebello — (Mexico) A fairly new cigar made in the same Tobaccos y Puros de San Andrés factory as the Cruz Real. Features San Andrés filler and binder with a Mexican-grown Sumatra seed wrapper.

Montecristo — (Cuba) A well respected, rich tasting cigar and one of the few Havanas in which all of the shapes, even the smallest, is completely made by hand. Because of its widespread recognition and fame, most smokers think the Montecristo brand is much older than it really is. (Actually, along with Cohiba, it is one of the few 20th century Cuban cigars that is still being produced.) Montecristo was started in 1934 by Garcia y Menendez, the same families who were then producing the famous H. Upmann cigar. In fact, when originally introduced, the cigar was called the H. Upmann Montecristo, but in 1935 the name was spun off as a separate brand for Great Britain so that it would not be confused with the regular line of H. Upmann Havanas. An enterprising fellow by the name of Jack Benham, a nephew of one of the importing company's directors, actually designed the art-nouveau Montecristo logo, which consists of six crossed swords forming a stylized triangle that was quite a shocking departure from the more traditional Victorian cigar logos still in use at that time. Originally sold exclusively by Dunhill, who gave it tremendous and well deserved exposure among serious cigar smokers the world over, the Montecristo quickly rose in prominence, partly due to its wonderfully re-fined taste and also because of the vast array of sizes that this brand offered (with the No. 2 being one of the all-time greats). The Montecristo A, which was first rolled in the 1970s, is still heralded as the most expensive cigar in the world (in Havana-less America that honor has now been handed over to the Davidoff Aniversario No. 1). By the end of the Cuban revolution, the Monte-cristo was irrefutably one of the very best thorough-breds in the Havana stables. Unfortunately, shortly after that, quality and taste began to slip, but thankfully, the cigar has again regained its image of excellence. For many cigar aficionados in Europe, it remains the hall-mark by which all other Havanas are judged. Because of this prominence, however, the Montecristo is also widely counterfeited. But for those who have ever smoked a genuine "Monte," the taste and aroma are unmistak-able. Once, while visiting the Partagás Factory in Cuba, I was given an unbanded cigar to smoke. I lit it up; the combination of the smooth, semi-rich taste and HPH 2.5 strength was like a calling card. "A Montecristo!" I immediately exclaimed, but not without some trepida-tion, as the Montecristo had always been made in the H. Upmann factory. A representative from Cubatabaco nodded in confirmation, and then told me they were making this famed cigar under license. Such is the un-mistakable character of this great cigar. Its name, as you might have guessed, is taken from the Alexandre Dumas novel, *The Count of Monte Cristo*, of whom Dumas wrote of his famous character, "I think he is an excel-lent host, that he has traveled much, and...he has some excellent cigars." Indeed, acquaintances may say the very same thing about a man today who chooses to keep this classic brand stocked in his humidor.

Montecristo — (Dominican Republic) In 1993-94, an all-new Dominican-made Montecristo cigar was launched by Consolidated Cigar Corporation as a continuation of one of the most famous brand names in cigar smoking history. For many years prior to this new cigar's ap-pearance, a limited number of Dominican-made Mon-tecristos (roughly 10,000 to 15,000 cigars), with a taste identical to the H. Upmann, had been distributed to a few select tobacconists in the United States. This newest cigar, however, is made with an entirely different blend, featuring Dominican grown Cuban seed filler and binder tobaccos matched with a Connecticut shade wrapper, all of which are substantially less heady (but no less full-flavored) than the Cuban version and spiced with a dark Connecticut shade wrapper. Connoisseurs will also appreciate the fact that the Dominican Montecristo is an aged cigar, which adds depth to its rich-tasting compliment of tobaccos.

Montecruz — (Dominican Republic) This cigar was created in 1964 for the U.S. Dunhill stores as an elegant alternative to the recently outlawed Cuban Montecristo. Consequently, the similarity of names, logo design, and label colors to the embargoed Havana product was not entirely accidental. Originally produced in Las Palmas of the Canary Islands by the same families (Menendez and Garcia) that had owned the H. Upmann factory in Havana prior to the revolution, the cigar is now handmade in the Dominican Republic. Montecruz was the first imported cigar in the U.S. market to be made with a Cameroon wrapper, which was exceedingly expensive at that time. (For an idea of what it cost to make this cigar, when it was first introduced, Connecticut shade was selling for $8 a pound, while Cameroon was fetching a hefty $23 a pound.) As a result, Montecruz became the most expensive cigar of its day. Currently, Montecruz is offered in no less than 23 different shapes with sun-grown wrapper and 9 natural Claro shapes, with the most popular being the 210, 220, and 230. True to its heritage, the Dominican-made Montecruz of today remains one of the most refined of the high grades, especially in its newest blends, combining Dominican grown Piloto Cubano and Olor with Brazilian tobaccos plus a Dominican binder. There are now two wrapper choices: an Indonesian wrapper (the original sun-grown Cameroon was changed in 1994 due to a scarcity of this African leaf) and a Natural Claro Connecticut shade. Although the filler ingredients of both cigars are the same, the proportions are changed to complement the different wrappers, with the Claro wrapper being lighter in taste. Either way, the Montecruz provides plenty of flavor in an already flavorful cigar.

287

Montenegro — (Mexico) Made with San Andrés tobacco, of long leaf filler, and packed in a sealed glass tube.

Montero — (Dominican Republic) Dominican filler and Havana seed binder with a Connecticut shade wrapper. Available in six sizes.

Montesino — (Dominican Republic) Originally made in the last century by Don Marino Montesino, today these cigars are manufactured by the Arturo Fuente family in their Moca factory for export to the United States, where it was reintroduced in 1981. This all-tobacco, 100% handmade cigar features a shade-grown Connecticut wrapper with a Nicaraguan binder and a Dominican and Brazilian filler. It is lighter tasting than the A. Fuente, rating a 1.5 to 2 on the Highly Prejudiced HackerScale. In a way, it might be called a premium bundled cigar that is put in a box, as not all of the wrapper colors will be evenly matched. But then, this cigar costs less than a Fuente. While many of us may prefer the fuller taste and more sophisticated appearance of the regular Fuente line, for a boxed cigar the Montesino is a real sleeper as far as smoking value is concerned.

Montiago — (Dominican Republic) Long filler cigars from the DR.

Moore & Bode — (United States) I hesitate to even mention this cigar, as it is extremely elusive. But then, this is *The Ultimate Cigar Book* so here goes... Made by Robert Moore and Sharon Bode since 1991 in Miami, two blends are offered, the Miami Blend, which is floral and light, and the Flamboyan (named after the flamboyan tree that is common to both Southern Florida and Cuba), which is heftier in taste. Extremely limited production and distribution, but the cigars are delicious, using aged leaf and keeping production down in order to maintain quality. The cigars are uncello'd and are packed in redwood boxes as Moore & Bode don't want cedar to affect the taste of their cigars.

Moreno Maduro — (Dominican Republic) A handmade cigar that comes in seven sizes, and as the name implies, all are maduro.

Mozart — (Austria) An excellent, high quality European-style cigar made and distributed by Austria Tabak.

Mild and of a sufficient ring size to make Americans feel comfortable, these cigars consist of a Java wrapper, Sumatra binder and Havana and Brazil filler. Obviously, not available in the U.S. but worth searching for in any of their various sizes when in Austria.

Muniemaker — (United States) Started in 1912 by the F.D. Grave Cigar Co, one of the few original American cigar manufacturing companies left. Original advertising for this cigar was the height of consciousness, and consisted of billboards that simply said the word, "Muniemaker." For more information, see F.D. Grave.

My Own Blend — (Honduras) Chances are you won't find this cigar anywhere else but in Denmark, although it may eventually work its way to a few other European countries. Made with Havana and Mexican leaf, it is currently available in four shapes.

Nat Sherman — (Dominican Republic) First introduced on the national market in 1993. Each band is color coded as to the type of cigar it is. Moreover, they all have names pertaining to the New York locale. For example the (telephone) Exchange Selection is a blend of Dominican and South American leaf with a Connecticut wrapper; the Landmark features a Cameroon wrapper; a Mexican wrapper graces the Manhattan series, the Gotham has a Connecticut wrapper and comes in a leather box, the City Desk is Maduro, and the elegant Host has a Cuban seed filler and Connecticut wrapper. From the mild tasting Gotham to the spicy Host to the rich V.I.P., the Big Apple of Nat Sherman has a smoke for every facet of city life.

New York — (Mexico) Made by Te-Amo, this brand was started in 1989 as a result of the tremendous popularity of the Te-Amo brand in the Big Apple. Each of the sizes are named for a famous boulevard, such as the 6 x 52 Wall Street, 7¼ x 48 Broadway, and the 6⅝ x 42 Park Avenue. The 1920's Art Nouveau designs on the wooden boxes almost make this reason enough for buying the cigars. But no matter what the size, the New York, with its all Mexican-grown Sumatra wrapper and San Andrés binder and filler, is extremely mild. In fact, it is one of the mildest cigars I have ever smoked, a definite 1 on the Highly Prejudiced HackerScale. The only way it could be milder is if you didn't light it. But if you are a new cigar smoker, or one who goes through a great number of Coronas in a single day, make an exploratory stop at New York.

Nicarillos — (Switzerland) A European cigar now owned by SEITA in France.

Niñas — (France) A popular machine-made small cigar by SEITA. Very mild, with Java, Dominican, and Havana tobaccos.

Nobel — (Denmark) Makers of the popular European-style "dry" cigars, Nobel is the largest cigar maker in Denmark, with 400 million cigars sold in 1990-91 alone. Extremely well known on the European Continent, their products are not as much in evidence in the United States, although the Nobel Petit and Christian of Denmark brands that are imported are making inroads with those who want a short, twelve to twenty-minute smoke. The company was founded in 1835 by Emilius Nobel and was instrumental in establishing the 100% tobacco mini-cigarillo in Europe. Launched in 1898, the Nobel Petit is now the oldest cigarillo brand in Denmark and one of the oldest in the world. In more recent times, 1985 marked the introduction of the Christian of Denmark mini-cigarillos, which feature a Dominican, Java and Brazil filler, Java binder and Sumatra wrapper. Unfortunately, the Long Cigarillo and Corona also have a touch of Havana in their otherwise identical filler contents, so you won't be seeing them on American shores for awhile. Likewise with the tubed Hirschprung Apostolado, a delicious full-bodied cigar that incorporates Brazil and Havana in its filler. Pick up a five-pack the next time you travel overseas, because that is the only way you are going to find them. But the Nobel Petit and the Christian of Denmark Mini-Cigarillos are a nice change of pace when you want a quick Continental smoke with your espresso or in between the first and second acts of Agatha Christie's *The Mousetrap*.

Nørding — (Honduras) Named after master Danish pipe craftsman Erik Nørding, who created this brand to augment his pipe smoking and reflect his own love for fine cigars. The Nørding cigar consists of a Dominican and Nicaraguan filler, Nicaraguan binder, and a Connecticut shade wrapper. The cigars are all housed in a unique cedar box that features a plastic "porthole." through which you can view your cigars without having to open the lid. Equally unique is the hollowed out cedar stick inside that is filled with moisture-holding clay pebbles that act as a humidifier for these medium-flavored HPH 2 cigars. Five shapes are available, a Corona Grande (6 x 50); Corona (5½ x 43); Robusto (4¾ x 52); Lonsdale (6¾ x 43); and the Presidente (7½ x 52). An HPH 2—2.5.

Old Port — (Canada) An inexpensive machine-made short-filler cigar with homogenized wrapper. This small, mild cheroot is very popular in the United Kingdom and Canada. It is very sweet tasting and boasts that not only is it rum flavored, but its tobacco leaves have been dipped in wine. I guess you shouldn't smoke this one while driving!

Onyx — (Dominican Republic) Introduced in 1992, this cigar gets its name from its dark Mexican Maduro wrapper. It is very mild, with a Java binder and filler of Piloto Cubano, Olor and Mexican tobaccos.

Optimo — (United States) At one time this cigar was made of all Havana tobacco. It is still a popular, mass-market machine-made cigar, utilizing homogenized tobacco and short filler.

Orient Express — (Honduras) Rather bland for a Honduran but suitable for those entry level smokers who want to start light and work their way up. The Nicaraguan and Mexican filler is supposedly aged for seven years. It is encompassed by a Dominican binder and an Ecuadorian wrapper, all of which are then aged for three months. With all these great components, you'd think this HPH 1.5—2 cigar, which was introduced in 1995, would pack a little more punch, but it does not. The fleur-de-lis band is elegant but sometimes cumbersome, as its die-cut design is prone to catch on inside coat pockets and cigar cases.

Ornelas — (Mexico) One of the better known Mexican cigars, made in Guadalajara.

Ortiz — (Mexico) Named after Jorge Ortiz Alvarez of Tabacos San Andrés, one of the cigar world's great gentlemen. Like him, this cigar is big and refined, without any roughness. An HPH 2—2.5.

Oscar — (Dominican Republic) First introduced in October, 1988 by Oscar Rodriquez, these superb smoking cigars originally came in six distinctive sizes, ranging from a 5 x 30 Prince all the way up to an elegant 9 x 46 Don Oscar, although the 8 x 48 Supreme remains a favorite anytime after dinner or late into the evening. This handmade cigar has a filler carefully composed of Dominican grown long leaf tobaccos, Dominican binder, and a Connecticut shade wrapper, all of which translate into a 2.5 on the Highly Prejudiced HackerScale. There is also a stronger-blended cigar produced for the European market and designed to compete with the Havanas. Oscar cigars are made in their own factory, which is located outside of the Free Zone, much like the Juan Clemente operation. In addition to the regular line of full-ring sized cigars, not to be missed are the excellent Oscaritos, small humidified mini-cigars that scale out to a 4 x 20. They come boxed in cedar cases of 26 cigars each and are the perfect apéritif cigar for those who like a full-bodied smoke in a small package. Oscar cigars are available in the U.S., South America, Australia, Hong Kong, and Europe. Unfortunately, Oscar became victim to the cigar boom in the early '90s and there were production problems in trying to keep enough cigars on the market to satisfy demands. Thus, it was very difficult to find for awhile. But now it's back in boxes of 25 and packs of 10. A Pyramid was introduced in 1994.

Padrón — (Nicaragua) Although their company logo contains a map of Cuba (the homeland of the Padrón family), their current cigars are handrolled in Honduras from tobacco grown on the family farms in Nicaragua. Thus, the geographical interpretation of this rich-tasting cigar can be a little confusing. But technically, it is Nicaraguan. José Orlando Padrón, a Cuban tobacco merchant who fled Cuba during the revolution, began life again in 1964 in Miami. With one roller working full time during the day, José would sell his cigars to various restaurants and cafeterias at night. As word of his quality cigars grew, so did his company. By 1969 the Padrón factory employed forty rollers. In an effort to expand, the family looked towards Nicaragua and an enlarged factory was started there in 1970. But the Sandinista revolution in 1978 literally burned them out. Later the factory was rebuilt, but just to be on the safe side, a second factory was started in Honduras. It proved to be a smart move, for when the U.S. embargo was enacted against Nicaragua, Padrón cigars could still be made in Honduras. Eventually the embargo ended and the company began to expand its line nationally throughout the United States. José Padrón has now been joined by his two sons, Orlando and Jorge, to help him run the company he started. Their current line contains twelve shapes, ranging from a 46 x 4⅞ Delicias all the way up to a giant 50 x 9 Magnum. In 1994 they introduced their 30th Anniversary limited edition cigars, which are aged for three years. Only five sizes are produced. Although relatively popular in Miami, the regular line of cigars is not as widely available as it should be. Delicious, rich, and spicy, with a flavorful oily wrapper, they are an excellent after-dinner smoke, especially in the larger ring sizes. Definitely an HPH 2.5.

Palais Royal — (Dominican Republic) This is the name of the Juan Clemente cigar sold in France.

Parodi — (United States) A Toscano-styled dry cigar made by the Avanti Cigar Company of Scranton, Pennsylvania, who purchased the brand in 1913. The motto on the side of the red, white and green (the Italian national colors) box says, "Not strong, not mild, but different." Actually, for a dry cigar, not bad.

Partagás — (Cuba) Please note the accent over the "a" on the Cuban brand, which is lacking (and hence affects the pronunciation) on the Dominican version. This cigar was "officially" born in 1845 (the years 1843 and 1867 have also cropped up in some 19th century writings, probably because Don Jaime Partagás first christened his very best cigars with his name in 1843; in 1845 he opened his own factory. And you won't find that dual year information in any other book, so if you see it elsewhere, you'll know where it came from). But no matter what the year, we do know the brand was created by Don Jaime. In 1876 Don Ramón Cifuentes and his partners, Cifuentes, Fernandez and Co., became sole owners of the brand. His son, the same Ramón Cifuentes featured in the current Partagás ads, carried on the tradition of this excellent Havana right up to the revolution, at which time he brought his family's famous cigar to the Dominican Republic. During the 1920s and '30s, the Cuban Partagás was one of the most fashionable cigars to smoke, especially in Great Britain. It was a favorite of novelist Evelyn Waugh, who thought enough of the Partagás to mention it by brand in his work, *Brideshead Revisited*. Today, the Partagás is still made in the same 19th century factory on a tree-lined boulevard located at 520 Industria Street in Havana. It is one of the oldest continuing operating cigar factories in Cuba; the only time it was closed down was from 1987 to 1990 for refurbishing. The Partagás line offers a rather extensive range of over 30 different shapes. Somewhat strong and harsh, they nonetheless have an equally strong (but not harsh) following. I particularly took a liking to their small Chicos, which are an ideal "carry anywhere" size that can satisfy one's need for a quick but definitely fulfilling smoke. And their No. 4 Series D Robusto along with the prominent Lusitania are classics among those who want a Havana with staying power. Depending on size, the strength of a Partagás will range anywhere from a 2.5 to a 3 on the Highly Prejudiced HackerScale.

Partagas — (Dominican Republic) No accent here; for the Dominican version, the emphasis is on the "Par" part of their name. These celebrated cigars, originally introduced through the Dunhill USA stores but now available throughout the country and in Europe, are made of Dominican, Jamaican, and Mexican filler, with a Mexican sun-grown binder and is one of the very few cigars still using costly Cameroon wrapper from Africa. Although it incorporates the same tobaccos in the filler as its sister cigar, Macanudo, the different percentages, plus the Cameroon wrapper, make the Partagas a more robust smoke. In fact, it is one of the finest, richest tasting cigars on the market, from the diminutive Purito to the No. 10, a can't-go-wrong choice for an after dinner treat. Their vintage Limited Reserve is one of the most handsomely boxed cigars on the market, and comes with a signed certificate noting their exact release date. Thankfully, bigger ring sizes of this great cigar were finally introduced in 1996. Of course, their 150th Anniversary

294

cigar (see the collectable cigar section elsewhere in this book), which was brought out in 1995 and snapped up so quickly hardly anything was left on the dealer's shelves by 1996, is a classic landmark in taste. Equally as desirable is the limited edition Cifuentes by Partagas, which was brought out in 1996 to commemorate the 120th anniversary of Don Ramón Cifuentes' acquisition of the Partagas brand back in Cuba. Only 150,000 of these cigars were made in the Jamaican factory. They were then aged for a full two years before being released, primarily only through the Dunhill stores. These creamy-mild cigars contain a spicy Cameroon flavoring that has obtained wonderful character through the aging process. Five sizes were offered: Petit Corona, Lonsdale, Pyramid, Churchill, and Corona Gorda. But if these cigars are gone by the time you read this, don't despair. Chances are Partagas will be repeating this limited edition aging scenario in the near future.

Pedro Iglesias — (United States) Originally created for one wholesaler but now sold nationally. This all-tobacco brand was started in the 1950s and is made in Tampa with a machine-bunched medium filler (neither short nor long). There was never anyone named Pedro Iglesias, but if there had been, no doubt he wouldn't mind smoking these popularly priced cigars.

Pedroni — (Switzerland) The European factory that makes these dry, Italian-looking small cigars has been in business since 1847. They are full-flavored for their size, using dark, fired-cured and aged tobaccos in their construction, which could be called a mini-pyramid. Rugged looking but great for topping off a morning cup of *café au lait* with some hard bread.

Peterson Hallmark — (Dominican Republic) Created by the good ol' Irish lads of Dublin, who have been making Peterson pipes ever since 1895. But these flavorful cigars do not hail from the Emerald Isle, even though every box is prominently stamped with the Kapp & Peterson hallmark. They are made with a Dominican filler, Ecuadorian binder and Connecticut shade wrapper. A mild cigar in the HPH 1.5—2 range, they were introduced in late 1995.

Petri — (United States) A dry cigar that is mainly found along the west coast. The San Francisco-based Petri Cigar Company was originally owned by the same folks who made Petri Wine, sponsors of those great old Sherlock Holmes radio shows back in the 1950s. Boy, talk about your trivia! The brand was purchased in 1963 by the Avanti Cigar Company, thus giving them almost total control of the U.S. dry-cured cigar market.

P.G. — (Dominican Republic) This cigar was first tested on a limited scale in the fall/winter of 1990 and officially launched on May 1, 1991. The P.G. doesn't stand for "pretty good," but rather, are the initials of Paul Garmirian, a cigar hobbyist who decided to get into the cigar business. Paul is now training his son Kevork to become the second generation in his enterprise. P.G. wrappers are Connecticut shade, with a Dominican binder and filler. There are more than twelve shapes in the line, most of which correspond to the original Cuban sizes and which run the range from the 4½ x 38 Petite Bouquette all the way up to the 9 x 50 Celebration. Made in the same factory as the Davidoff and Avo, these are cigars for the experienced smoker. Although they are a bit pricey, they are full of flavor, averaging out to a 2.5 on the Highly Prejudiced HackerScale.

Peter Stokkebye — (Dominican Republic) The original Stokkebye Santa Maria was one of Winston Churchill's many favored smokes. However, the present Dominican product is obviously not the same blend as the pre-embargo cigar. Made for today's "moderate" statesman, it is an extremely mild cigar, a 1 on the Highly Prejudiced HackerScale. Constructed of Brazilian and Cuban seed tobaccos for the filler and with a Dominican binder, the strength of this cigar is greatly subdued so that the pure taste of the lightly fermented Connecticut shade wrapper is allowed to come through. Although Peter is Danish and his cigars are sold in America, in keeping with the brand's past history, three popular British sizes are offered: a Churchill, a Lonsdale, and a Corona.

Petrus — (Honduras) No relation to Chateau Petrus wine. The name means Peter in Latin and this cigar is laced with subtle Christian symbols, not only in its name but in its logo and band design. Established in 1990, it has a pleasantly mild mixture of Honduran filler and binder with an attractive Ecuadorian wrapper, all of which brings it to an HPH 2. However the Honduran Maduro version, which is a "puro," soars up in strength to a rich, fudge-like HPH 2.5. A special red-banded vintage edition called Etiquette Rouge has a much milder but equally rich mixture of Nicaraguan filler, Honduran binder and a Dominican wrapper.

Phillies — (United States) Not surprisingly, this popular mass-market machine-made cigarillo was originally made in Philadelphia, PA. It is now made in Selma, Alabama.

Picadu — (France) A popular machine-made cigar from SEITA.

Pintor — (Costa Rica) Long filler from Costa Rica, Honduras and the Dominican Republic.

Playboy — (Dominican Republic) Officially known as the Playboy Cigar by Don Diego, this well constructed premium smoke was first introduced to the public in my article, "Gentlemen (And Ladies), You May Smoke," which appeared in the September 1996 issue of *Playboy* magazine. An HPH 2.5, it is actually Don Diego's European blend, which is aged. The result is an elegantly flavored upscale cigar that is a personification of the Playboy lifestyle — smooth and rich in taste, with an undercurrent of spice. Playboy by Don Diego is available in five sizes: Double Corona, Robusto, Churchill, Lonsdale, and Gran Corona. A distinctive marbleized band sports Hef's gold and silver embossed monogram and signature. And somewhat indicative of the magazine covers, both box and band are subtly accented with the Playboy Rabbit; you have to look for it, but it's there. Also introduced in the fall of '96 was a sub-brand, the Leroy Neiman Selection (named after the well-known artist and creator of many Playboy-inspired paintings), a limited edition super-premium cigar that is only available by the box, not individually. Each shape in this line was personally selected by Neiman, and each box is a definite work of art.

Pléiades — (Dominican Republic) This Caribbean product has the distinction of being the only French cigar that is not made in France. And yet, it is packaged and shipped from there, which is ample tribute by the French marketing agency SEITA to the excellence of Dominican tobacco and workmanship. Pléiades is actually made in two different factories in Santiago, with each factory making up specific sizes. After being handrolled in the DR, the cigars are shipped — unboxed, but in protective containers — to France, where they are carefully unpacked and aged for six months (although sometimes this aging period is less, if the demand outweighs the supply). Then they are color sorted, boxed in the SEITA-owned Strasborgen factory, and finally shipped to tobacconists in various countries. The reason for all of this extra care, according to French tobacco officials, is to maintain control over cigar quality and packaging. SEITA prefers to use their own design of cedar boxes, which are made in Holland and include a unique rechargeable Credo humidifier, thus enabling the Pléiades box to be reused again. Indeed, the boxes make an ideal travel humidor and I often take mine on trips with me, fully stocked, of course. When first introduced, Pléiades were extremely popular, but a series of problems with getting available supplies soon caused many smokers to abandon the brand when they could not find it on dealer's shelves the second time around. Then the blends were changed, which did not help matters. Today, however, this Dominican/French cigar seems to have left its past behind it (whether in France or the DR, it doesn't matter) and is once again a consistent and very mild cigar, ranging from a 1.5 to a 2 on the Highly Prejudiced HackerScale. The wrapper is Connecticut shade, the binder is Dominican, and the filler is Olor and Piloto Cubano. These cigars can be found in the U.S., France, Canada, Hong Kong, Singapore, Switzerland, and Germany, where they are very popular, especially with people who do not own humidors.

Por Larrañaga — (Cuba) One of Cuba's oldest brands, this famous cigar had its beginnings in 1834 and for a time was one of the most celebrated of all the Havanas. It was a favorite cigar of Rudyard Kipling, and perhaps he was referring to his Por Larrañaga when he wrote, "A woman is only a woman, but a good cigar is a Smoke." Production is much reduced today, and many of the smaller shapes are now made by machine. Somewhat difficult to find, the Por Larrañaga is nonetheless a deliciously medium-heavy flavor with just an undertaste of spice. One must work at opening a new box, as the lid is secured by no less than three seals.

Por Larrañaga — (Dominican Republic) Now being made for non-Havana smokers, with Dominican filler and binder and a Connecticut wrapper, blended to give this cigar a medium to full-bodied flavor.

Primo del Rey — (Dominican Republic) A popular cigar that is machine bunched, with a Dominican and Brazilian filler, DR binder, and now an Indonesian wrapper.

Punch — (Cuba) Started in 1840 by Manuel Lopez (whose name still appears on some of the historic bands) of J. Valle & Co., this cigar was originally created for a British importer. Its name was derived from the popular British magazine, *Punch*, whose cartoon mascot was the comical character from the famous Punch and Judy duo. This harlequin appeared prominently on the label and his presence is still there today (not only on Havanas, but also on some of the Honduran varieties as well), unchanged from the original. Not surprisingly, Punch soon became one of the most sought after cigars in Britain (and America, where it was also imported) and remains popular in the U.K. and Europe to this day. Punch has the little known distinction of being the first cigar to come out with a half corona size. It is a medium powerful cigar — one of my favorites — and offers a wide assortment of shapes and varying blends to give the connoisseur an ample range from which to choose, from the 4 x 40 Petit Punch to the 7 x 47 Churchill, which is a cigar to be reckoned with. The brand was eventually purchased by the owners of the Hoyo de Monterrey factory and the Punch cigar-making operations were subsequently moved there. It is a wonderfully smooth HPH 2.

Punch — (Honduras) If you are a fan of richly cured and expertly rolled Honduran cigars, this is the one to purchase by the box. The filler is of Honduran, Dominican and Nicaraguan long leaf, tucked into a Connecticut binder and topped off with a smooth, oily Ecuadorian grown Sumatra EMS wrapper. The Maduro versions of this cigar are not overly dark, but rather, a smooth chocolate brown. There are 12 shapes in the regular series, including a Rothschild, double corona and the famous Punch shapes. Then there is the Selección Deluxe, in natural and Maduro, which offer 5 shapes distinct to this line (otherwise, they have the same tobacco blends as the regular series), including a Corona, the full, rich Chateau L (my personal favorite), and the 8½ x 44 Raja. Then there is the Premier Grand Cru Selección, a premium, double-banded cigar with four full-bodied shapes in 48 and 50 ring sizes; the largest, a 7½ x 54 Diademas, is the perfect post-banquet cigar and the Monarcas, at 6¾ x 48 is one of the largest (ring size) tubed cigars available today. In all, this eminent Punch family is an ideal way to discover what the best Honduran long leaf premium cigars are all about. Always easy drawing and full flavored (a 2.5 to 3 HPH in the Maduro, a 2 to 2.5 HPH in the EMS wrappers), it doesn't get much better than this.

Puros Indios — (Honduras) Made by Rolando Reyes, the same skilled roller who started the Cuba Aliados brand. Now ably assisted by his son, Rolando Reyes, Jr. The first cigars hit the humidors in the winter of 1996. With a well blended filler of Brazil, Dominican, and Nicaragua tobacco, plus a well fermented Ecuadorian binder and wrapper, these full-flavored cigars have achieved a well deserved word-of-mouth reputation. HPH 2.5.

Quai D'Orsay — (Cuba) This is the only Cuban cigar that has a French name. So it should not be too surprising to learn that you won't find this cigar in too many places other than France. It was created in 1970 by SEITA, the French tobacco monopoly. The romantic sounding name, by the way, means "the bridge of D'Orsay." D'Orsay is a street in Paris, so this area must be a fantastic place to smoke a cigar. But more realistically, it is also the commonly referred-to name of the home office of the French Foreign Office, which thereby gives us a clue as to the brand name's inspiration. Quai D'Orsay has the distinction (along with Cohiba, Diplomáticos and Montecristo) of being one of the few Havana cigars in which every single shape is handmade. This French/Cuban cigar has a very hefty and spicy taste and a typical three-hour French lunch, followed by a Quai D'Orsay Churchill, is a sinfully pleasant and self-indulgent way in which to while away most of the afternoon. I suppose the only thing better would be to actually smoke a Quai D'Orsay on the quai d'Orsay. Or within the hallways of the Quai D'Orsay.

Quintero y Hermanos — (Cuba) A strong tasting, machine-made cigar that is one of the best selling Havanas in Germany. One shape, the Panetela, however, is machine bunched but it is handrolled, for a different look.

Rafael Gonzalez — (Cuba) Another 20th century Havana that is still with us. It was started in 1928 by George Samuel and Frank Warwick, who wanted to create a special cigar for the British market. The factory used only the best Cuban tobaccos, and this brand was the originator of the Lonsdale shape, which was made on special order for the Earl of Lonsdale. In fact, the earl's photograph and signature still adorn the box to this very day. Also worthy of note is the inscription on every box that states, "These cigars should be smoked within one month of shipment or should be carefully matured for one year." These instructions were originally written on a box of Rafael Gonzales cigars by an English importer back in the 1930s. Never one to take such concern lightly, the Cuban makers have kept this notation on every box produced since. Owing to their light taste, I would opt for the latter part of the instructions. Cubatabaco's blend for this cigar today is relatively mild (an HPH 1.5—2), but it still manages to make its presence felt with a sweet and sour accent and the strength increases to as much as an HPH 2.5 as you smoke it on down towards the band.

Ramón Allones — (Cuba) Made in Havana since 1837, this is the second oldest Cuban brand in existence, and the year of its birth is proudly printed on the band (not only on the Cuban cigar, but on the Dominican version as well). A very innovative cigar maker, Ramón Allones was the first to utilize full color labels on his boxes. He also originated the 8-9-8 method of packing cigars in a box, so that there would not be a full row of cigars pressuring the row beneath it, a system designed for those who like their cigars "in the round," (i.e., not squared in shape). This is another of the original Cuban brands that has maintained its strength through the years. It is definitely not a novice's cigar, even in the smaller ring gauges, but one of the best for a lingering late night repast by the fireside after one has eaten too many servings of smoked roast boar. Expect a rousing HPH 2.5—3. Today, Ramón Allones is made in the Partagás factory.

Ramón Allones — (Dominican Republic) Formerly made in Cuba by the Cifuentes family (yes, the same skilled artisans who also made the Partagas and Macanudo), these excellent cigars are now being made by hand in Santiago. First reintroduced in America as a semiprivate brand in the 1970s, Ramón Allones has now gone national, and is available in the Alfred Dunhill shops as well as other selected tobacconists. The filler blend is a recipe of Jamaican, Dominican and Mexican tobaccos, with a Mexican binder and a beautiful Cameroon wrapper. To me, it tastes like a mild Partagas. In case you're wondering, the "Seleccion Privada" subtitle under the Allones logo simply means, "Private Selection." The Seleccion Privada is a pressed cigar; that is, it has been purposely squared in the handmaking process. However, for those of us who like our cigars in the round, the Ramón Allones Trumps feature this elegant cigar in its more natural shape, with a slightly deeper taste in the filler, and packed without band or cellophane in a stylish cedar box that can double as a desktop pencil caddie when you are through smoking the contents. It is a mild 2 HPH cigar that has potential for aging.

Rigoletto — (United States/Dominican Republic) Their Black Arrow and Dominican Lights are now being handmade in the Dominican Republic; other sizes are still being machine made in Tampa.

Ritmeester — (Holland) One of the world's premiere Dutch-type cigar-making companies in which 100% tobacco is used. Jochem van Schuppen, who started manufacturing cigars in 1887, introduced the Ritmeester trademark in 1915 and the company has since become a major player in the worldwide manufacture of quality dry cigars. You can find their Elites, Livardes, and Royal Dutch Panetelas and cigarillos in the U.S. and their tinned Livarde small cigars are specially popular in the British Isles, as well as South Africa and Scandinavia.

302

Robt. Burns — (United States) An economical cigar that has been around since Teddy Roosevelt was President. The Cigarillo and Panetela were two of the most popular cigars of their day. In those early years, the entire line boasted Havana filler and Connecticut wrappers. Today these are mass-market cigars that utilize HTL and are machine made in Dotham, Alabama. Only 2 sizes are made.

Rolando — (Dominican Republic) A handmade cigar available in six shapes.

Romeo y Julieta — (Cuba) This famous cigar started out in 1875, with the company of Alvarez y Garcia making cigars only for the local Havana market. However, like the unknown Hollywood starlet who needs a good agent, it got a boost to stardom when Rodriquez "Pepin" Fernandez, former manager of one of Havana's largest cigar factories, bought the brand in 1903. At that time Romeo y Julieta was little known outside of Cuba, but within two years Pepin had made it into one of the largest selling premium Havana cigars in the world. A great promoter, he produced a wide range of personalized cigar bands for celebrities of the day and even named his race horse Julieta. He always referred to his cigars as "my children." Romeo y Julieta achieved additional fame by being credited as the cigar that originated the Churchill shape, which was really their tubed Clemenceau (named after a highly respected French diplomat of the time). In fact, in later years, this was one of the many cigars that England's celebrated statesman, Sir Winston Churchill, is said to have smoked on a regular basis, which is how it eventually came to be named after him. Up until recently, cigars continued to be made at the old Alvarez y Garcia factory, where many of the Dunhill Havanas were also manufactured. Today it is made by Cubatabaco in the Partagás factory. It is a full, rich, but not overpowering cigar, with a very pleasing aroma that women seem to like. A 2—2.5 on the Highly Prejudiced HackerScale.

Romeo y Julieta — (Dominican Republic) Up until recently, this had always been a quiet, unassuming cigar, savored by those who liked it and ignored by those who did not. When Castro came into power, the owner of this famous brand left Havana, as did so many other legendary cigar makers, and established his cigar elsewhere in the Caribbean. And that was part of the problem, for at one time it was actually being produced in three countries: Cuba, the Dominican Republic and Honduras. This did not cause any problems in Europe, where only the Havanas were available, but it was responsible for a lot of confusion in the U.S., as Dominican and Honduran cigars are decidedly different in taste. And so it was that the Romeo y Julieta violated the first rule of a good cigar: always be consistent. As the Honduran cigar is no longer being made on a national scale, the Dominican-made Romeo y Julieta has made a dramatic comeback. With its Indonesian wrapper, Connecticut broadleaf bunch, and Dominican and Cuban seed filler, it is a mild yet flavorful and aromatic cigar. Moreover, the Romeo y Julieta is now achieving a new pinnacle of excellence and taste with the Vintage series, which features one of the best Connecticut shade wrappers on any cigar, and a pleasant blend of Dominican and Brazilian tobaccos, all of which meld together to produce a wonderfully refined taste that measures a 2 to 2.5 HPH. These cigars can be easily identified by their distinctive wrappers and the gold lining on the otherwise standard red and white Romeo y Julieta band. The Vintage series was introduced in 1993 with five shapes, of which the No. III (4½ x 50) and the No. IV (7 x 48) are my undisputed winners for a lasting smoke anytime after 5 p.m. You might also want to try the new No. VI Triangular (7 x 60). The Romeo y Julieta Vintage cigars come in a handmade Spanish cedar box which is fitted with its own Credo humidifier, one of the best devices available. All the more reason to check out this great cigar for yourself.

Royal Jamaica — (Jamaica) One of the original all-Jamaican cigars made for export. But in 1989, after Hurricane Gilbert devastated the factory, the company moved to the Dominican Republic. Finally in 1996, it returned to its homeland. This mild tasting cigar (HPH 2) features filler from Jamaica and the DR, with a Cameroon binder and up until 1992 it had a Cameroon wrapper, which has now been changed to Indonesian leaf. The Maduro version of this cigar has the same filler blend and binder, but utilizes Mexican leaf for the wrapper. It is interesting to note that the Jamaican filler tobacco is still being grown by the same family that founded this cigar.

Royal Manna — (Honduras) An inexpensive and extremely mild handmade cigar, unique in its uncured wrapper. One of the best cigars of its type for the money.

Saint Luis Rey — (Cuba/Germany) This complete range of cigars and cigarillos is unique in that it has a dual nationality, as some shapes are handmade in Havana, while others, such as the Corona and small Panetela, are machine made in Germany by the Villiger company. The cigars from both countries are medium strong in flavor, with a sweet undertaste which reminds one of Cuban coffee.

Saint Luis Rey — (Honduras) Originally slated to come out in 1993, it took three additional years to finally get everything working right, but the wait was definitely worth it. The taste is milk chocolaty thick, creamy and rich, but like hardened taffy, you sometimes have to pull a bit to get a draw. Which means the first few cigars I smoked in the Spring of '96 were rolled perfectly but some later sticks were just a tad too tight. Yet even with a hard pull, it is worth the effort as far as flavor goes. Made of all Cuban-seed Honduran tobaccos, this is not a cigar for the meek; it jump starts your palate with an HPH 2.5—3. Be sure to smoke this one with a full stomach and you'll enjoy it even more.

San Angelo — (Dominican Republic) An old Dominican brand that was resurrected in 1996. This new version features a Dominican filler of Cuban seed and Olor, a Dominican binder and a Connecticut shade wrapper.

San Pedro Sula — (Honduras) The name given to the Honduran-made Punch cigar that is sold in Europe. San Pedro Sula is one of the largest cities in Honduras and is near the factory where the Punch cigars are manufactured.

Sancho Panza — (Cuba) A mild smoke from an old Havana brand that still retains a loyal following.

Santa Clara 1830 — (Mexico) Made by Santa Clara S.A. De C.V., the date on this cigar is that of the factory's founding. These cigars are 100% handmade of long leaf filler. After manufacture, the cigars are aged, which results in a surprisingly medium-mild flavor that is endowed with substance. A slightly coarse 2 on the HPH scale, you'll find these cigars in the U.S., Australia, and Germany.

Santa Cruz — (Jamaica) Handmade, long filler cigars made with Jamaican, Dominican and Mexican tobaccos.

Santa Damiana — (Dominican Republic) Introduced in London in January 1992 and brought to the U.S. in September of that same year, this cigar has rapidly become a much sought after commodity, even among the Havana smokers of the UK and some parts of Europe. It is an old brand, but has been upgraded for today's sophisticated tastes with a blend of Dominican filler and binder and a handsome Connecticut shade wrapper. This is an unexpectedly mild, super-premium cigar.

Santa Fe — (United States) Not named for the picturesque town in New Mexico. Chances are more probable that this old-time cigar was named after the highly regarded Menendez y Garcia tobacco farm in pre-revolutionary Cuba. Today it is machine made in Alabama of short filler and homogenized tobacco for the mass market.

Santa Rosa — (Honduras) Introduced in 1984, this medium-flavored cigar is very popular in some areas of the country, due to its attractive Connecticut shade wrapper and competitive pricing. Very pleasantly blended, it comes in at a 2 to 2.5 on the HackerScale. These are the perfect cigars for retired gunfighters, for I have found some of them to be a little slow on the draw.

Santiago Cabana — (United States) Key West, Florida was one of the first anchoring spots for Cuban refugees just before and shortly after the Spanish American War. They quickly established a cigar making colony that, although past its prime, still thrives today in many "buckeye" operations. But this cigar is worthy of the best that Key West or any other cigar making region has ever produced. In fact, it is made in Key Largo. "Pleasant" is the best one-word description of its taste. But it's more than that. For a medium-tasting cigar, it is one of the best of the "new breeds." With Dominican, Honduran and Nicaraguan filler, Ecuador binder and a wonderful Ecuador wrapper, it smoothly sails in as a perfect HPH 2. Eight shapes are offered with the 7¾ x 52 Presidente bringing out the full flavor of this excellent cigar. Definitely worth buying by the box.

Savinelli — (Dominican Republic) Introduced in 1994, this mild-tasting cigar (also called the ELR, for Extremely Limited Reserve) is made by the A. Fuente factory. It is named after the company founded by Achille Savinelli, a master pipemaker in Italy.

Schimmelpenninck — (Holland) Made in Wageningen. Holland, this is one of the most prestigious of the small Dutch-type cigar manufacturers. The company was started in 1924 by two brothers and their uncle, who began making cigars under the Schimmelpenninck name. The brand was derived from the name of one of Holland's 19th century governors. This has resulted in the longest name in this entire book, and the more one has to drink, the easier it is to pronounce. Nonetheless, the cigars have become extremely popular in over 160 countries, with 90% of their production being shipped outside of Holland. In the United States, which is traditionally not a Dutch-type cigar market, the Schimmelpenninck brand nonetheless accounts for 50% of "dry" cigars sold in America. Their popular Duet is the world's best selling thin Panetela, with a blend of more than 20 different types of short filler tobaccos from Indonesia, Brazil, and Cameroon. And for an unusual shape with a Rothschild-type smoke, try one of their Grand Luxe, a short, squat torpedo shaped cigar with a full-bodied Cameroon wrapper. The Florina is another full-tasting cigar in a small shape, but that is because it has Havana tobacco blended in with its Brazil and Java tobacco fillers; best to pick these up at the duty-free shops on your next overseas travels. But my all-time favorite, is the V.S.O.P. Corona De Luxe, which I find good enough to smoke with a cognac.

Shah-ow-shu-ma — (China) An all-tobacco Chinese cigar first made in the 1940s, and now sold throughout China, as well as Japan. A few were exported to the U.S. in 1992. A variety of tobaccos are grown in China, but the various cigars within this brand are made in different factories located within a specific growing area, so that they each have a distinctive taste, according to the province in which they were made.

Signet — (Dominican Republic) A high end cigar introduced in 1996 in three shapes. Components are: Dominican filler and binder with a Connecticut shade wrapper.

Sosa — (Dominican Republic) Arriving from Havana in the last century, the Sosa family eventually set up their own cigar making operation in Miami's Ybor City in 1964. Ten years later Juan Sosa created his own cigar in the Dominican Republic. This was one of the very first mass produced cigars from the DR. Today it is made with a Dominican filler and binder and a Connecticut shade wrapper. Its taste is rich and mellow, like chocolate pudding. An HPH 2—2.5 chocolate pudding to be exact.

Tabacalera — (Philippines) A mild tasting cigar that was discontinued in 1996, but you still may find a few wayward boxes on dealer's shelves.

Tabantillas — (Spain) Reportedly the best selling cigar in Spain. Which makes me wonder who's smoking all those Havanas that are shipped there each year.

Tabaquero — (Dominican Republic) Introduced to the U.S. in 1995.

Te-Amo — (Mexico) Originally brought out in the 1960s, this brand has become one of the best-selling cigars from south of the border. It is especially popular in New York. The name means "I love you," in Spanish, and a box of Te-Amo's would be an appropriate gift on Valentine's day. Offered in Mexican-grown wrappers of Natural Sumatra seed and Maduro, they are handmade in the San Andrés Valley. Although already very mild in flavor (a 1.5 on the HPH scale) there is also a Te-Amo Light, which refers to the flavor, rather than what you do to it with a match.

Temple Hall — (Dominican Republic) This is an old 19th century brand that was named after one of the Jamaican tobacco plantations established by Cuban growers in 1876. In fact, the Temple Hall estates still exist, but the cigar is now made in Santiago. It was relatively low key, but was reintroduced in 1992 with an updated image and a new blend, consisting of a Connecticut shade wrapper and a Dominican, Jamaican, and Mexican filler.

Tesoros de Copan — (Honduran) With its characteristic green band, this is one ecology-friendly cigar I encourage everyone to buy because the proceeds go to the Ruta Maya Foundation, which was started by former National Geographic editor Bill Garret to help preserve Central America's rain forests and Mayan culture. Anyone who has walked through the thick forested jungles of Honduras or explored some of the hidden and crumbling Mayan ruins as I have, knows that these irreplaceable entities are in need of all the help they can get. The cigar's name means Treasure of Copan, and the Mayan frieze from the town of Copan (near some of the recently excavated ruins) stamped on each box helps explain the cigar's noble purpose. It's not a bad smoke either, with a spicy-mild HPH 2.

The Ultimate Cigar — (Honduras) Absolutely no relationship to *The Ultimate Cigar Book*, even though it is one of the best cigars I have smoked in quite a while. Once a private mail order brand, it is now available nationwide. I first had one of these cigars, in their No. 1 shape (a 7¼ x 54), when visiting the factory near San Pedro Sula where they are made. At the time, I did not know what they were, as they were unbanded. However, its rich, creamy texture of flavor and faintly sweet undertaste made me return the next day to learn its identity. And to acquire a box. These cigars are all aged for a full year and are handmade of Cuban seed tobaccos grown in Honduras. A 2—2.5 on the HPH, The Ultimate Cigar is available in sixteen different sizes, and in almost as great a variety of wrappers: Claro, Double Claro, and variations of EMS and Maduros. In keeping with the well aged connoisseur quality of this cigar, it comes un-cellophaned in cedar boxes.

Thomas Hinds — (Honduras) First manufactured in 1994, this cigar is the product of brothers Mel and Tom Hinds, who used to own the Cubatabaco concession in Canada. After they sold their interest in this concern in 1993, they set about creating a full-bodied Honduran cigar and this is it. You can identify it by its green band (as opposed to the white banded Nicaraguan described below). With a meaty Honduran filler and binder and an excellent Ecuadorian wrapper, it rates a 2—2.5 HPH but is never overpowering. Still, it is definitely an after-the-meal smoke for most palates.

Thomas Hinds — (Nicaragua) This is the one with the white band. Brought out in 1995 hot on the success of their Honduran entry, this all-Nicaraguan "puro" is one of that country's finest products. It is available in a natural wrapper and an extremely flavorful naturally aged Maduro, which clocks in at an HPH of 2.5.

Tiparillo — (United States) A small, mass-market, plastic-tipped cigar that created a mini-revolution in smoking mores when it was introduced in 1962 with the advertising slogan, "Should a gentleman offer a lady a Tiparillo?" Then, thanks to the Surgeon General's report (when he said what we already knew about the healthful aspects of cigar smoking), within a few years of its introduction, Tiparillos were selling at the rate of 1½ billion a year. Machine made of homogenized tobacco, it is still selling. Only now the ladies ask if they should offer a Tiparillo to a gentleman.

Topper — (Dominican Republic) Called the Topper Centennial, this cigar was introduced in 1995 — one year early — to commemorate the Topper Cigar Company's 100th anniversary in the cigar making business. It features a Dominican filler, Mexican binder and a Connecticut wrapper. A very pleasant HPH 2. For a history of one of the last of the American cigar companies, see below.

Topper — (Honduras) Known as the Topper Handmade, this cigar was actually a little ahead of its time, coming out before the huge cigar boom of the 90s. It has a Dominican, Mexican, and Honduran filler, and a Honduran binder and wrapper.

Topper — (United States) One of the last of the old time American cigar making companies. B.P. Topper, after apprenticing at one of the many Pennsylvania cigar companies that were flourishing around the latter part of the 19th century, started the Topper Cigar Company in 1896. It has been family owned and run ever since. In fact, the Topper cigar was one of the last of the handmade cigars to be produced in the U.S.; it had a 73-year run, lasting until 1969. By that time the high cost of labor and the fact that most of the experienced cigar rollers were either gone or too old to continue their trade finally caught up with this venerable company. Not willing to sacrifice their commitment to producing a quality cigar, they changed with the times and went to a short filler machine made version, but still keeping it all-tobacco. They remained especially strong along the eastern part of the United States. In 1980, under B.P.'s grandson Frank, a Honduran cigar, the company's first handrolled product in eleven years, was brought out. In 1994, B.P.'s great grandson Chris joined the firm and one year later, to keep up with the new growth in the cigar business, they introduced their second handrolled cigar. Only this time it was made in the Dominican Republic. But Topper's U.S. production continues, with their line of Connecticut Broadleaf short-filler cigars, thereby keeping alive an American cigar-making legacy that I might not have known about, had I not stumbled into Chris's brother Dave at a cigar dinner I was speaking at a few years ago in New Hampshire.

Top Stone — (United States) Originally manufactured by E. Waegeman & Sons of Bridgeport, Connecticut in 1903. In true entrepreneurial fashion, one of Waegeman's customers liked the cigar so much, he ended up buying the factory from the last surviving heir of the founding family. The operations were moved to Tampa in late 70s. Prior to the embargo this cigar was made with Broadleaf wrapper and binder and the filler was Cuban. Later, this was replaced with Dominican and domestic tobaccos. Today, Top Stone remains an all-tobacco cigar, made with Connecticut broadleaf wrapper and binder and machine-bunched long-leaf filler. It is one of the better values on the market for a good, medium-grade American cigar with a wide variety of Claro, Colorado and Maduro wrappers.

Toraño — (Dominican Republic) Tobacco broker Carlos Toraño has made so many cigars for other people, he finally decided to make one for himself. Handcrafted in a small village that is home to the Cuevas y Hermanas factory, it is constructed of Piloto Cubana filler, Ecuadorian binder, and a Connecticut shade wrapper. There are eight sizes to choose from ranging from the Carlos I to the Carlos VIII, all of which are named in memory of Carlos' father (also named Carlos), who was instrumental in introducing Cuban seed tobacco to the DR.

Toraño — (Honduras) This is the Virtuoso line of the Toraño cigar. It features a Nicaraguan, Honduran, and Costa Rican filler, Honduran binder, and a Connecticut seed Ecuadorian wrapper. It comes in eight sizes and is an HPH 2.5

Travis Club — (United States) An historic, long-filler Texas-made cigar that is still being produced by the original company. The Travis Club cigar was named after a private club in San Antonio, Texas. Henry William Finck, owner of the Finck Cigar Company in San Antonio, was a charter member of the Travis Club, which was founded in 1909. As this exclusive organization's only cigar manufacturing member, it was felt that his club should have its own cigar. And so it came to pass. When World War I rolled around, the patriotic members of the Travis Club opened their doors to the military officers who were stationed in San Antonio. Soon the Texas-based American doughboys were extolling the virtues of Travis Club cigars, and the demand for these homegrown smokes soon changed the Travis Club cigar from a private brand into a public one. In addition to the current Travis Club line of fourteen different shapes (many stemming from the earliest years of the company's existence), May of 1993 saw the introduction of the Travis Club Centennial Cigar, created to commemorate the 100th anniversary of the founding of the Finck Cigar Company (see Chapter 2), which has now been making Travis Club cigars for over a century. Housed in a commemorative cedar box with its own humidifier, this special cigar is similar to Finck's turn-of-the-century Senator, only its 6⅞ x 45 size provides a fuller flavor. These all-tobacco cigars are made of Connecticut shade wrapper, Connecticut broadleaf binder, and a blend of Dominican, Piloto, Olor and Brazil long leaf filler. Today, the Travis Club and the Elks Club building that housed it on the top floor are both long gone, but their image is preserved in the artfully nostalgic label of a cigar that is too good to die.

Tresado — (Dominican Republic) An excellent entry-level cigar, with a mild taste and a mild price. A very well made, handrolled cigar with a Java shade grown wrapper, Cameroon binder, and long leaf Dominican filler. HPH 1—1.5.

Trinidad — (Cuba) The phantom cigar of Havana. Trinidad (named after a town in Cuba) has replaced Cohiba as the official government cigar, now that Cohiba is publicly available. But officially, no one in Cuba claims to know anything about the Trinidad, (even though these elusive stogies were given out at a major $1,000-a-plate "Dinner of the Century" in 1995 in Paris, where some entrepreneur paid $250,000 for ten boxes of the non-existent cigars!). High ranking dignitaries and guests of the government are supposedly the only ones who have ever smoked it. I am happy to say that since the first edition of *The Ultimate Cigar Book* was published I have finally experienced the Trinidad (they wouldn't give me another one to take back and photograph; I had to smoke it *there!*) and found its taste to be rich and vinegary, almost acidic. In short, it is a very carefully honed strength, like a tempered steel blade and easily qualifies for an HPH 2.5 and not as a 3 as some have suggested. However, the intensity of the tobacco can be tamed by smoking it outdoors. But for all its elitist posturing, the Trinidad is still only available in one size, a 7½ x 38. Having said all that, the fact remains that few people in Cuba even want to talk about the mysterious Trinidad cigar for the record. So forget you ever read this.

Troya — (Cuba) A famous brand whose name was inspired by Helen of Troy.

Troya — (Dominican Republic) A well-made, medium-tasting and very mild cigar, garnering a 1.5 HPH. Produced in the same factory as the Davidoff, and made with Dominican filler and binder and a Connecticut shade wrapper. The Troya Classico, which contains the same tobaccos, is aged slightly longer and comes in at around an HPH 2.

Tueros — (Canada) A Havana leaf, short filler cigar with homogenized binder that is machine-made in Montreal, Canada for distribution in that nation only. Only one size, a corona, is made and each cigar is individually packaged in a tube. Extremely mild, rating a 1.5 HPH.

313

Tulum — (Mexico) A handmade long leaf cigar first brought out in 1994. Rather refined and woodsy in taste. An HPH 2—2.5.

V Centennial — (Honduras) The "V" stands for the Roman numeral five, which signifies five centuries since Columbus first discovered tobacco in the New World. With a complex Dominican, Honduran, and Nicaraguan filler, a Mexican binder and a Connecticut shade wrapper, this well constructed cigar embodies the best of all five of those tobacco-producing countries. An HPH 2, it is sweet tasting and smooth, perfect for after lunch or afternoon.

Veracruz — (Mexico) First appearing in 1977, this mild and delicately flavored long filler cigar takes its name from the state in which the famous San Andrés tobacco-growing region is located. The Veracruz cigar is the inspiration of Mexican entrepreneur Oscar J. Franck Terrazas. It is handmade of tobaccos from San Andrés Tuxtla and Oaxaca. The Veracruz features one of the most elaborate individual packages of any cigar made today. There are two sizes, the 6¼ x 42 Reserva Especial and a 7⅞ x 50 Magnum. Both come encased in an amber glass tube, which is topped off with a foam spacer and sealed with an airtight rubber cap. The tube is then hand wrapped in tissue and slipped into a thin cedar box. These cigars are sold individually and you don't have to put them in a humidor, as the importer guarantees them to stay fresh for up to six months. I think Oscar is being judiciously cautious. Don't try this at home, but I once left a packaged Veracruz cigar on my desk for a full two years before I finally discovered it under a pile of papers (this gives you an insight into the lifestyle I lead when writing a book). Not wishing to wait a moment longer after its excavation, and thrilled at finding a cigar just when I needed it, I immediately uncorked this Latin treasure and smoked it. To my surprise, it was as fresh as if I had just plucked it from my humidor. In fact, if you don't have a humidor, or plan to be traveling for an extended period of time, this is a perfect cigar to take along with you, as long as you like the limited sizes that are offered and the comparatively subdued flavor. Not readily found because of its somewhat lofty price, it is nonetheless a super premium smoke that is distributed in the Continental U.S. and Hawaii.

Villa de Cuba — (United States) In spite of its name, this cigar has always been made in Tampa ever since it began in the 1930s. It is now a mass-market cigar, machine bunched, with a homogenized binder.

Villiger — (Switzerland/Germany) One of the very few European cigar making firms that is still owned and operated by the original founding family. The Villiger brand was started in 1888, when Jean Villiger, a Swiss bookkeeper, decided he wanted a better quality cigar than what was available in his local town of Pfeffikon, and so, he started making cigars for himself. These private cigars were a favorite shape for the region, called *Stumpen* (which we would call cheroots today) and it wasn't long before word of his tasty cigars traveled throughout the village and surrounding countryside. Soon Villiger had more than 50 people manufacturing his cigars in a small factory and their reputation gradually spread throughout Switzerland and neighboring Germany. Since those early years, the Villiger family has continued to inherit Jean's love of tobacco, and the company has managed to survive two world wars and numerous personal obstacles. In 1950, Jean's grandson Heinrich entered the family business and in 1966 his brother Kaspar joined him, although he had to leave this post in 1989 when he was elected to the Swiss Federal Government. However, Heinrich remains as president of the famous company and his sister, Monika is in charge of the marketing operations. Up until the late 1960s, you rarely saw a Villiger cigar outside of Switzerland and Germany. But today, Villiger has factories in Switzerland, Germany and Ireland and employs about 900 people who produce over 450 million cigars and cigarillos, of which 20% are exported to over 70 countries, including all of Europe and the United States. In addition, Villiger cigars are quite prominent in duty-free shops as well as being supplied to the Diplomatic Corps. They were the first company to introduce the now familiar five-pack to the Swiss market. Originally handmade, today the Villiger factories utilize state-of-the-art machine making techniques. Their cigars are made with tobaccos that have been aged from two to three years, from countries such as Brazil, Columbia, Dominican Republic, Java, Mexico, Peru, Ecuador, Sumatra, and Africa. Havana is also used for many of their cigars that are not exported to the U.S. Villiger produces a vast array of European-type cheroots, cigars and cigarillos. Especially notable in Europe are their all-Havana Romeo y Julieta cigarillos and Saint Luis Rey cigars (made under license from Cubatabaco) and their 100% tobacco Backgammon cigars. In the U.S., the most popular brands are Export, a unique square-shaped Swiss cigar with Sumatra wrapper, and Kiel, a long, slender Villiger shape that dates from the early 1900s. This European favorite originally had a built-in goose quill tip, which in German is called "Gänse Kiel"; the "kiel" part stuck, so to speak, and thus begat the name of this popular cigar. Ecological concerns (and no doubt lobbying efforts by the geese) have since dictated that a distinctive yellow plastic mouthpiece be substituted for the goose quill. Also worth searching out during your travels are the mild Rio and Tobajara small cigars, as well as Braniff which is made from the finest Mexican tobaccos from the San Andrés Valley. Some Villiger cigars are all tobacco while others utilize homogenized leaf so that they can more effectively be made on machines. In addition to their extensive lineup of cigars and cigarillos, Villiger also makes pipe tobacco and has recently diversified into bicycle manufacturing. Perhaps the ideal European vacation would be peddling through the lush Swiss countryside on a Villiger bike while puffing a Villiger cigar, which continues to provide smokers the world over with a variety of very Continental shapes and blends.

Vueltabajo — (Dominican Republic) Yes, I know Vuelta Abajo should actually be two words. But current maps and guidebooks aside, the manufacturers insist this is the more historically correct spelling for Cuba's fabled tobacco growing region. But don't let this minor technicality dissuade you from trying this fine cigar. It is a real "sleeper" — one of the truly great tastes of the newer brands. It first made its appearance in October 1993 and has proven extremely popular with "those in the know." Cuban seed Dominican-grown filler, Dominican Olor binder and a fine Connecticut shade wrapper all combine to produce a multi-faceted taste-treat when you first light up. Especially satisfying in the 6 x 50, 8½ x 52, and Pyramid sizes, it rates a 2 to 2.5 HPH and can be at home anytime after 3 p.m.

W. Ascot — (United States) A short filler cigar made with Honduran, Dominican, and Ecuadorian tobaccos.

White Owl — (United States) This early American brand started out in 1887 as Owl Brand cigars. Then it was changed to Brown Owl. Finally in 1902 it became White Owl. In the earlier part of this century, an eighteen million dollars a year ad budget made it a best seller nationwide. Today, with its short filler and HTL binder, it remains a popular and affordable mass-market cigar.

Willem II — (Holland) Established in 1916, this is the leading brand in Holland and also one of the more popular small Dutch type cigars in more than 100 countries. It is made of Indonesian and South American tobaccos, with a Sumatra wrapper and homogenized binder. From the small Wee Willems to the short Dutch Wiffs to the lengthy Long Panetelas, they are a comforting and versatile smoke that can usually be found in most metropolitan smokeshops.

Wm. Penn — (United States) A cigar that was born during the Roaring '20s, it is still being made today, although now it is manufactured by machine, with homogenized leaf. The Perfecto and Panetela are classic shapes that have been in the line since its beginning. Still one of the most popular mass-market cigars in the Mid-West and New England.

Zino — (Holland) Known as their Specialty Series of cigars, this Davidoff product is of the dry, European-style variety. Offered in both Indonesia (light) and Brazil (dark) wrappers, they are made of 100% tobacco and are among the mildest of the Davidoff line. Milder yet are the foil-wrapped Zino Relax in light and dark wrappers, and the Zino Classic.

Zino — (Honduras) This is the Honduran line of humidified Davidoff cigars, named after the late Zino Davidoff. The Zinos, which are 100% handmade, were introduced in Europe in the late 1970s and were first sold in the U.S. in 1983. There are three categories of Zinos: Mouton Cadet, one of the mildest and the cigars that were specifically selected for Baronne Philippine de Rothschild (the torpedo, which was introduced in 1996, is especially notable in this blend); Honduran Series, a medium blend in a wide range of sizes; and the Connoisseur Series, a full, rich tasting cigar that was launched in 1987 to celebrate Davidoff's opening of their New York store but was quietly discontinued until 1997, when it was brought back with an even heavier blend.

A Listing Of All Currently Exported Cuban Cigars

One of the most frequently asked questions I receive relates to whether or not a specific brand of Cuban cigar is still being produced. While many Havana cigars have been discontinued, others remain in the line, while new ones are being introduced. So here, personally gleaned from the files of Cubatabaco, for the very first time, is every brand that is currently being exported by Cuba.

Bolivar
Caney
Cifuentes
Cohiba
Diplomáticos
El Rey del Mundo
Fonseca
Gispert
H. Upmann
Hoyo de Monterrey
José L. Piedra
Juan López
La Corona
La Escepción
La Flor de Cano

La Gloria Cubana
Montecristo
Partagás
Por Larrañaga
Punch
Quai D'Orsay
Quintero y Hermanos
Rafael Gonzales
Ramón Allones
Romeo y Julieta
Saint Luis Rey
Sancho Panza
Siboney
Stantos de Luxe
Troya

Chapter 10

CigarSpeak

A dictionary of terms you're not likely to use outside the realm of fellow cigar connoisseurs who have also read this book, but which are fun to drop into a conversation when you are visiting a cigar factory or when you want to impress friends at the next smoker.

Aging Room — Also called Marrying Room (which gives one cause to ponder); the room, usually cedar lined, where the completed cigars are permitted to rest, so that their various tobaccos can reach a constant humidity level while their flavors blend.

A.M.S. — American Market Selection, a term used to define the light and relatively mild Claro Claro, Jade, or Candela type of wrapper that once was very popular in America.

Artificial Head — No, this is not an anatomical part of a politician. It is a method of using a separate tobacco cap for the head of a cigar, but making it appear as if it was a part of the wrapper leaf. This is done by cutting a flag shaped piece of tobacco and inserting the pole of the flag into a small slit in the wrapper, then proceeding to make the head in a normal fashion.

Barrel — The body of a cigar. Also called a cañon.

Belicoso — A relatively thick cigar, usually of 52 ring gauge, with a shaped (i.e., Panetela) head. One of the easiest cigars to clip for smoking, even while under the influence of potent liquors.

Biddies — A term for a small East Indian cigar. Also used by Agio as a brand name for one of their 100% tobacco miniatures.

Binder — The leaf that is rolled around the filler to hold it together.

Booking — A method in cigar making where the leaves of the bunch are folded in half, as if they were pages of a book. Booking the bunch is not desirable in cigar making, as it tends to produce a heavy concentration of all the filler leaves along the folds (or spine of the book), impairing the smoker's ability to get a complete, evenly distributed taste of every tobacco in the blend. This linear concentration can also cause a cigar to burn unevenly down the side.

Box Press — The old-time Cuban art (now practiced in other cigar making countries as well) of pressing or squaring off cigars, so that they are not round. The original purpose of box pressing was to keep the cigars from rolling off the table. (This bit of trivia is a "ringer"; at the time of this writing, there is nowhere else in the world where you can read this tidbit of information, so if you see it in another book after August 1996, you will know the source from whence it came.)

Buckeye — A term used to designate a small cigar-making (i.e., a "Mom and Pop") operation.

Bunch — The group of leaves that comprise the filler and binder before they are rolled into a wrapper.

Bunchbreaker — The person in a cigar factory who makes bunches.

Bunchmaker — Same as a Bunchbreaker.

Burros — Cuban term for the bales of tobacco in which leaf fermentation takes place.

322

Butt — The small tied ends of a hand of tobacco. Can also be used to describe someone who doesn't agree with your choice of cigars.

Cabinet Box — A thick cedar box in which all of the wood is exposed and not covered with stickers or labels. Ink stampings are used instead.

Cañon (pronounced "canyon") — The body of a cigar between the tuck end and the head.

Cap — The piece of tobacco that forms the covering for the head; the end that you will ultimately clip.

Casing — The process of spraying newly-arrived hands of tobacco, dry from storage, with water, so that the re-moisturized tobacco becomes pliable and easy to work.

Chaveta — The flat rounded blade used by cigar rollers to trim the various tobacco leaves during the construction of a cigar. Today's chavetas are usually handmade out of old saw blades.

Cigarden — A landscaped backyard environment that has been specifically designed for cigar smoking.

Clear Havana — An American term used for a 100% all-Havana cigar.

Corte Caracol — Spanish for "seashell cut"; the technique of hand-cutting a rounded circle of tobacco and leaving it attached at the end of a wrapper, so that the end of the leaf can be used for the head without having to remove it from the wrapper. (See Finished Head).

Criollos (Cree-oh-yoss) — A Cuban term for descendants of the original Spaniards, but it is also a strain of Cuban tobacco from which filler blends and binders are derived. A third definition is the name given to the harsh cigars smoked by Cubans locally.

Culebra — A twisted cigar, usually three, corkscrewed into a rope-like shape. Culebras originated in the 19th century as a means to stop workers from stealing the cigars they were rolling. It was decided to allocate three cigars per day to each worker, and to have them twisted together while they were still wet. In that way, it would be easy to spot which cigars were not supposed to be leaving the premises. Today, these interesting shapes can be found in brands such as the Cuban H. Upmann, Honduran Hoyo de Monterrey, Calixto López from the Philippines and the Swiss-made Villiger. People in law enforcement might appreciate this crime-prevention smoke.

Curly Head — The twisted end of tobacco on the head of a cigar. It had its origin as a "quick fix" by cigar rollers who were making cigars for their personal use, so that they would not have to bother cutting and affixing a separate cap. However, today the curly head is found on a variety of premium cigars, including certain shapes by Davidoff, El Rico Habano, and Cohiba.

Cutting Board — The laminated hardwood table of the bench on which cigars are made. Also referred to as La Tabla.

Desbotonar — Process of trimming the suckers off of the tobacco plant so that more strength goes into the main leaves.

Dress Box — A cedar plywood box, in which you rarely see the wood because of the total coverage by labels and colorful border trimmings.

Dry Cigars — An American term for the non-humidified Dutch and Swiss cigars that are so very popular on the European Continent. Usually made with Sumatra, Brazil and Java tobaccos. In Europe these cigars are sometimes referred to as small, light, or specialty cigars.

Dutch Cigars — Also referred to as "dry cigars," most of these normally small-sized smokes are made from Indonesian (Sumatra and Java) leaf, while a percentage are also made from Brazilian and Cuban tobaccos. Obviously, the Cuban blends are not sold in the U.S. All Dutch cigars are made of short filler and one of their benefits is that they require little or no humidification.

E.M.S. — Stands for English Market Selection. A rich brown in color (see Chapter 3), it was named after the wrapper color that was preferred by British smokers and is now quite popular in America as well.

Fancy Tail — Another name for the curly head.

Figurado — Any cigar with a nontypical shape, such as a Torpedo, Pyramid or Culebra.

Filler — A blend of tobacco that forms the thick center of a cigar and provides much of its taste.

Finished Head — A technique of utilizing the wrapper leaf to continue on up around the cigar and form the head or cap of the cigar, without having to cut a separate piece for the cap.

Flathead — A cigar in which the head is flat.

Foot — The end of the cigar that you light. Also called the tuck end.

Frog Stripping — The act of hand striping the lower portion of a stem, leaving approximately 1/3 to 1/2 of the upper tobacco leaf intact, with two gradually tapering "legs" of leaf on either side, so that it looks like a frog that has been squashed by a semi. This technique is used in the making of long filler cigars.

Frontmark — The name of a cigar's shape that is printed on the outside of a box. Thus, a "frontmarked cigar" is a boxed cigar of a designated shape.

Full Cut — Same as a guillotine cut.

Fuma — Another name (although not so widely used anymore) for the curly head or pig's tail of a cigar. It comes from the phrase that came to symbolize the twisted "signature" head of the cigar maker's smoke: La Fuma de Tabacalera (the smoke of the cigar maker). The name "fuma" stuck.

Galera — Of Cuban derivative: the huge room in a cigar factory where cigars are rolled.

'Gar — Newspeak slang for cigar.

Guayavera — A traditional four-pocket shirt worn by cigar makers throughout the Caribbean. The long sleeved version of the guayavera is considered formal enough to wear to a wedding without a tie.

Hand — A hand of tobacco is a group of similar leaves, usually 20, that have been tied together at the bottom of their stems. A hand of tobacco can measure anywhere from 15 to 21 inches in length.

Handmade — A cigar that has been bunched and rolled entirely by hand.

Handrolled — A cigar in which the wrapper has been rolled onto the bunch by hand. Sometimes loosely used to designate a handmade cigar.

Head — The end of the cigar that is clipped.

Hecho a mano — Spanish for "made by hand," denoting a handrolled cigar.

Homogenized Tobacco — An artificially produced tobacco that is used as a binder and occasionally as wrapper on many lower priced European cigars as well as in a number of mass-market humidified cigars. Homogenized tobacco is made by mixing powdered tobacco with pure cellulose, fibers and water to create a pulp, which is pressed into long, thin sheets which are dried and then wrapped in rolls. These rolls of tobacco are subsequently fed into cigar-making machines.

HPH — Highly Prejudiced HackerScale, a system of measuring cigar strength (not quality) on a scale of 1 to 3, with #1 being the mildest and #3 being the strongest.

HTL — Homogenized Tobacco Leaf, an artificial tobacco process now owned by General Cigar.

Keep — British term for a private cigar locker.

La Tabla — See Cutting Board.

Lieberman — A hand-operated bunching device that utilizes a rubber sheet to roll the filler up into the binder. Named after the inventor.

Marble Head — A cigar that has a rounded head.

Marrying Room — See Aging Room.

Mass-Market Cigar — A generic term for a relatively low priced cigar that is made in extremely large quantities by machine.

Miniature Cigars — The term sometimes used for Dutch-type small cigars such as cigarillos, whiffs, etc. Outside of Europe, these are often called "dry cigars."

Mulling — Another term for fermentation, or the aging of tobacco leaves to bring them to color. It has nothing to do with hot Christmas wine.

Mulling Room — A fermentation or steam room, where the tobacco leaves are allowed to "sweat," which is what you should be doing in a steam room.

Natural Head — Using an attached part of the wrapper leaf to form the head, without having to cut off a separate piece.

Perfecto — One of the all-time classic shapes: a straight cigar with a reverse flare, or tapered end.

Pig Tail — Same as curly head, in which the tobacco covering the head is twisted at the tip.

Plume — The crystallization of oils from the tobacco of a cigar; it takes on the appearance of a light grayish-white dust on the surface of the wrapper. The formation of plume is activated by the dark, moist confines of a humidor over a long period of time. It is not harmful; some even believe it is beneficial to a cigar's taste. Not to be confused with mold.

Puros — In Havana it means any high-grade export-type cigar, but outside of Cuba, the term has come to mean a cigar whose filler, binder and wrapper are made with tobaccos that are all grown in the same country. For example, a cigar made with 100% Honduran tobacco is a puro. It would not be a puro if it had an imported U.S. grown Connecticut wrapper.

Premium Cigar — A generic term for a high-grade, 100% tobacco, long filler, handmade cigar.

Priming — The act of harvesting the leaves off of a tobacco plant.

Private Label Cigar — A cigar that is made for just one company and which is sold exclusively by them.

Pyramid — A cigar that gradually goes from a very narrow ring size at the head and flares out to a large foot. Almost always incorrectly referred to as a "torpedo," which it is not.

Ring Gauge — A unit of measurement divided into 1/64ths of an inch, and used to calibrate the diameter of a cigar. Thus, a cigar that is a 32 ring is 32/64ths of an inch, or 1/2 inch thick.

Sandwich Filler — A technique in which the filler is composed of "chopped" short leaf tobacco, which is rolled in long leaf outer filler leaves. Sounds more like a burrito than a sandwich.

Scrap Filler — The leftover tobacco cuttings used in the manufacture of inexpensive cigars. Not to be confused with short filler, which can be smaller cuts of premium long filler leaves, so that cigars can be machine made for economy.

Serones — A bag made of woven Cana palm tree leaves and used to transport dried tobacco from the fields. Each serone is filled with roughly 60 kilos (about 103 pounds) of tobacco.

Shaded — A term used to describe the sorting out of cigars by color, prior to boxing.

Smokeasies — A term originally coined by the author to generically describe any room or facility that caters strictly to cigar smokers, permitting them to light up and relax without incurring the wrathful glares of less sophisticated individuals. A modern-day version of the speakeasies of Prohibition infamy.

Smokers — The term loosely applied to a "cigar smoking event." It can be a dinner, a cognac or whiskey and cigar tasting combined, or simply a randomly scheduled gathering where people from all walks of life get together to smoke a cigar, without regard to race, creed, religion or politics. There aren't many other conclaves that are so broadly open to humanity as this one pastime.

Sticks — A semi-slang term for cigars, used among manufacturers and distributors when describing the number of cigars they want, as in, "Send me one hundred sticks of your new Honduran."

Stogy — A long thin, inexpensive cigar, often with a twisted end. Originally invented about 1827 by a tobacco merchant named George W. Black in Washington, Pennsylvania as an inexpensive smoke for the teamsters and settlers heading west. Because it was believed they looked like the spokes of a Conestoga wagon wheel, frontiersmen began referring to these cigars as "Conestogas," then "Conestogies," and finally the name was shortened to "stogy." Today, this term is often used incorrectly by journalists to mean any cigar, no matter what the shape or price or in what direction of the country the smoker may be heading.

Straight Cigar — A cigar with the same ring size running throughout the length of its body or cañon.

Super Premium — Not a gasoline, but definitely a high octane cigar. Normally priced substantially higher than even the premiums, and relying on image as well as good tobacco.

Torcedor — Cuban term for a cigar roller. It means "one who twists" but is used almost exclusively for cigar making.

Torpedo — A cigar in which the body flares (widens) and then narrows near the tuck where it is to be lit.

Tuck — The end of the cigar that is lit. Also known as the foot.

Tuck Cutter — A grooved wooden trough with a spring-loaded slicing blade at one end that determines the length of the cigar.

Vega — Another word for "plantation."

Whiff — A Dutch-type cigar that is smaller than a cigarillo.

Wrap Box — This has nothing to do with music. It is a relatively inexpensive cardboard or plywood box for mass-market cigars, in which a series of large labels are used to cover the entire box. Do not confuse this with the more artistic dress box, in which a number of individual border strippings and labels are put on manually for the more expensive handmade premium cigars.

Wrapper — The outer leaf of a cigar that is rolled around the binder.

XL — The designation for a tobacco leaf that is broken or cracked. Not used in Cuba, where the number 17 designates a broken leaf.

Addendum

Practically every cigar and accessory in this book can be found in some tobacco shop somewhere in the world. But occasionally there are suppliers and individual craftsmen who prefer to sell to their customers directly. Try your tobacconist first. If you can't find it there, here are those few products that are not usually found through cigar retailers:

Custom-made Leather Cigar Cases

Wild Bill Cleaver
P.O. Box 13037
Burton, WA 98013 USA

Cigar Smoker's Ties

Marc Hauser
Hauserwear
1810 W. Cortland
Chicago, IL 60622 USA

Nicole Miller
525 Seventh Avenue
New York, NY 10018

Sailcloth & Leather Saddlebag Briefcase

Pusser's Ltd.
Box 626, Road Town
Tortola
British Virgin Islands, West Indies

Custom-made Humidors

D. Marshall, Inc.
P.O. Box 3841
Tustin, CA 92681 USA

Cigar Band Cufflinks & Fashion Jewelry

Pop Art
(800) 567-6727

Cigarden Consultants

LandPlan
10573 West Pico Blvd., #178
Los Angeles, CA 90064 USA

Antique Reproduction Electric Lighters

Pioneer Manufacturing Company
501 Lake Street, Box 436
Battle Lake, MN 56515 USA

Index

336

CigarNotes

A place to enter new brands, tasting experiences and other miscellanea, as may have been inspired by this book.

Brand	Size	Blend	HPH	Observations

Brand	Size	Blend	HPH	Observations

Brand	Size	Blend	HPH	Observations

Brand	Size	Blend	HPH	Observations

Brand	Size	Blend	HPH	Observations

Brand	Size	Blend	HPH	Observations

Brand	Size	Blend	HPH	Observations

Brand	Size	Blend	HPH	Observations

Brand	Size	Blend	HPH	Observations

Brand	Size	Blend	HPH	Observations

Brand	Size	Blend	HPH	Observations

Brand	Size	Blend	HPH	Observations